Praise for

THE
FIVE

A No. 5 *Sunday Times* bestseller (UK)
Winner of the Baillie Gifford Prize for Nonfiction,
Short-listed for the Crime Writers' Association Gold Dagger
for Nonfiction, and the Historical Writers' Association
Nonfiction Crown Award

"Hallie Rubenhold's hard-edged, heartbreaking biographies of the
five women killed by Jack the Ripper over two months in 1888 offer
a blistering counter-narrative to the 'male, authoritarian, and middle
class' legend of a demonic superman preying on prostitutes . . . Her
riveting work, both compassionate group portrait and stinging social history, finally gives them their due."   — *Washington Post*

"Rubenhold has produced a significant study of how poor and working-class women subsisted in an unforgiving age."
      — *New York Times Book Review*

"The five London women murdered by Jack the Ripper, in 1888,
were long assumed to be prostitutes. This history shows otherwise,
presenting deeply researched portraits of the victims as they lived:
they were all poor, some to the point of homelessness; they were all
apparently killed while asleep; and, with one exception, they were
known by family and acquaintances not to be prostitutes. Each had
a distinct story that has never been fully or truthfully told. Why Victorians preferred to embrace the myth is one question that guides
the book; why *we* continue to do so is another."   — *The New Yorker*

"Deeply researched and powerfully told, *The Five* unearths the truth behind the Victorian Age's most sensational crime: the 1888 murder spree of Jack the Ripper. Hallie Rubenhold reaches beyond 130 years' worth of lurid headlines and misleading reports to humanize the victims and explore their lives—and tragic, untimely deaths. *The Five* is a coruscating gem of a book, as necessary as it is compelling."
— Karen Abbott, *New York Times* best-selling author of *Liar, Temptress, Soldier, Spy*

"*The Five* is a long-overdue investigation that shines the spotlight on [the victims], giving context to who they were and what circumstances molded their lives."   —*Hypable*

"Meticulously researched and beautifully executed, *The Five* is a powerful and timely retelling of a story you think you already know. Rubenhold strips away decades of myths and misconceptions so that the women who were ruthlessly murdered by Jack the Ripper are no longer one-dimensional characters in a Penny Dreadful, but real human beings with very real struggles, hopes, and fears. With this important book, Rubenhold proves she is a master of narrative nonfiction: a historian with a novelist's soul."
— Lindsey Fitzharris, author of *The Butchering Art*

"Devastatingly good. *The Five* will leave you in tears, of pity and of rage."   — Lucy Worsley, BBC presenter, chief curator at Historic Royal Palaces, and author

"A Ripper narrative that gives voice to the women he silenced; I've been waiting for this book for years. Beautifully written and with the grip of a thriller, it will open your eyes and break your heart."
— Erin Kelly, best-selling author of *He Said/She Said*

THE
FIVE

Books by Hallie Rubenhold

THE
FIVE

THE UNTOLD LIVES
OF THE WOMEN KILLED BY
JACK THE RIPPER

Hallie Rubenhold

MARINER
BOOKS

An Imprint of HarperCollins*Publishers*
Boston New York

First Mariner books edition 2020
Copyright © 2019 by Hallie Rubenhold

Mariner Books
An Imprint of HarperCollins Publishers, registered in the United States of America
and/or other jurisdictions.

www.marinerbooks.com

Library of Congress Cataloging-in-Publication Data
Names: Rubenhold, Hallie, author.
Title: The five : the untold lives of the women killed by Jack the Ripper /
Hallie Rubenhold.
Description: Boston : HarperCollins Publishers, [2019] |
Includes bibliographical references and index.
Identifiers: LCCN 2018038562 (print) | LCCN 2018041373 (ebook) |
ISBN 9781328664082 (ebook) | ISBN 9781328663818 (hardcover) |
ISBN 9780358299615 (PBK.)
Subjects: LCSH: Jack, the Ripper. | Murder victims — England — London —
Biography. | Working class women — England — London — Social conditions
— 19th century. | Whitechapel (London, England) — History — 19th century.
Classification: LCC HV6535.G6 (ebook) | LCC HV6535.G6 L6578 2019 (print) |
DDC 362.88 — dc23
LC record available at https://lccn.loc.gov/2018038562

Book design by Chrissy Kurpeski

Printed in the United States of America
23 24 25 26 27 LBC 12 11 10 9 8

Map by Liane Payne, based on 1851 edition of *Reynolds's Map of London*

For
Mary Ann "Polly" Nichols,
Annie Chapman,
Elisabeth Stride,
Catherine Eddowes
&

Mary Jane Kelly

CONTENTS

I write for those women who do not speak, for those who do not have a voice because they were so terrified, because we are taught to respect fear more than ourselves. We've been taught that silence would save us, but it won't.

— *AUDRE LORDE*

THE FIVE'S LONDON

P *Polly Nichols*
A *Annie Chapman*
E *Elisabeth Stride*
K *Catherine "Kate" Eddowes*
M *Mary Jane Kelly*

0   5 miles

Regents Park

69 Gower Street **E**

Kirby Street **P**

Bridgewater Gds

K

M

St James's
Restaurant

E St Giles Church

P Shoe
Lane

M The Alhambra

South Bruton Mews **A**

Trafalgar Square

Hyde Park **E** Wells St **A**

Hyde Park

M

P

Café de l'Europe

P

A Raphael Street

Stamford Street
Peabody buildings

A Montpelier Place

WESTMINSTER

M Brompton Square

LAMBETH

A KNIGHTSBRIDGE

K

Onslow Mews

Bell Street

K

Lower George Street

Trafalgar Street **P**

RIVER THAMES

Rosehill Road, Wandsworth (3½ miles

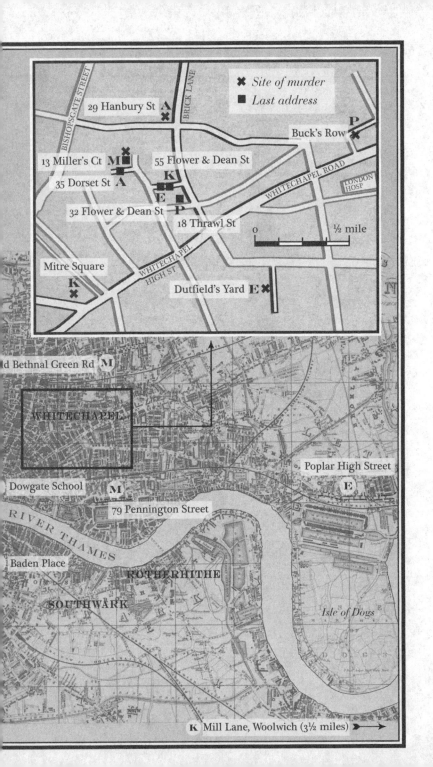

Site of murder ✖
Last address ■

29 Hanbury St **A** ✖

BRICK LANE

BISHOPSGATE STREET

Buck's Row **P** ✖

13 Miller's Ct **M** ✖
55 Flower & Dean St **K**

35 Dorset St **A**

WHITECHAPEL ROAD

LONDON HOSP

32 Flower & Dean St **E**

18 Thrawl St **P**

0 ½ mile

Mitre Square **K** ✖

WHITECHAPEL HIGH ST

Dutfield's Yard **E** ✖

N

Bethnal Green Rd **M**

WHITECHAPEL

Poplar High Street **E**

Dowgate School **M**

79 Pennington Street

RIVER THAMES

Baden Place

ROTHERHITHE

Isle of Dogs

SOUTHWARK

K Mill Lane, Woolwich (3½ miles) ➤

INTRODUCTION:
A TALE OF TWO CITIES

There are two versions of the events of 1887. One is very well known, but the other is not.

The first version, more frequently featured in history books, is the one that those who lived in late-nineteenth-century Britain wished to recall, the version they recounted to their grandchildren with a wistful smile. It is the story of Queen Victoria and a summer of celebrations for her Golden Jubilee. No more than a teenage girl when the nation's weighty crown was placed upon her head, she had become, a half-century later, the embodiment of empire, and a suitably grand series of events had been planned to commemorate her fifty-year reign. On June 20, the precise day she had first mounted the throne, the crowned heads of Europe, Indian princes, dignitaries, and representatives from all corners of the empire, and even the Hawaiian queen, Lili'uokalani, converged upon London. West End shopkeepers adorned their windows in red, white, and blue; Royal Standards and Union Jacks, festoons of flowers, and colored garlands could be seen hanging from every somber stone edifice. At night, the embassies and clubs, the hotels and institutions throughout St. James and Piccadilly threw the switches on the electric lights and turned on the gas jets, illuminating the giant crowns and the letters *V* and *R* affixed to their buildings. Her Majesty's loyal subjects came to the center of the city from the suburbs and tenements; they punched their rail tickets from Kent and Surrey and pushed their way into the crowded streets, hoping to catch a glimpse of a royal coach or a princess in diamonds. They placed candles in their windows when the long summer twilight faded away, and toasted their monarch's health with beer and champagne and claret.

There was a service of thanksgiving at Westminster Abbey, a state banquet, a military review at Windsor, and even a children's fete in Hyde Park for twenty-five hundred boys and girls. They were entertained by twenty Punch and Judy puppet shows, eight marionette theaters, eighty-six stereoscope displays, nine troupes of performing dogs, monkeys, and ponies, as well as bands, toys, and "gas inflated balloons," before being treated to a lunch of lemonade, cake, meat pies, buns, and oranges. Throughout the summer there were commemorative concerts, lectures, performances, regattas, picnics, dinners, and even a yacht race. As the jubilee corresponded with the traditional London "season," there were also lavish garden parties and balls. Ladies dressed up in that summer's fashions: lace-trimmed, bustled dresses in black-and-white silk, and hues of apricot yellow, heliotrope, and Gobelin blue. A magnificent ball was held at the Guildhall, where the Prince and Princess of Wales entertained their visiting regal relations, as well as the prince of Persia, the papal envoy, the prince of Siam, and the Maharaja Holkar of Indore. All of high society danced beneath banners and cascading arrangements of perfumed flowers. Tiaras and tie pins sparkled in the mirrors. Young debutantes were introduced to suitable sons. The whirl of Victorian life spun round and round to the dreamy melody of a waltz.

Then there is the other version.

This is the tale of 1887 that most chose to forget. To this day, only a scant number of history books recount it, and surprisingly few people know that it occurred. Yet in that year, this story filled more newspaper column inches than did the descriptions of royal parades, banquets, and fetes put together.

That jubilee summer had been exceptionally warm and rainless. The clear blue skies that presided over the season's carefree picnics and al fresco parties had shriveled the fruit harvest and dried out the fields. Water shortages and an absence of seasonal jobs in agricultural labor exacerbated an already growing employment crisis. While the wealthy enjoyed the fine weather from beneath their parasols and from under the trees of their suburban villas, the homeless and poor made use of it by creating an open-air encampment in Trafalgar Square. Many had come to the center of town, looking for work at Covent Garden Market, where Londoners bought their produce, but a drought meant fewer boxes of plums and pears to lift and haul. With no money for lodgings, these migrants slept rough in the nearby square, where they were joined by an increasing population of unemployed workers who would rather live on the street than face the deplorable and demeaning conditions of the workhouse. Much to the horror of more fortunate observers, these campers could be seen making their morning ablutions and scrubbing their "vermin infested" clothing in the fountains, directly beneath the nose of Lord Nelson, high atop his column. When the autumn chill began to move in, so too did the socialists, the Salvation Army, and various charitable organizations, handing out Bibles, admission tickets to lodging houses, coffee, tea, bread, and soup. Tarpaulins were erected to create makeshift bivouacs; each day, impassioned speakers declared their messages from between the paws of the square's mighty bronze lions. The excitement, the sense of community, and the free refreshments swelled the number of outcast Londoners, which attracted the police, which in turn brought the journalists. The newspapermen roamed among the square's bedraggled population, collecting their names and stories.

"Mr. Ashville" called himself "a painter and glazier by trade." Out of work for twelve months, he had spent thirty-three nights sleeping on the Embankment until the weather grew too cold. Then he moved to Trafalgar Square, hoping it might prove a bit warmer. Dejected and visibly worn down by his experience, he attempted to remain positive about his prospects of finding employment again one day.

A soldier's widow circled Trafalgar Square, selling matches to support her young son, but she hadn't always lived like this. After failing to pay the final installment on her rent-to-own sewing machine, she lost her livelihood and the single room she had called home. She knew that going into the workhouse meant that her child would be separated from her. It seemed a better option to rough it in the square each night, with the boy curled up under her shawl.[1]

An "elderly couple," who had never before faced adversity, now slept on a stone bench in the square.[2] The husband had been employed as a musical director at a theater, but an accident had left him unfit to work. With no savings, the couple soon fell behind on their rent and eventually were forced to make their bed under the stars. The thought of throwing themselves upon the mercy of their local workhouse was too shameful and frightening to consider.

Hundreds, each with a similar tale to tell, came to Trafalgar Square to lay their head against the paving stones. It did not take long for political agitators to recognize that this congregation of the downtrodden was a ready-made army of the angry with nothing to lose. Londoners had long realized that Trafalgar Square sat on an axis between the east and west of the city, the dividing line between rich and poor; an artificial boundary, which, like the invisible restraints that kept the disenfranchised voiceless, could be easily breached. In 1887, the possibility of social revolution felt terrifyingly near for some, and yet for others it did not seem close enough. At Trafalgar Square, the daily speeches given by socialists and reformers such as William Morris, Annie Besant, Eleanor Marx, and George Bernard Shaw led to mobilization, as chanting, banner-waving processions of thousands spilled onto the streets. Inevitably, some resorted to violence. The Metropolitan Police and the magistrate's court at Bow Street, in Covent Garden, worked overtime to contain the protesters and clear the square of those whom they deemed indigents and rabble-rousers. But like an irrepressible tide, soon after they were pushed out, they returned once more.

On November 8, the police made a fatal decision. Sir Charles Warren, the commissioner of police, banned all meetings in Trafalgar Square. Those who had come to see this site, in the heart of London, as a rallying place for the common man and a forum for political action interpreted this as a deliberate act of war. Plans were made for a demonstration on the thirteenth of the month. Its pretext was to demand that the Irish MP William O'Brien be released from prison, but the grievances expressed by the protesters extended far beyond this particular cause célèbre. More than forty thousand men and women gathered to make their point, and two thousand police, along with the Queen's Life Guard and the Grenadier Guards, were there to meet them. Almost immediately, clashes erupted. The police, wielding truncheons, fell on the protesters. Those participating in the march had been advised to demonstrate peacefully, yet many had come equipped with lead pipes, knives, hammers, and brickbats. Forty protesters were arrested, more than two hundred were injured in the riot, and at least two were killed. Unfortunately, Bloody Sunday, as it came to be known, did not signal the end of the conflict. The tinkling sound of smashing glass and the outbursts of public rage continued well into the start of the following year.

Through these two disparate scenes moved two women whose lives and deaths would come to define nineteenth-century Britain; one was Victoria, who gave her name to the years 1837–1901. The other was a homeless woman called Mary Ann, or "Polly," Nichols, who was among those encamped at Trafalgar Square in 1887. Unlike the monarch, Polly would be largely forgotten, though the world would remember with great fascination and even relish the name of her killer: Jack the Ripper.

Roughly twelve months lay between the Queen's Golden Jubilee summer and Polly Nichols's murder on August 31, 1888. She would be the first of Jack the Ripper's five "canonical" victims — those whose deaths the police determined were committed by the same hand in the district of Whitechapel, in London's East End. A few days later, on September 8, the body of Annie Chapman was discovered in a yard off Hanbury Street. In the early morning hours of the thirtieth of that month, the Ripper managed to strike twice. In what became known as "the double event," he claimed the lives of Elisabeth Stride, who was found in Dutfield's Yard, off Berner Street, and Catherine "Kate" Eddowes, who was killed in Mitre Square. After a brief pause in his spree, he committed his final atrocity on November 9: a complete mutilation of the body of Mary Jane Kelly as she lay in her bed at 13 Miller's Court.

The brutality of the Whitechapel murders stunned London and newspaper readers around the world. The Ripper had cut the throat of each victim. Four of the five were eviscerated. With the exception of the final killing, these violent deaths occurred in open places, under cover of darkness. In each case, the murderer managed to abscond, leaving not a trace of his or their or her identity. Given the densely populated district in which these killings occurred, the public, the press, and even the police believed this to be remarkable. The Ripper always seemed one ghostly, ghoulish step ahead of the authorities, which bestowed upon the murders something extra terrifying and almost supernatural.

The Whitechapel-based H Division of the Metropolitan Police did the best they could with their resources, but having never before faced a murder case of this scale and magnitude, they quickly found themselves overwhelmed. House-to-house inquiries were conducted throughout the area and a wide variety of forensic material was gathered and analyzed. The police were besieged with statements and letters from those who claimed to be witnesses, those offering assistance, and others who just liked spinning tales. In all, more than two thousand people were interviewed and more than three hundred were investigated as possible suspects. Even with assistance from Scotland Yard and the City of London Police, none of these efforts yielded anything useful. Genuine leads were certain to have been lost among the swirling wash of paper that the investigators had to process. In the meantime, as the constables scribbled into their notebooks and followed potential malefactors down dark alleys, the Ripper continued to kill.

As the "Autumn of Terror" wore on, Whitechapel filled up with journalists. They hovered over this seam of sensationalist gold with pencils sharpened. Their presence amid the ongoing police investigation and an East End population living in a state of fear proved explosive. In the absence of any conclusive information offered by the police, the newspapers posited their own theories about the killer and his modus operandi. As the papers continued to fly off the newsstands, journalists became hungry for more content and new angles on the story. Inevitably, embellishment, invention, and "fake news" found their way onto the page. However, printing rumors and hotheaded opinion pieces that disparaged the efforts of the police did little to quell the anxiety of those who lived in Whitechapel. By the middle of September, residents were described as "panic-stricken"; most were too terrified to leave their homes at night. "Hooting and shouting" crowds gathered outside the police station on Leman Street, demanding the arrest of the killer, and local tradesmen, eager to take matters into their own hands, founded the Whitechapel Vigilance Society. All the while, the press speculated wildly about the identity of the culprit: he was a Whitechapel man; he was a wealthy "swell" from the West End; he was a sailor, a Jew, a butcher, a surgeon, a foreigner, a lunatic, a gang of extortionists. The inhabitants of the neighborhood began to attack anyone who fit these descriptions; doctors toting medical bags were set upon, and men carrying parcels were reported to the police. Sickened by the grotesque events, many people nonetheless found themselves compulsively intrigued by them. Just as crowds grew outside Leman Street police station, so they also gathered around the sites of the murders. Some stood staring at the places where the vicious deeds had been committed in the hope of finding answers, while others were simply entranced by the horror of the spectacle.

Because the police failed to apprehend and charge a suspect for any of the five murders, the itch to see justice meted out in the form of a trial was never salved. Instead, that which served to offer a few answers and a degree of closure was the series of coroner's inquests, one for each killing. These were held publicly in Whitechapel and in the City of London in the wake of each murder and covered extensively by the newspapers. At a coroner's inquest, as at a criminal trial, witnesses are called before a jury to give an account of events; the objective is to piece together a clear and official picture of how a death occurred. Most of the information that currently exists about Jack the Ripper's five victims appears in witness statements given during the inquests; however, these accounts are problematic. The examinations lacked thoroughness, the juries asked few follow-up questions, and inconsistencies and vagaries in the testimonies were rarely challenged. Ultimately, the information disclosed over the course of the inquests only skims the surface of a far deeper and murkier well of potential answers.

Investigations into the Whitechapel murders did, however, explicitly and convincingly expose a disturbing set of facts: the poor of that district lived in unspeakably horrendous conditions. The encampment and riots at Trafalgar Square were a conspicuous manifestation of what had been chronically ailing in the East End and other impoverished parts of London. It was a cough hacked in the face of the establishment. The emergence of Jack the Ripper was a louder and more violent one still.

For most of Victoria's reign, journalists, social reformers, and Christian missionaries had been decrying the horrors that they observed in the East End, but the situation grew even more acute during the 1870s and '80s, as "the Long Depression" bore down on the economy. What work there was for London's vast army of unskilled laborers — those who sewed and laundered the textiles, carried the bricks, assembled the goods, peddled in the streets, and unloaded the ships — was poorly paid and insecure. Casual work on the docks might pay no more than fifteen shillings a week; "sandwich board men" who carried advertisements through the streets might make one shilling, eight pence per day. To worsen matters, rents had been steadily climbing and lodgings were harder to come by. Large areas of lower-income housing across the capital had been destroyed to make way for railroads, and the creation of broad new thoroughfares, such as Shaftesbury Avenue, decanted London's poor into fewer and more densely packed spaces.

Whitechapel was one of the most notorious of these, but was by no means the only sink of poverty in the capital. As the social reformer Charles Booth's extensive study of London's impoverished areas in the 1890s revealed, pockets of destitution, crime, and misery flourished throughout the metropolis, even within otherwise comfortable areas. Still, Whitechapel's reputation trumped even Bermondsey, Lambeth, Southwark, and St. Pancras as the most sordid. By the end of the nineteenth century, seventy-eight thousand souls were packed into this quarter of common lodging houses, "furnished rooms," warehouses, factories, sweatshops, abattoirs, pubs, cheap music halls, and markets. Its overcrowded population represented diverse cultures, religions, and languages. For at least two centuries, Whitechapel had been a destination for immigrants from many parts of Europe. In the late nineteenth century, a large number of Irish, desperate to escape the rural poverty of the mother country, had arrived. By the 1880s an exodus of Jews, fleeing the pogroms of eastern Europe, joined them. In an era highly suspicious of those of other nationalities, races, and religions, integration, even within the slums, did not occur naturally.

Nevertheless, Booth's social investigators regarded these various residents as fairly uniform in terms of their social class. With a number of middle-class exceptions, a significant percentage of the inhabitants of Whitechapel were identified as "poor," "very poor," or "semi-criminal."

The throbbing dark heart at the center of the district was Spitalfields. Here, near the fruit and vegetable market and the soaring white spire of Christ Church, some of the worst streets and accommodations in the area, and perhaps in all of London, were situated. Even the police feared Dorset Street, Thrawl Street, and Flower and Dean Street, and the smaller thoroughfares contiguous to them. Lined with cheap, vice-riddled lodging houses (known as "doss houses") and decrepit dwellings, whose crumbling interiors had been divided into individual "furnished rooms" for rent, these streets and their desperate inhabitants came to embody all that was rotten in England.

Those who strayed into this abyss from the safety of the middle-class Victorian world were struck dumb by what they encountered. The broken pavement, dim gaslights, slicks of sewage, stagnant pools of disease-breeding water, and rubbish-filled roadways foretold the physical horrors of what lay within the buildings. An entire family might inhabit one vermin-infested furnished room, eight by eight feet in size, with broken windows and damp walls. On one occasion, health inspectors found five children sharing a bed alongside a dead sibling awaiting burial. People slept on the floors, on heaps of rags and straw; some had pawned all their clothes and owned barely a scrap to cover their nakedness. In this circle of hell, alcoholism, malnutrition, and disease were rife, as was domestic violence — along with most other forms of violence. Girls, having barely reached puberty, turned to prostitution to earn money. Boys just as easily slipped into thieving and pickpocketing. It appeared to moral, middle-class England that in the face of this level of brutal, crippling want, every good and righteous instinct that ought to govern human relations had been completely eroded.

Nowhere was this state of affairs more apparent than in the common lodging houses, which offered shelter to those too poor to afford even a furnished room. The lodging houses provided temporary homes for the homeless, who divided their nights between the reeking beds on offer here, the oppression of the workhouse casual wards, and sleeping on the street. They were the haunts of beggars, criminals, prostitutes, chronic alcoholics, the unemployed, the sick and the old, the casual laborer, and the pensioned soldier. Most residents would fit into a number of these categories. In Whitechapel alone there were 233 common lodging houses, which accommodated an estimated 8,530 homeless people.[3] Naturally, those on Dorset Street, Thrawl Street, and Flower and Dean Street bore the worst reputations. Four pence per night could buy someone a single hard, flea-hopping bed in a stifling, stinking dormitory. Eight pence could buy an equally squalid double bed with a wooden partition around it. There were single-sex lodging houses and mixed lodging houses, though those that admitted both sexes were acknowledged to be the more morally degenerate. All lodgers were entitled to make use of the communal kitchen, which was open all day and late into the night. Residents used this as a gathering place, cooking meager meals and quaffing tea and beer with one another and anyone else who cared to drop in. Social investigators and reformers who sat at these kitchen tables were appalled by the rude manners and the horrific language they heard, even from children. However, it was the violent behavior, degrading filth, and overflowing toilets, in addition to the open displays of nakedness, free sexual intercourse, drunkenness, and child neglect to which they truly objected. In the "doss house," everything offensive about the slum was concentrated under one roof.

The police and reformers were especially concerned about the link between common lodging houses and prostitution. As long as a "dosser" could pay the pence required for a bed, the lodging-house keeper asked few questions. Many women who regarded prostitution as their main source of income lived in or worked out of lodging houses, especially in the wake of the 1885 Criminal Law Amendment Act, which saw the enforced closure of many brothels. The result of this meant that a large number of prostitutes were forced to ply their trade in places separate from where they lived. A lodging house with eight-penny doubles was a convenient place to take a man who had been solicited on the street. Other prostitutes chose to sleep in a cheaper four-penny single but see to their customers in dark corners outside, where quick sexual encounters, which frequently did not involve full intercourse, took place.

Lodging houses provided shelter for a wide variety of women facing an assortment of unfortunate circumstances. While some resorted to what has been called "casual prostitution," it is categorically wrong to assume that all of them did so. These women were inventive when it came to scraping together their "doss money." Most took on poorly paid casual labor, doing cleaning and laundering or hawking goods. Generally, they supplemented the little money they earned by borrowing, begging, pawning, and sometimes stealing. Pairing up with a male partner also played an essential role in defraying costs. Often these relationships, formed out of necessity, were short-lived; some, however, endured for months or years without ever being sanctified in a church. The nonchalance with which poor men and women embarked upon and dissolved these partnerships horrified middle-class observers. Whether or not these unions produced children also seemed to be of little consequence. Obviously, this way of life diverged considerably from the acceptable moral standard and threw another layer of confusion over what exactly it was that the female residents of these wicked lodging houses were doing in order to keep a roof over their heads.

During the Ripper's reign of terror, newspapers, eager to scandalize the nation with graphic details of slum life, regularly asserted that Whitechapel's lodging houses "were brothels in all but name" and that the majority of women who inhabited them, with very few exceptions, were all prostitutes. In the grip of such terrible events, the public were willing to believe it. Hyperbole became enshrined as fact, although some within the police had come to perceive the situation in another light. An altogether different perspective is offered in a letter written by Sir Charles Warren, the commissioner of the Metropolitan Police, at the height of the murder spree. After doing some rough calculations, Warren estimated that approximately 1,200 prostitutes inhabited Whitechapel's 233 common lodging houses. More importantly, he qualified this statement by admitting that the police "have no means of ascertaining what women are prostitutes and who are not."[4] In other words, the newspapers were in no position to make this determination when even the police found distinguishing a prostitute from among her sisters an impossibility. Warren's figures present another intriguing prospect. If the lodging-house population was comprised of 8,530 people and a third, or 2,844, of those residents were female, and if it were to be accepted that 1,200 of these women could be identified as prostitutes, that would still indicate that the majority of them, or 1,644, were not engaged in any form of prostitution at all.* Much like the inhabitants of Whitechapel's common lodging houses, the victims of Jack the Ripper and the lives they led became entangled in a web of assumptions, rumor, and unfounded speculation. The spinning of these strands began over 130 years ago and, remarkably, they have been left virtually undisturbed and unchallenged. The fibers that have clung to and defined the shape of Polly, Annie, Elisabeth, Kate, and Mary Jane's stories are the values of the Victorian world. They are male, authoritarian, and middle class. They were formed at a time when women had no voice, and few rights, and the poor were considered lazy and degenerate: to have been both of these things was one of the worst possible combinations. For over 130 years we have embraced the dusty parcel we were handed. We have rarely ventured to peer inside it or attempted to remove the thick wrapping that has kept us from knowing these women or their true histories.

Jack the Ripper killed prostitutes, or so it has always been believed, but there is no hard evidence to suggest that three of his five victims were prostitutes at all. As soon as each body was discovered, in a dark yard or street, the police *assumed* that the woman was a prostitute killed by a maniac who had lured her to the location for sex. There is, and never was, any proof of this either. To the contrary — over the course of the coroner's inquests, it became known that Jack the Ripper never had sex with a single victim. Additionally, in the case of each murder there were no signs of struggle and the killings appear to have taken place in complete silence. There were no screams heard by anyone in the vicinity. The autopsies concluded that all of the women were killed while in a reclining position. In at least three of the cases, the victims

---

*Joseph O'Neill, *The Secret World of the Victorian Lodging House* (Barnsley, 2014), p. 117. Women were believed to make up under half of the total lodging-house population in London.

were known to sleep on the street and on the nights they were killed did not have money for a lodging house. In the final case, the victim was murdered in her bed. However, the police were so committed to their theories about the killer's choice of victims that they failed to conclude the obvious — the Ripper targeted women while they slept.

Unreliable source material has always been the obstacle to discovering the truth about these murders. Although a handful of police records exist, the coroner's inquests provide most of what is known about the actual crimes and the victims. Unfortunately, in three of the five cases, the official documentation from these inquests is missing. All that remains is a body of edited, embellished, misheard, reinterpreted newspaper reports from which a general picture of events can be teased. These documents have been approached with care on my part, and nothing contained within them has been taken as gospel. Similarly, I have also refrained from using unsubstantiated information provided by witnesses who did not know the victims personally prior to their deaths.

My intention in writing this book is not to hunt and name the killer. I wish instead to retrace the footsteps of five women, to consider their experiences within the context of their era, and to follow their paths through both the gloom and the light. They are worth more to us than the empty human shells we have taken them for; they were children who cried for their mothers, they were young women who fell in love; they endured childbirth, the death of parents; they laughed, and they celebrated Christmas. They argued with their siblings, they wept, they dreamed, they hurt, they enjoyed small triumphs. The courses their lives took mirrored that of so many other women of the Victorian age, and yet were so singular in the way they ended. It is for them that I write this book. I do so in the hope that we may now hear their stories clearly and give back to them that which was so brutally taken away with their lives: their dignity.

PART I

POLLY

August 26, 1845

August 31, 1888

THE BLACKSMITH'S DAUGHTER

THE CYLINDERS TURNED. The belts moved, and gears clicked and whirred, as type and ink pressed against paper. Floors rattled; lights burned at all hours. In some rooms, lengthy sheets of words hung from the ceilings on drying racks; in others stood towers of wooden boxes filled with tiny pieces of metal type. There were rooms where men bent and molded leather, tooled gold leaf onto covers, and stitched bindings. There were sheds in which copper plates were etched and lettering was forged. There were shops stacked high with books and newspapers and magazines, redolent with the delightful scent of fresh paper and sharp ink. Fleet Street, and all the smaller byways surrounding it, was a multichambered hive of printing. Filthy canvas smocks and smeared aprons were the only fashion; the sootier and blacker, the harder the worker. Printer's boys ran their errands arrayed head to toe in ink dust. Hardly a man in the publishing parish of St. Bride's could boast of unstained fingers, nor would he wish to. This was the home of the author, the printer, the newspaperman, the bookseller, and every other profession related to the written word.

Fleet Street and its tributaries flowed constantly with human traffic. As one writer commented, it was possible to look back on the street from Ludgate Hill, near St. Paul's Cathedral, and see "nothing but a dark, confused, quickly-moving mass of men, horses and vehicles" without "a yard of the pavement to be seen — nothing but heads along the rows of houses, and in the road, too, an ocean of heads."[1] Between this broad thoroughfare and that of High Holborn, which paralleled it, a network of smaller alleys and passages was lined with rotting wooden structures and old brick buildings all crushed together. These had been the homes and workshops of printers, thinkers, and impoverished writers since the seventeenth century. Neighbors were close enough to hear a wail, a sneeze, or even a sigh from next door. In the summer, when the windows were thrown open, the thumping and the churning of presses — steam-powered and those run by hand — could be heard along nearly every street.

Amid this cacophony, in a cramped old room, Caroline Walker brought her second child, Mary Ann, into the world. She arrived on August 26, 1845, a day that the surrounding newspapers described as "fine and dry." The home into which she was born, a dilapidated two-hundred-year-old house known as Dawes Court, on Gunpowder Alley, off Shoe Lane, bore an address worthy of any of Charles Dickens's heroines. Indeed, the author of *Oliver Twist* had come to know these dingy courts and fetid alleys intimately in his youth while he worked as a shoeblack, and later scribbled away in nearby rooms. Polly, as Caroline Walker's daughter came to be called, would spend her first years in lodgings just like those of the fictional Fagin and his pickpocket boys.

The Walkers had never been a wealthy family, nor, given the limitations of her father's profession, were they ever likely to be. Edward Walker had trained as a blacksmith in Lambeth, on the opposite side of the Thames, until work along the "Street of Ink" beckoned him north across the river. He had turned his skills at first to making locks and then, quite probably, given his location, to the founding of type, or the creation of typeface.* Although blacksmithing was a respected skilled trade, it paid only a passable living. A journeyman blacksmith at the start of his career might be paid three to five shillings a day, a sum likely to rise to at least six shillings and sixpence when he gained

---

* The printing trade relied heavily on the skills of blacksmiths for its machinery and typeface, and it is likely that Walker moved the family to the area for this reason.

a permanent position, though the expansion of a man's family would stretch the extra pennies more thinly.*

Edward and Caroline and their three children — Edward, born two years before Polly, and Frederick, four years after — made a humble but steady life together on these wages. In the early decades of the Victorian era, this was not a simple task. Illness or the sudden loss of work might send a family into rent arrears and then just as quickly into the workhouse. The average weekly expenditure for a medium-sized family like the Walkers was about one pound, eight shillings, and one penny. The rent for one large room or two smaller rooms in central London ran from four shillings to four shillings and six pence a week. A further twenty shillings would be spent on food, while one shilling and nine pence was the least one might expect to pay for coal, wood, candles, and soap.[2] A skilled laborer like Edward Walker would be expected to put aside at least several pennies in savings, in addition to an estimated one shilling and three pence for his children's education.

Although schooling would not become compulsory until 1876, more prosperous working-class parents often sent their boys and sometimes their girls to local charity schools or even to schools requiring a fee. This was especially true among the families associated with the printing trade, where literacy was not only highly valued but considered essential. Some employers, such as Spottiswoode & Co., one of the era's largest publishers, went as far as to offer schooling on site for boys under fifteen and also ran a lending library for its staff in order to encourage literacy in the home. While Polly and her brother Edward might not have had access to such a resource, it is likely they attended either a National School or a British School. National Schools, such as the City of London National School, based on nearby Shoe Lane, were organized by the Anglican Church and offered part-time instruction for children who had to bring home an income. British Schools, favored by working families who considered themselves a cut above the poorest in the community, offered what was thought to be a slightly

---

* By 1861, Walker was describing himself as a blacksmith and engineer — one involved in the creation of much larger machinery — possibly, given the family's location, equipment used in printing.

more rigorous learning experience; there, older children taught younger pupils under the auspices of the school's master or mistress. Edward Walker apparently was a firm proponent of education. Polly, quite unusually for her gender and class, was permitted to remain in school until the age of fifteen. During this period, when it was conventional to teach reading but not writing to working-class girls, Polly mastered both skills. As the Walkers could have afforded little in the way of luxuries, it's likely that access to the printed word was the only advantage that Polly enjoyed from growing up near the Street of Ink.

The homes of her youth could offer few other comforts. The Walkers never lived far from Shoe Lane or High Holborn. From Dawes Court they moved to Dean Street, Robinhood Court, and Harp Alley. Space and privacy were almost unknown in the dwellings clustered along the slender medieval streets in the parishes of St. Bride's and St. Andrew's. An 1844 inquiry undertaken into the state of housing in populous London districts found that buildings situated in enclosed courts and narrow alleys, like those in which the Walkers lived, were some of the "worst conditioned . . . badly ventilated and filthy . . . in the entire neighbourhood." Most families shared one room; the average size "measured from 8 to 10 feet, by 8 feet, and from 6 to 8 feet from floor to ceiling."[3] In these compact rooms entire families were squeezed together. Dawes Court, once a large half-timber-and-plaster house, had been subdivided into three separate dwellings, before being apportioned once more into individually rented rooms, inhabited by no fewer than forty-five people. One bed may have sufficed for an entire household, with younger children sleeping on makeshift truckle beds stowed beneath. A table and a few chairs served as parlor, dining room, and wardrobe. Every corner would contain something of use, from brooms, pots, and buckets to sacks of onions and coal. Social campaigners worried about the impact that such living conditions had on the morals and sense of decency of the hardworking artisan class. Parents, children, siblings, and members of the extended family dressed, washed, engaged in sex, and, if no "adjacent conveniences" were available, defecated in full view of one another. As one family member prepared a meal, a sick child with a raging fever might be vomiting into a chamber pot beside them, while a parent or sibling stood by half-naked, changing their clothes. Husbands and wives made future children while lying beside present ones. Little about the human condition in its most basic form could be concealed.

Even at a rent of four shillings a week, these buildings had little to recommend them. Tenants might expect damp interiors, soot-blackened ceilings with peeling plaster, rotting floorboards, and broken or ill-fitting windows with gaps that allowed in the rain and wind. Blocked chimneys blew smoke back into the rooms and contributed to a host of respiratory illnesses. The internal corridors and stairwells were not much better; some were positively hazardous. One such building was described as having "a handrail broken away" and the stairs no better, "a heavy boot has been clean through one of them already, and it would need very little . . . for the whole lot to give way and fall with a crash."[4]

However, what concerned the inhabitants most frequently was not the crowded living conditions or the ramshackle buildings, but rather access to clean water, sufficient drainage, and fresh air. The city's little courts suffered the worst, and inspectors regularly found that only one source of water served a number of households. Almost all of the barrels were tainted by "a filthy accumulation on the surface." In some cases, residents had to use "refuse water," gathered from stationary pools that stank in the summer, for cooking and cleaning. Many of these buildings lacked cesspools, so the contents of emptied chamber pots "ran into the courts or streets where they remained until a shower of rain washed them into the gutters."[5] Unsurprisingly, deadly outbreaks of cholera, typhus, and what medical inspectors described broadly as "fever" were rife, especially in the warmer months.

As the capital's laboring classes knew too well, filthy, overpopulated dwellings made a comfortable home for nothing but disease. Smoke-filled rooms, as well as London's noxious yellow "fogs," further impacted the health of the overworked and undernourished. Polly was to learn of this even before she had reached her seventh birthday. In the spring of 1852, her mother began to sicken. At first, Caroline would display the symptoms of what appeared to be the flu, but the cough she developed would grow worse. As the tuberculosis, which had settled in her lungs, gradually began to consume them, her dreadful hacking became blood-laced. Feverish, thin, and weary, Caroline continued to waste away until November 25.

At her death, she left behind a widower and three children; the youngest of whom, Frederick, had not yet passed his third birthday. At a time when workingmen were not expected to undertake the sole care of small children, it is a testament to Edward Walker's affection for his family that he persisted in doing so. Rather than leave his sons and daughter with relations or even at the local workhouse (a not uncommon eventuality), Walker was determined to give them a home. As he never remarried, it appears that Caroline's elder sister, Mary Webb, may have taken on the task of rearing of the children and tending the hearth.*

At the time of Caroline's demise she did not know that she had communicated her illness to her son Frederick, nor endangered her children by her constant close proximity to them. Little about the pathology of tuberculosis would be understood until the end of the nineteenth century. The disease, spread via airborne particles over a period of regular exposure, remained one of the Victorian era's greatest killers, especially within family groups. Women, who assumed the burden of nursing their ailing relations and neighbors, often unwittingly introduced the infection into their own household. Less than eighteen months after his mother's death, Frederick too began to sicken. Sensing that the boy would not live, Edward and Mary had him baptized on March 14, 1854. A month later, Frederick was laid to rest alongside his mother at St. Andrew's Church, in Holborn.

Despite the support of her aunt or other female relations, Polly had to grow up quickly. According to commentators of the era, the daughter of a bereaved husband was expected "to be a comfort to her widowed father" and "to keep his house and take care of his family." In the absence of her mother, Polly's first duty, even above acquiring an

---

* Following Caroline's death, a Mary, along with Edward, is cited in Frederick's baptismal record as being his "parent." It is also possible that Edward, as a widower, may have formed a temporary relationship with another woman of this name, though he was not known to have any further children, nor is there any record to indicate that he lived with another woman.

education, was to the home, whether she herself wished to fulfill the role of the "woman of the house" or not. This expectation also would exclude her from seeking full-time employment, especially in domestic service, with its requirement that she live elsewhere.[6] Certainly by the age of nine, Polly had mastered the basic skills necessary to keep house and cook meals for the family. Much as convention dictated, she apparently remained beneath her father's roof throughout her teenage years, rather than take work eventually as a servant, as girls of her age and class regularly did. Edward Walker's wages covered the expenses of his reduced household, so Polly's days were divided between her household duties and the luxury of prolonged schooling into her teenage years.

It seems that misfortune fostered a strong bond between Polly and her father, one that endured for most of her life. While Polly was expected to assume the physical burden of her mother's former role in the home, Victorian society also looked to the widower's daughter to provide her father with the emotional support he now lacked. The era's literature regularly depicted the daughters of bereaved men as paragons of selfless devotion: perfectly behaved, devoid of childish cares, resourceful, gentle, and innocent. Charles Dickens's Florence Dombey, of *Dombey and Son,* a story written the year after Polly's birth, was one such irreproachable character. Having lost her mother, Florence strove successfully to win and secure her widowed father's love through her moral strength and self-sacrifice. In the case of Polly and Edward Walker, evidently the devotion and moral strength were equally distributed between the two.

For most of her life, Polly rarely strayed far from her father, even in her choice of spouse. In 1861, nineteen-year-old William Nichols was living in a men's lodging house at 30–31 Bouverie Street and working as a warehouseman, most likely in the printing trade. Nichols was the son of a herald painter. By tradition, this type of artisan applied coats of arms to carriages and signs; over the course of the nineteenth century, herald painters moved into printing stationery and bookplates. At some time prior to the spring of 1861, William had set out from his birthplace in Oxford to begin a career as a printer. Bouverie Street placed him directly at the heart of the scene. No fewer than seven magazines and newspapers had offices between numbers 10 and 25, including the *Daily News,* once edited by Dickens, and *Punch* magazine, cofounded by the journalist and social reformer Henry Mayhew. The London chronicled by both of these writers was the London of William Nichols and the Walkers. Mayhew, like Dickens, had experienced debt and poverty, had known the precariousness of life along with much of the area's print fraternity. The world of "Grub Street," as the area had been called since the seventeenth century, was comprised of a close community of men from a variety of backgrounds who scribbled, read, produced, and sold text, who drank together, borrowed money from one another, and married into one another's families.

In this Dickensian story, the motherless blacksmith's daughter, who dutifully kept house for her father and elder brother, met William Nichols, a young man with a broad, sunny face and light hair. Aware that he needed to ingratiate himself to the two male guardians of this small, dark-haired, brown-eyed young woman, William would have carefully sought their friendship and approval. And he succeeded. Shortly before Christmas in 1863, a marriage proposal was made and accepted. The banns were read, and on January 16, 1864, eighteen-year-old Polly and her beau were married at St. Bride's, also known as "the Printer's Church." William proudly entered that precise profession as his on the register.

Polly and William's marriage brought change to everyone in the family. Polly's father and brother, who had come to rely on her, had to welcome another man into their household, with the full understanding that a succession of children would likely follow. The newly expanded Walker-Nichols clan moved to lodgings at 17 Kirby Street, situated in the down-at-heel area known as Saffron Hill, just north of High Holborn. As two households living as one, they would have sought two, if not three, separate rooms, so that the married couple might enjoy some degree of privacy. However, the building on Kirby Street, with three floors each occupied by one family, would not be much of an improvement.

Much as anticipated, three months after the nuptials, Polly was expecting the couple's first child. On December 17, 1864, the cries of William Edward Walker Nichols filled the rooms of 17 Kirby Street.[7] By the autumn of 1865, Mrs. Nichols was pregnant once more, and the need for larger accommodation grew as obvious as her maternal belly.

By the 1860s a working-class family's budget would have been better spent living south of the Thames in Southwark, Bermondsey, Lambeth, Walworth, or Camberwell than it would have near Fleet Street in the areas of Holborn and Clerkenwell. For four to five shillings a week, one might rent a small house, with three to four rooms and possibly a yard at the back. However, the quality of the housing south of the river was not entirely superior to that of the north, nor would it be an economical choice unless equally well-paid work could be procured close by. By the summer of 1866, the Walker-Nichols household went to Walworth, the part of London where Polly's father, Edward Walker, had spent his youth. The family, now six in number, took a house at 131 Trafalgar Street, on what was described as "a terrace of two-story brick cottages." Although the road and its dwellings had been constructed relatively recently, shortly after 1805, they had not weathered the passage of sixty years especially well. The insatiable demand for affordable housing meant that homes once designed for the Georgian middle classes were now, in the Victorian era, divided up and occupied by multiple households. William and Polly's neighbors were carpenters, machinists, shopkeepers, and warehousemen whose large families lived in homes only marginally more spacious than those she would have known in Holborn. The Walker-Nicholses, with three male wage earners — Polly's husband, brother, and father — were more fortunate than many. They could afford to inhabit all four rooms of their house. However, this situation was not to last.

In the Victorian working-class household, a family's level of comfort rose and fell like the tide with each birth or death. As the Nicholses' brood of children expanded, their means of supporting themselves would be stretched. Infants arrived and, tragically, departed at intervals. Polly and William's eldest child failed to live more than a year and nine months, but the family was soon joined by others. Edward John was the first child to be born at the home on Trafalgar Street, on

July 4, 1866. He was followed two years later by George Percy, on July 18, and by Alice Esther in December 1870. Shortly after the birth of this daughter, Polly's brother left home to begin a family of his own. The loss of Edward's financial contribution, and the addition of another mouth to feed, tightened the household's purse strings and caused the Nicholses to fret about their future prospects.

THE PEABODY WORTHIES

IN JANUARY 1862, it was difficult to be an American in London. Only a few months earlier, the Civil War had erupted in the United States, dividing the country into the Union and the Confederacy. In the drawing rooms of Mayfair, London's small expat community of Yankees and Southerners underwent a similar split. To complicate matters, recently, in November 1861, the Union navy had forcibly boarded a British ship, the *Trent,* in order to apprehend Southern envoys traveling to London. Parliament, the press, and the newspaper-reading public were up in arms at the Union's flagrant act of aggression. As Virginia businessmen based in Grosvenor Square broke off their friendships with New York investors and as Londoners cursed the name of Abraham Lincoln, the American financier George Peabody sat in his Broad Street office, despairing. Shortly before the *Trent* affair, Peabody had intended to make a generous philanthropic gift to his adoptive city's "poor and needy . . . to promote their comfort and happiness."[1] A variety of possibilities had been discussed — a donation to charity schools or an investment in municipal drinking fountains — but Peabody wished to directly address what he felt to be the most pressing concern among the working classes: housing.

Peabody himself had come from humble beginnings; he had worked his way up from an apprenticeship at a Massachusetts dry goods store to ownership of an international import and export business. In 1838, he moved his headquarters to London and eventually expanded into banking. Upon his retirement, in 1864, control of his merchant banking firm, Peabody & Co., was assumed by his partner, J. S. Morgan, of the Morgan family of bankers. As Peabody neither married nor had legitimate children, he wished to bequeath his own considerable fortune to good works and alighted on the idea of creating a number of low-cost dwellings for London's laboring families. Preparations were being made to announce his gift of £150,000 in the newspapers when the *Trent* affair so soured relations between the United States and the UK that Peabody feared his donation might be rebuffed.

In his founding letter, George Peabody made only a handful of stipulations as to who should benefit by his new model of social housing. He required that in addition to being a Londoner "by birth or residence," "the individual should be poor, have moral character, and be a good member of society." "No one," he further stated, "should be excluded on the grounds of religious belief or political bias." The Peabody Buildings would offer housing for all.

After several anxious months, Peabody finally disclosed his intentions to the press on March 26, 1862, and work began on the first block of Peabody Buildings, to be situated on Commercial Street in Spitalfields. Ultimately, George Peabody's gift of £150,000 grew to £500,000, a sum worth roughly $60 million today. His generosity humbled the British public, helped heal a rift in Anglo-American relations, and prompted a personal letter of gratitude from Queen Victoria. It also would eventually help over thirty thousand Londoners out of the slums.

The Peabody trustees received more than one hundred applications for the fifty-seven available apartments before the Commercial Street block was opened in 1864. Much as George Peabody had imagined, demand was intense. More sites were acquired and ground broken for further tenement blocks in Islington, Shadwell, Westminster, and Chelsea. In 1874, work began on a site in Lambeth, off Stamford Street, just adjacent to the large print works owned by William Clowes and Sons.

Because Peabody's aim was to promote the health, happiness, and moral well-being of the working classes, he intended that his tenements should offer accommodation superior to anything otherwise available to the laboring population. Unlike the moldering ceilings and verminous interiors of most housing for artisans, the Peabody Buildings were built from brick, with board floors and white cement walls. At Stamford Street, the four-story blocks, consisting of one-, two-, three-, and four-room gaslit apartments, were arranged around a courtyard and boasted modern conveniences. "There are several cupboards, one in the kitchen having over it a meat safe, with doors of perforated zinc. In the passage outside is a coal-bin of neat and ingenious construction, capable of holding half a ton," wrote the *Daily News* of Stamford Street's neighboring development on Southwark Street. In the multiroom tenements, one room was "fitted up for a kitchen . . . with a range in it, an oven, boiler, etc."[2] Stamford Street even provided residents with picture rails, "to avoid the necessity of driving nails into the walls." With a central room designated for cooking, eating, and living, family members could enjoy the privacy afforded by separate bedrooms, or might even choose to use a room as a parlor.[3] Although middle-class journalists often remarked on the smallness of the rooms, which ranged from "14 or 15 feet long by 11 to 12 feet wide," these dimensions offered a considerable improvement on the living space that most of the residents had contended with in slum dwellings.

Hygiene factored significantly into the design of George Peabody's tenements, especially at Stamford Street, where "closets" (indoor toilets) as well as "water sinks" were installed in the corridors, each to be shared by two apartments. The ground floor of each block also contained "a spacious bath"; its gas-heated water was provided "at the expense of the trustees." The tenants could enjoy access to this facility "free of charge and as often as they please, there being no other necessary preliminary than that of calling at the superintendent's office for the key." As one journalist reported, the residents "will have no excuse for not keeping themselves and their clothes thoroughly clean," especially as an extensive laundry room was provided in the attic, which was at least one block in length in each development. At Stamford Street, this space included not only "tubs with water taps . . . and three large coppers for boiling" but also a tiled room with "8 large light windows" designated for clothes drying.[4] It was believed that residents of the Peabody Buildings, inspired by their well-scrubbed bodies and fresh-smelling clothes, would maintain their healthful surroundings by decorating their apartments with wallpaper and whitewash and by keeping them tidy and free of filth. To this end, Cubitt and Co., the architects of the Lambeth development, patented a waste disposal system consisting of a shaft that ran through the center of each building. There, residents could dispose of their rubbish, which was captured in a hopper below. This system was necessary to preserve standards of health, wrote the *Circle,* particularly "when considering the very large number of persons who will all be living upon the same premises."

Wishing to secure the best possible outcome for their social experiment, the Peabody trustees took pains to ensure that only the "most deserving of the working poor" — those with the appropriate moral character as well as the means to meet the weekly cost of their rent — were admitted as residents. The screening process was rigorous. All male heads of household had to produce a letter of character from their employers in order to demonstrate that their jobs were not only relatively secure but that "there was nothing in [their] conduct . . . to disqualify [them] from partaking in the benefits of the fund."[5] The trustees then visited an applicant's home. Anyone who was found to be a "habitual drunkard" or had been entangled with the law was disqualified. Equally, those judged to have too comfortable an income or a family too large for the accommodations were also refused. Finally, to gain admission, each household member needed to provide proof of inoculation against smallpox.

In 1876, the Nichols family was judged to be an ideal match for the Peabody Buildings on Stamford Street. When the trustees called upon them at their home on Trafalgar Street, they would have found William, Polly, and their three children washed and dressed in their Sunday best, their rooms swept and tidy. There was no indication of low morals or alcoholism, and William's employer, the printing house of William Clowes and Sons, which lay just opposite the gates of the Stamford Street estate, endorsed him as an industrious family man.

As one of the trustees' aims was to provide housing for residents convenient to their places of work, it is likely that the firm directed its employees' attention to the Peabody scheme. William Clowes and Sons was a formidable operation by the time William Nichols began drawing his salary of thirty shillings a week. Its Duke Street premises contained six composition rooms, where type was assembled, and no fewer than twenty-five steam-driven printing machines, which Nichols assisted in operating. By the middle of the century, the company employed over six hundred members of staff and was engaged in printing some of the era's most memorable books, including many works of Dickens, who until his death in 1870 used to come to Duke Street to correct his proofs. Like its staff members, the company prided itself on its reputation as a trustworthy and respectable business. Even its compositors insisted on wearing top hats and starched collars to work until the end of the nineteenth century.

After spending most of her life in ramshackle dwellings, Polly must have been thrilled at the prospect of making a home in the clean, modern rooms on Stamford Street. To have a proper stove on which to cook, a working indoor toilet, and a place to dry laundry where it didn't gather soot or the scent of smoke would seem a luxury. The children would have a separate bedroom, and the married couple might even enjoy some occasional privacy. Just as the Peabody trustees had hoped, William's home was no more than a few minutes from his workplace, enabling him to return for dinner with his family. Work, community, family, health, industry, and moral well-being would all come together as the era's social reformers intended.

On July 31, 1876, the Nicholses took up residence on the second floor of D block, at number 3. For the first time in her life, Polly would not be sharing a home with her father. Edward Walker had gone to live with his son, also named Edward, and his young family on nearby Guildford Street. The new apartment, with its four rooms and abundant space, would be occupied exclusively by Polly, her husband, and their children.

The six shillings and eight pence the Nicholses paid in weekly rent allowed them to experience a remarkably innovative living environment. Unlike the managers of the privately operated slum dwellings they had known, at Stamford Street, the superintendent and porters enforced regulations concerning cleanliness and order. Tenants were charged with keeping communal spaces clean; the corridors, steps, and "closets" were to be swept every day before ten o'clock and washed every Saturday. Children were allowed to play outside in the courtyard but were forbidden to make a ruckus on the stairs, in the passageways, or in the laundry. Residents could not sublet their apartments nor open a shop on the premises. Women were barred from "taking in laundry" to make a few extra shillings from the tubs and basins on the attic floors. Should tenants break the rules, they were threatened with "being turned out."[6] However, in many cases, it seems some regulations were very loosely applied. When a journalist from the *Telegraph* came to visit the Stamford Street buildings, he reported children "playing at hide and seek along the passages." He commented on their cheerfulness and that in spite of being "poorly clad . . . most of them were clean and tidy and had their hair nicely arranged." The superintendent remarked to the reporter that most families new to the buildings arrived with bad habits acquired as a result of slum living. But they soon learned that dirty windows and barefoot children incurred the disapproval of fellow Peabody residents. "Poor people like to be as good as their neighbours," he stated. Another visitor noticed "flowers in the windows and bright, happy faces looking from them." Neither were there any "quarrelling or fighting children, no drunken women, or discouraged looking men."[7] Stamford Street's superintendent credited this to the buildings' distance from public houses; it kept women at home, tending to their responsibilities. "Most husbands," he said, were pleased to think that their wives would not be "gossiping about from court to court" after a few glasses of beer, "but minding the children and keeping the place clean."[8]

But gossip they did, as well as occasionally flout the rules, and lead lives that were no more or less complicated than if they had inhabited lodgings on the opposite side of the buildings' gates. The Nicholses' neighbors in D block hailed from a number of different professions and circumstances. Among those who shared their building were railway porters, packers, policemen, widows, laborers, warehousemen, charwomen (day servants doing general housework), carpenters, and numerous employees of William Clowes and Sons. The three children of Cornealus Ring, who lived next door at number 2, would have run and tumbled with the Nicholses' own brood. Having lost his wife in childbirth, Cornealus had asked his sister to look after the family, including a three-month-old infant. At number 9, William Hatch's family continued to grow. The six children placed the family at the outer limit of occupants allowed by the Peabody Buildings; however, Hatch's bachelor brother, Arthur, who lived next door at number 8, took in the overflow. Polly and the other women would have kindly kept an eye on the building's widows: Anne Freeman at number 7, Emona Blower with her two children next door in 4, and Eliza Merritt, who had a pension (perhaps unbeknownst to her neighbors) of sixty-five pounds per year, in number 1.[9]

This close community, who shared walls and water closets, who would have whispered over the mangles in the laundry rooms, bred no small amount of drama. The records of the Peabody Buildings tell tales of hopes and losses, of love and ruin, and the characters who made their homes beside the Nichols family. Walter Duthie was a Scottish railway porter, but his wife, Jane, had been born in Ambala, India. The Gaytons at number 10 aspired to a better life. While Henry Gayton worked as a picture packer, he also began a side business as an art dealer, eventually saving enough money to immigrate with his family to Australia. In 1877, Polly and her neighbors would have discussed poor John Sharpe, who had not only lost his wife but his two children to illness. Sharpe had been made to leave number 6 and move to number 8, a single room. Devastated by his misfortune, he was unable to manage. By September, the superintendent was forced to turn out the grieving widower for his "dirtiness." There were celebrations and love stories too. Jane Rowan, a widow with four children who worked as a laundress, was about to move to the buildings in Southwark when another resident, Patrick Madden, asked her to marry him.[10] Then there were the secrets, the acts that occurred behind closed doors or in snatched moments, which were never noted in the superintendent's record book.

Sarah Vidler was one of the many widows who successfully secured a place for her family in the Stamford Street buildings. On April 19, 1875, she and four of her five children — eleven-year-old Sarah Louise, fourteen-year-old Jane, and sixteen-year-old William, moved into number 5, in D block, along with her eldest daughter, twenty-one-year-old Rosetta. Rosetta's situation was not a happy one. The year before, on January 4, she had married a ship's cook called Thomas Woolls (or Walls). The date of the wedding may have anticipated her husband's next job, aboard the *Russia,* a screw steamer that would sail from Glasgow on February 2.[11] Undoubtedly, Woolls assured his new bride that their separation was to be only temporary, and for a time the couple would have lived together for the short weeks or months when he was in port. However, Thomas's absences gradually grew longer, and the pair drifted apart.

Rosetta's separation from her husband left her in a difficult position. While she was still legally bound to Woolls, she could not remarry. She remained a dependent in her mother's household, both of them taking employment as charwomen, the most poorly paid and worst regarded of all service occupations. Rosetta accepted whatever work became available, so when her neighbor Polly Nichols required assistance around the time of the birth of a new son, in December 1878, Rosetta was in no position to refuse.

The summer before, the Nicholses had found it financially expedient to exchange their four-room tenement for three rooms, and they moved into apartment number 6, next door to Sarah Vidler and her family. At the time, Polly was about four months pregnant with Henry Alfred, the child who would become her fifth.* At the end of 1876 she had given birth to Eliza Sarah, whose arrival likely prompted this domestic belt-tightening.†

Three rooms, four children, and another on the way would have made the home environment busier and more hectic, though the Vidler girls, who were old enough to assist with the Nicholses' smaller

---

* Henry Alfred would be her fifth child to survive.
† It has been suggested that Eliza Sarah was born in 3 J block, but this is a misreading of the faded handwritten script on her birth certificate, which reads 3 D block.

children, would have lent a hand when required. The two families appeared to have got on well together; Sarah's son, William, secured a position as a porter at W. Clowes and Sons, while her two girls took on book-folding work, possibly on the recommendation of William Nichols. The internal adjoining doors of apartments 5 and 6, as well as the shared water closet, would foster a strong sense of intimacy between the two families, who would have been regularly in and out of each other's homes, with hardly an inch of space between each other's business.

It is impossible to know when the arguments began between Polly and William Nichols, or what precisely lay at the heart of their initial difficulties. Their closer quarters, larger family, and greater financial pressures may have played some role. As with any domestic dispute, there are at least two sides to the story. William later asserted that their disagreements arose because of his wife's sudden affinity for drink. Yet any change in Polly's habits could not be as dramatic as William implied. If such was true, it would have come to the attention of the superintendent and been noted in the family's records. Steps would have been taken to remove the Nicholses, as had been the case for other tenants who developed a drinking problem. Later, Edward Walker, Polly's father, offered another explanation: he claimed that William, his son-in-law, had begun an affair with Rosetta Walls.

Walker would have heard these accusations from his daughter, who, it seemed, had begun to make regular appearances at the house on Guildford Street that he shared with his son. Polly did so to escape her increasingly toxic home environment. In the wake of the birth of Henry Alfred on December 4, 1878, the couple's disagreements had escalated; each of their shouted grievances shared through the wall with the Vidlers, scarcely a room away.

Perhaps jealousy and suspicion, rather than firm evidence of an affair, motivated Polly. She may have seen a warmth growing between her husband and the younger, curly-haired, blue-eyed woman next door. With four children and a newborn to rear, Polly would be exhausted, and possibly suffering from postnatal depression. Perhaps her new affinity for the bottle was not simply William's invention, but rather a means of coping with her feelings of estrangement from her husband.

It will never be known what Polly witnessed transpire between her own husband and Rosetta — or indeed if she saw anything at all. Awake in the middle of the night, cogitating on the woman who slept on the opposite side of the wall, she may have found it difficult to interpret a fleeting touch, a look, or an affectionate word. Whatever the case, whatever suspicions Polly may have harbored, the Nichols family's physical proximity to the Vidlers meant that Rosetta's presence would have been constant and therefore a perpetual source of agitation and concern to Polly. Even the sound of Rosetta's voice, whether echoing from the corridor or the rooms adjacent to their own apartment, would have been inescapable. Whomever Polly blamed for her woes, whether it was her husband or her neighbor, she could never have entirely escaped the reminder of them.

Daily, the couple's rows and accusations increased. William would later claim that between the birth in December 1878 and the first few months of 1880, Polly stormed out of their home "perhaps five or six times," to land herself on her father's doorstep. According to Edward Walker, by then Polly's husband "had turned nasty."

This level of disruption could not continue. Polly's father or her brother would remind her of her duty to her five children, one of whom was still a tiny infant. There was no room for her at Guildford Street. She would have to return to her family, and she and William would have to work out their problems.

But they couldn't. Polly would limp back to Stamford Street, and another round of angry confrontation would begin.

That which must have dawned upon her one day was a simple fact; Rosetta Walls could not be removed from their lives. So long as the two families lived beside each other, so long as they inhabited D block, so long as they continued to reside in the Stamford Street Peabody Buildings, Rosetta would be there. To Polly it must have seemed that William had made his choice, and now she had to make hers.

On March 29, 1880, the day after Easter, Polly finally tired of arguing. Whether she had made plans to depart on that day or whether anger had suddenly pushed her to it, Polly Nichols decisively turned her back on her family home. She walked through the gates of the Peabody Buildings, never to return, leaving behind the life she had known and handing her children over to their father, the only person able to support them.

AN IRREGULAR LIFE

O N JULY 31, 1883, the couple at 164 Neate Street, with their five children, attired themselves in their Sunday best. "Mrs. Nichols," as her neighbors called her, fastened the little ones' buttons and adjusted their uneven ribbons. She had learned over the years which of the children sat still and which had to be coaxed into good behavior. She knew which were most likely to cry and how to soothe them when they did. It was she who cooked their dinners and mended their clothes. It was she who assumed the role of mother, and she who would have felt entitled to lead the children around the corner to the church on Coburg Road. As she did so, she proudly carried in her arms little Arthur, not quite three weeks old, wearing his white christening gown. He was the first child to be born to William and Rosetta Nichols, at the house they had taken almost exactly one year ago to the day. It is unlikely the neighbors or shopkeepers or even the clergyman who performed the rite of baptism guessed at their true circumstances. Instead, they stood before the font with their newborn between them and witnessed his acceptance into the Church of England. On that day too, five-year-old Henry Alfred, Polly's youngest, was also christened, his name entered beside those of his "Christian parents," William and Rosetta, on the parish register.[1]

The comfortable domestic arrangement that the couple enjoyed was not one that would have been open to them had they wished to remain at the Peabody Buildings. A decision had to be made as to their future together and what they were willing to risk in order to secure it. Although living in adjoining apartments was convenient, ultimately, it would not have been an ideal situation for a man and a woman in love, who wished to share a home and a bed, despite being married to other people. If both the Nicholses and the Vidlers were aware of the affection that existed between the couple, then it would not be long before their neighbors discovered it too and word would find its way to the superintendent. "Irregular unions," the term for couples who lived together without benefit of marriage or who carried on extramarital relationships, went against the strict regulations of the Peabody Buildings. The Stamford Street ledgers document many such situations; invariably, when they were discovered, the tenants involved were ejected. In 1877, two of the Nicholses' neighbors, George Henry Hope and Fanny Hudson, were asked to leave after both had parted with their spouses. Arthur Scriven in K block lost his housing because he had been "living apart from his wife with another woman," while Mary Ann Thorne had been ejected for being "a widow who gave birth to a child." While William and Rosetta pursued their relationship, they were gambling with the reputation and the secure living circumstances of both the Nicholses and the Vidlers. In the meantime, how William explained Polly's absence to the Peabody authorities, who were bound to have noticed it, is anyone's guess.

According to her own account of events, when Polly left 6 D block in March 1880, she went directly to Lambeth Union Workhouse on Renfrew Road.[2] However, it's far more likely that she first went to the house where her father and brother lived. One who had never before passed through the gates of a workhouse would do so only with extreme reticence and after all possible alternatives had been exhausted.

It is difficult to paint an accurate picture of the Victorian working-class experience without the foreboding and ever-present shadow cast by the austere brick edifice of the workhouse. In 1834 the Poor Law Amendment Act sought to bring an end to what the government saw as the abuse of the system of charitable relief offered, up to that time, by local parishes. The poor were judged to be lazy and immoral paupers who refused to do honest work and bred bastards and enormous families while "living off handouts." Now the government wished to compel the indigent to lead moral, hardworking lives by reducing what was called "outdoor relief," or charity that was paid to impoverished families while they inhabited their own lodgings. Rather than giving them the opportunity to drink away parish funds or indulge in illicit sexual behavior that led to more illegitimate children, a new system of highly regulated "indoor relief" was to be meted out inside the workhouse. It had two main goals: to regulate the lives of the poor by forcing them to earn a meager sustenance within the filth-ridden workhouse walls and ultimately to frighten them into leading upstanding, industrious lives outside, in the community.

One of the workhouse's primary functions was to humiliate those who were forced to rely upon it. Regardless of their circumstances, the old, infirm, the sick and abandoned, the able-bodied but unlucky were treated with equal disdain. If the head of a household lost his income, he and all of his dependents had to join him under the workhouse roof. Upon entering, families were divided by gender and made to live in separate wings. Young children were allowed to remain with their mothers, but those over age seven were placed in the workhouse school and isolated from their parents. All new inmates were stripped of their clothing and whatever personal belongings they possessed. They were then required to enter a communal bath and scrub themselves in water that had been used by every other person who had gained admission that day. Following this, much like prisoners, inmates were clothed in a functional workhouse uniform, which never truly belonged to them. Their diet was basic: watery porridge known as skilly, as well as small portions of poor-quality bread, cheese, and potatoes, and occasionally meat. Though minor improvements were made to the workhouse diet later in the century, by 1890, complaints about the need to pick rat droppings out of the skilly were still being heard.[3]

At the workhouse, no able-bodied person received anything for free. Both men and women were assigned work considered gender-appropriate. Men were generally tasked with stone-breaking (creating aggregate for making roads), pumping water, milling corn, chopping wood, or picking oakum. This latter activity was also often assigned to women. It involved using a spike and bare hands to pull apart old ships' ropes, so that the fibers could be mixed with tar and used to caulk ships. Other tasks deemed suitable for female inmates included cleaning, working in the laundry, and preparing food. Life inside the workhouse entailed constant hunger, frequent illness, and poor sleep in a dormitory of pallet beds. Violence, including brutal coercion by staff, was common. Poor sanitation, restricted access to water, and exposure to vermin and contaminated food ensured that inmates suffered regularly from diarrhea and infections, which could spread quickly.

Conditions inside the workhouse were well known among those who gazed at its walls from the outside. The Poor Law Board of Guardians, who administered the system, wanted it that way. Just as the guardians had hoped, self-respecting working-class families came to pride themselves on avoiding indoor relief, crediting themselves with resourcefulness as they looked down on those who apparently lacked it. Within laboring communities, the social stigma of time spent at the workhouse was so great that many would rather beg, sleep rough, or become a prostitute than place themselves at the mercy of this institution. Neighbors rarely forgot those who had been tarred by misfortune, and many families continued to suffer the humiliation that followed a stay in the workhouse long after they had departed.

All her life, Polly would have feared the workhouse, and heard it reviled. Both the Walkers and the Nicholses were hardworking families who could hold up their heads, knowing that they earned a respectable living. Winning a place in the Peabody Buildings would have made them proud of their status and even more likely to look down their nose at those whose lack of industry or moral vice led them into the yard of Renfrew Road or Prince's Road. However, in an era when divorce was an option only for those who could afford the exorbitant court fees, a working-class wife who wished to "officially" separate from her husband had to first demonstrate her desperation and destitution. Entering the workhouse was the only means of achieving this. Nonetheless, it would have cost Polly dearly. Many wives in similar circumstances described it as "the most humiliating experience of their lives," which left "a permanent stigma."[4]

In 1880, when Polly turned her back on her husband and walked out of her matrimonial home, she would have understood the consequences. It was an enormously bold step. While separation from a husband was not uncommon among the working class, it spelled the end of a woman's status as a respectable member of that class. Culpability did not matter; according to the moral tenor of the day, even if a woman left her husband for good reason, she had failed. A decent wife was "enduringly, incorruptibly good; instinctively, infallibly wise," and not simply for the sake of "self-development, but for self renunciation." Her duty to her husband was "to never fall from his side."[5] Her responsibility as a mother was likewise fixed: to never forsake or abandon her children. Leaving the familial home rendered her unfit, immoral; a specimen of broken womanhood. In parting with her husband, she was also committing herself to the embrace of poverty and further degradation. Earning a living was barely possible. Traditional women's labor, such as domestic service, laundry work, sewing, or home-assembly piecework, did not yield a livable wage. Unless a woman could take refuge with another male family member, she would hardly be able to support herself.

To a limited extent, the law recognized the situation in which separated working-class women found themselves, though it very reluctantly offered solutions. A wife needed to remain with her family, and the government, parish officials, and the law did not wish to encourage or make it easy for women to leave their marriages. Even if Polly had been able to afford the costs of a divorce, in 1880 a wife could not cite adultery alone as a grounds for ending her union. While a man could divorce his wife for a sexual liaison outside the marital bed, a woman had to prove her husband was guilty of adultery *in addition* to another crime, such as incest, rape, or cruelty. This Victorian double standard was enshrined in law, permitting a man to enjoy as many sexual dalliances as he wished, so long as he did not also rape the servants, have sex with his sister, and beat his wife too severely. Had Polly possessed the means to bring a suit against William, and even if she had been successful in gathering evidence that he was having an affair with Rosetta, she would still lack grounds for divorce. However, by 1878 there was another means by which women could extricate themselves from a marriage that had failed. Under the terms of the Matrimonial Causes Act, if a man had been violently abusive to his wife and had been charged before a magistrate with such crimes, the court would uphold the wife's right to secure a legal separation from him. Fortunately, and yet unfortunately for Polly, William Nichols had done no such thing.

The reality was that most working-class women who wished to end their marriages had no other choice but to attempt to secure a type of unofficial separation with the assistance of the workhouse by claiming they had been deserted by their spouse. According to the Poor Law, a man could not simply turn his wife or children over to the workhouse and expect the ratepayer to foot the bill for their maintenance. Just as a woman had the duty to remain with her family, so the law viewed the husband as responsible for her upkeep, whether or not both spouses lived at the same address. If an able-bodied man refused to pay for his wife's maintenance, the Poor Law guardians would seek to recover the costs. They would bill him for the expenses, and if the delinquent husband did not discharge his obligation, he would suffer the indignity of being dragged before the magistrate. This rule was the working-class woman's only friend — up to a point. Workhouses were wary of becoming an instrument to domestic breakdown. Guardians were taught to be skeptical about women who turned up at the workhouse gates claiming "desertion." "Continual quarrelling," claimed the 1876 *Handy Book for Guardians of the Poor*, "the root of which is almost invariably drink on both sides," was "most common among these cases of desertion." A thorough investigation into such a woman's circumstances was required before she could be viewed with any sympathy.

Polly would have learned, somehow, what was required in order to initiate this type of unofficial separation from William. Only then would she venture to the workhouse, planning to make her stay there as brief as possible.

As part of the admission process, Polly would undergo a verbal "examination" by one of the relieving officers. These officials determined what type of assistance the applicant was worthy of: indoor or outdoor relief. Polly likely endured an intimidating and censorious inquisition. She would have stood, in her drab uniform and cotton cap, before this man and been told to account for herself. She would have been asked to provide her complete name and her age, as well as information about where she had been living, her marital status, the number of children she had, and who supported her, along with details of his occupation and wages. She would be asked if she had ever received outdoor relief, had ever been inside the workhouse, had any savings, or had ever been convicted of a crime. The legitimacy of her children would be questioned. Finally, she would report whether "she has any relatives who are legally bound to support . . . her, and whether such relatives were able to support her."[6] Here, the particulars of her separation from her husband would be probed. In Polly's case, the relieving officer was Thomas Taverner. He scribbled down these details with the intention of interviewing William Nichols.

Mr. Taverner, who rode about town in his own private coach, was noted for conducting business according to his own methods. William Nichols may have been summoned to the workhouse or the relieving officer may have taken the liberty of paying him a visit. However it came about, whether in front of his fellow employees, his neighbors, or inside the gates of the workhouse, Nichols would have found this meeting to be a mortifying experience. When questioned, Polly's husband was certain to have asserted what he would always claim: that his marital breakdown was due to his wife's drinking. Thomas Taverner, however, was not convinced by this story. Had William's account been entirely true, Taverner would not have ultimately made the decision to allow Polly to receive outdoor relief rather than enter the workhouse. As the guardians' handbook suggested, "Whenever it is found that a deserted wife is known to drink . . . out-door relief should not be given, but the workhouse alone offered."[7] Instead, Mr. Taverner, on behalf of the Poor Law Board of Guardians, awarded Polly Nichols a weekly maintenance of five shillings. Her husband was to pay over this sum, to be collected by Polly in person from Thomas Taverner at the workhouse every week.[8]

Ideally, in such a situation it would be expected or at least hoped that a woman separated from her husband yet receiving a maintenance from him would be taken in by a relative. But, whether through her own choice or as a result of a family disagreement, Polly did not go to live with her father and brother. Instead, she struck out on her own. For a woman who had never before lived independently and who had always been surrounded by male protectors, this new mode of life would have come as a profound shock, both practically and emotionally. If rent for one room in a down-at-heel part of town cost four shillings a week, Polly would have virtually no money on which to subsist, unless she wished to take her chances at an insalubrious lodging house, where a bed might be had at four pence per day. She would also have to find work. While this was not impossible, the employment she was likely to have found would have paid poorly in exchange for seventy to eighty hours per week of grinding, ceaseless, repetitive labor, like that offered in London's many large-scale laundries. Here, women who "worked at the tub" might receive "from 2 to 3 shillings a day," while shirt and collar ironers, who slaved away in overheated rooms, were likely to earn 8 to 15 shillings a week.[9] Polly might instead opt to take on "slopwork," earning six shillings a day for sewing together cheap clothing: trousers, coats, skirts, and waistcoats. She would be paid by the piece and could expect to work from the earliest hours in the morning until late at night, with scarcely a break. Various types of home assembly work, such as making "fancy boxes" or artificial flowers, were also available to women. All of these tasks required nimble hands and speed; a woman might expect to work ten hours a day for as little as 2½ pence per hour.[10] Factory work, which was no better than the other options, tended to favor younger female employees, and cleaning, or "charring," was badly paid, poorly regarded, and demoralizing.

Whichever choice she made, Polly faced a loss of identity and complete isolation in a society that viewed a woman without a family, or a husband, with deep suspicion, or even incomprehension. The sexes had distinctly defined roles, and Polly, like every other female, would have internalized the belief that a woman required a man to guide her, govern her, and bestow meaning on her life. Tennyson explained this in his poem *The Princess:*

Man for the field and woman for the hearth;
Man for the sword and for the needle she;
Man with the head and woman with the heart:
Man to command and woman to obey;
All else confusion.

The "confusion" occasioned by a woman of Polly's age, living apart from her husband and family, would have caused people to have concluded one thing alone; she was an aberration, a failure, and invariably, where the character of a woman was compromised, sexual immorality was also assumed. Regardless of whether or not she could support herself with laundry work or charring, the concept of a woman of childbearing age living and enjoying a single life was anathema to the Victorian era, regardless of one's class. Without a man, a woman had no credibility, no protection against the schemes and violence of other men, and no purpose in life. Similarly, a man without a woman had no one to tend to his practical and sexual needs. It was therefore expected that men or women who found themselves alone would attempt to establish themselves in a new relationship as soon as possible. However, what was permissible for the husband was not legally permissible for the wife.

With Polly no longer present, William and Rosetta grew weary of maintaining the pretense that they were not in love, and early in 1882, they found the opportunity to remedy their situation. At some point during the late winter or early spring of that year, Rosetta learned that her legal husband, Thomas Woolls, had immigrated to Australia on February 8.[11] The possibility that Woolls might suddenly reappear and assert his matrimonial rights was no longer a threat, which freed the lovers to set up a home together. They would have weighed their options carefully and calculated the expense. As an unmarried couple, they could not remain in the Peabody Buildings, and finding suitable accommodation elsewhere would increase the pressure on William's finances. The five shillings he was paying to Polly was apt to make a big difference in his ability to afford a fresh start.

It's unlikely that before he set out with the explicit intention of terminating his wife's maintenance payments, William was well-versed enough in the law to know precisely what steps to take. After making inquiries, he would have learned that it was possible to cut Polly's support by demonstrating that she was living with another man. According to the Matrimonial Causes Act, "no order for payment of money by the husband . . . shall be made in favour of a wife who shall be proved to have committed adultery, unless such adultery has been condoned." Magistrates and officials recognized that couples like William and Rosetta might wish to cohabit with other partners (though immorally) following a separation; however, where the separated wife was concerned, this could only occur with the husband's consent.

It is possible that over the years William had become aware that Polly had attached herself to another man. The 1881 census notes a Mary Ann Nichols living with a George Crawshaw in a room at 61 Wellington Road, in Holloway, North London. Crawshaw's occupation is listed as "scavenger" and Mary Ann Nichols's as "laundry work." They both are recorded as being married, though not to each other.* Although she was living across the river from Lambeth, she would have returned there weekly to collect her five shillings and been seen frequently by those who knew her. Gossip would have reached William's ears and now it was in his interest to discover the truth of the matter, a task that was easily enough accomplished with professional assistance.

Newspapers in London regularly featured advertisements placed by "Confidential Inquiry Offices" and "private investigation agents." For a fee, lower or higher depending upon the complexity of the task, these businesses would "discreetly investigate family matters requiring secrecy." Procuring evidence for divorce cases was always listed prominently among their specialties, as was having "suspected persons watched." In order to confirm his suspicions about Polly's living arrangements and wriggle free of a crippling financial obligation, William Nichols hired one such "spy." His agent evidently followed Polly long enough to determine that she was living with another man in a state of adultery. Now, with this confirmation, William promptly refused to hand over Polly's weekly sum and made plans to leave block D with Rosetta.

When Polly went to collect her maintenance, Mr. Taverner would have informed her that William was delinquent in paying it. Eventually, at the behest of the Lambeth Poor Law Union, Nichols was summoned to the magistrate's court to explain himself. He had prepared his answer well in advance. He produced the skillfully gathered evi-

---

* Although this census record cites her age as four years older than she actually was, her place of birth, in the Finsbury Ward of London, accords with someone who claimed she was born near Shoe Lane. Age discrepancies are common on census returns.

dence of his wife's "adultery without consent." According to Edward
Walker, his daughter denied that she was living with another man, but
the judge seemed convinced by the material.[12] He ruled that William
was now absolved of his financial responsibilities to Polly, and on July
28, 1882, William and his paramour packed their belongings, took his
children by the hand, and bid goodbye to the Peabody Buildings on
Stamford Street. The superintendent duly noted in the ledger, at the
time of his departure, that William Nichols had been a "good tenant"
but "left in debt." The words "good tenant" were later struck through.*

It is likely that Polly's defense — that she was not "living in adultery" at the time the case came before the magistrate — was in fact
true. Had she still been living with George Crawshaw, or under the
protection of another partner, she would not have found herself completely destitute, as in fact she did, upon the withdrawal of her allowance. On April 24, 1882, Polly had no choice but to enter Lambeth
Union Workhouse, this time for an indefinite stay. With the exception
of a short period spent in the infirmary in January, she remained there
for exactly eleven months, and discharged herself on March 24, 1883. It
appears she attempted to find her feet, only to return for another stay,
from May 21 until June 2.

Inmates in a workhouse, unlike those in a prison, were free to remove themselves from the care of the Poor Law Union whenever they
chose. However, without an offer of employment or any money at
their disposal, it could prove impossible to extract oneself from the
cycle of poverty. Those who were discharged left with a final meal in
their stomach and some bread. In theory, this meager provision was
to tide them over until they were able to find work and earn enough to
pay for shelter and sustenance. In reality, inmates frequently stepped
from life in the workhouse directly into life on the streets — begging,
prostituting themselves, or stealing in order to earn enough to pay for
food and a night's lodgings. Many others ended up sleeping rough.

On this occasion, it was fortunate that when Polly left the workhouse her father and brother had a home for her. The house at 122

---

* It is possible this strike-through was made after Nichols's private affairs were made public
over the course of the inquest into his wife's death.

Guildford Street, not far from the Peabody Buildings, was already a tight squeeze for Edward, his wife, his five young children, and his father. Whatever obstacles had prevented Polly from living with her family in the past had now been surmounted. Edward Walker later claimed with great emotion that he would have never turned his daughter out so long as he had a roof over his head. Nonetheless, life with his grown child did not always prove easy.

If Polly, in the final throes of her marriage, had acquired a taste for drink to dull her pain, her thirst for this medicine had grown only more acute since her separation. Since alcohol was largely prohibited in the workhouse, her stay there likely staved off dependency, at least for a time. After her discharge Polly was free to resume whatever habits she may have acquired earlier. Although Edward Walker never revealed what sort of work his daughter assumed while she lived with him, he did suggest that she spent a good amount of time in the local public houses. As her brother's family continued to grow, Polly may have wished to escape when she could from her increasingly awkward position at home. Her sense of shame too cannot be overestimated; she had lost her home, her husband, and her dignity. More excruciating still, she had lost her children, and the sight of her nieces and nephews could not fail to serve as a constant reminder of her worthlessness as a mother. Drink offered a way out.

The arguments began. Polly's drunkenness, even if not habitual, could not have contributed to a pleasant domestic environment in a small house. Although Walker insisted that his daughter "did not stay out particularly late" and "was not fast," nor had he "heard of anything improper" happening among the group of "young women and men" that "she used to go with," Polly's behavior at home eventually rendered life impossible.[13] It was said that after one disagreement in 1884, Polly simply decided to leave. "She thought she could better herself," said her father, "so I let her go."[14]

When Polly left the protection of this family home, she likely did so to take up with a man she had met. In March 1884, Thomas Stuart Drew, a blacksmith who lived on neighboring York Street, had been widowed. Now alone, in his late thirties, with three daughters to care for, Thomas found himself in a position identical to that of Edward

Walker when he lost his wife. Thomas's girls needed a mother, and perhaps their situation, so similar to Polly's childhood experience, attracted her to the widower and his family. Thomas apparently offered Walker's daughter a settled home and an opportunity to feel, once more, a sense of usefulness in the roles of wife (though without benefit of marriage) and mother. Although Polly and her father were not on speaking terms, Edward Walker noted that when he saw Polly in June 1886, she appeared respectable in both dress and demeanor.

The solemn occasion on which they met called for such propriety. Earlier that month, at around midnight, Polly's brother and his wife had been sitting in the kitchen, chatting. Just as Mrs. Walker left the room to go to bed, she heard a sudden explosion behind her. When she raced back to the kitchen, she found her husband's hair ablaze; the kerosene lamp he had gone to extinguish had burst into a fiery ball. The couple's screams alerted their lodger, who attempted to put out the flames, but by the time he did so, Edward had suffered third-degree burns to the right side of his face and chest. They rushed him in a cab to Guy's Hospital nearby, at which point he slipped into a coma. By early the following evening, he had died.

For Polly, the shock of her only surviving sibling's death was the first in a series of misfortunes to befall her that year. It is likely no coincidence that her stable relationship with Thomas Drew soon began to falter. If Polly had been able to manage her drinking in her new domestic arrangement, Edward's unexpected demise may have driven her once more to the bottle. Come November, she and Thomas were no more, and by the following month, he had taken another bride; a woman whom he could legitimately marry, and with whom he did not have to live in sin.

The consequences of separation in the nineteenth century were judged by many to be "a living death," for while the law sanctioned a split between a married couple, it never permitted them to move their lives beyond that. Any future relationships would always be considered adulterous, while any children of those unions would always be regarded as illegitimate. With divorce and remarriage an impossibility among the working classes, communities and families were often inclined to turn a blind eye to middle-aged couples who wished to cohabit, but as the social reformer Charles Booth remarked, even this level of toleration had limits. "I do not know exactly how far upwards in the social scale this view of sexual morality extends," he wrote, "but I believe it to constitute one of the clearest lines of demarcation between upper and lower in the working class."[15] For men like Thomas Drew and Edward Walker, proud skilled laborers who earned a respectable wage, this mode of living was ultimately beneath them.

Unfortunately, neither living with a husband nor a common-law spouse was an option for Polly in the autumn of 1886. Without the maintenance William had once paid her, without a home, and without the means of sufficiently supporting herself, she had nowhere left to retreat to but the stony embrace of Lambeth Union Workhouse once more.

"HOUSELESS CREATURE"

BY OCTOBER 1887, autumn had begun to spread its chill over those who passed the night in Trafalgar Square. Some curled up on the benches, while others slumbered on the flagstones, partially covered with yesterday's newspapers in a vain attempt to keep warm. Weary old men and women in ragged, battered bonnets propped themselves against the wall below the National Gallery. Shoeless children rolled themselves into balls in the corners and slept like small dogs. W. T. Stead, the editor of the *Pall Mall Gazette,* walked through the scene in the square one night, shaking his head and scribbling onto his pad. "Four hundred sleepers, men and women, promiscuously side by side, I count in the shadows of the finest hotels in the world."[1] Slumped at the base of a bronze lion or lying with her head against a bench was Polly Nichols, cold and anonymous.

When morning came, the rough sleepers were joined by a steady trickle of the unemployed and the "friends of Socialism." Daily that autumn they gathered in their thousands at the base of Nelson's column. They came with their red flags and banners, singing songs and shouting slogans about workingmen's rights. Speakers mounted a makeshift dais and addressed the assembled to rousing cheers, jeers, or hissing. The poor weather, even the blinding sulfurous fogs that fell like a curtain over the spectacle, failed to discourage the audiences. They came, men and women, the threadbare and the "respectably dressed," in billycock hats and low-slung flat caps, and stood attentively with hunched shoulders and hands in their pockets, or balancing a child on a hip. Among those who gathered in the square with Polly in the last weeks of October was the writer, textile designer, and socialist William Morris, along with several of his associates from the Socialist League, including John Hunter Watts and Thomas Wardle. They came to observe and debate and, in the case of Watts, to take his place at the base of the column in order to pontificate.

The speeches and demonstrations drew curious spectators along with the do-gooders. Some helped with the distribution of bread and coffee to "the homeless creatures" who had made Trafalgar Square their parlor. Others handed out Bibles or tickets to lodging houses, which were already filled to bursting. This congregation of the sympathetic, sensitive to the plight of the poor and downtrodden, provided beggars with a rich harvest. The ranks of police, significantly outnumbered by the crowd, kept an anxious distance — patrolling, listening, watching, and waiting, expecting the scene to explode into violence. This it did, with some regularity. Toward the end of October, the daily marches and processions grew more aggressive. The police were put on notice as speakers in Trafalgar Square hollered threats of violence. Some promised to set the city alight, to smash the windows of fashionable Regent Street, and to storm the Mansion House, the residence of London's Lord Mayor. On their marches, the protesters tried to outfox the police escort that followed them. On October 19, a crowd burst onto the Strand, a major thoroughfare, in an attempt to march toward the City of London, the central financial district. The police pushed them back into the yards around the train station at Charing Cross. Railings collapsed; demonstrators were injured and trampled. The crowd hurled rocks at the officers; some were kicked and beaten. The following day marches set off toward the shops of Bond Street. Terrified shopkeepers rushed to shutter their windows at the approach of "King Mob." On October 25, the procession made it as far as Belgravia, bellowing revolutionary songs at the windows of high society.

Numerous attempts were made to clear the square of its "troublemakers," especially in the wake of these violent events. The commissioner of police used the Vagrancy Act as he took "steps to arrest . . . all rogues and vagabonds throughout the Metropolis who are found wandering or sleeping in the open air at night during the cold weather." Inspector Bullock was on duty during the night of the twenty-fourth when the clearance began. Trafalgar Square had been his beat, and he had come to recognize many of those who bedded down there. At around ten o'clock, a charity worker had turned up, offering bread, coffee, and lodging-house tickets to "170 outcasts" in the square. As the night was looking to be particularly cold, most of those gathered went to the lodging houses listed on the tickets, "but several returned saying they were full."[2] Bullock offered to escort them to the casual ward of the workhouse at St. Giles, where a short stay was allowed in exchange for work, "but many of them said they could not think of going there." The officer then made it clear that he would arrest them if they remained, and sent thirty of them, with two constables, to the workhouse on Macklin Street. En route, eleven of them slipped away down the side streets of Covent Garden. Bullock was not at all surprised when the missing turned up again, "sitting and smoking in the Square, lounging about, and taking part in the scrambles for money thrown down by people passing on the terrace."[3] It was then that he took ten of them — "six women, two girls and two youths" — into custody. Polly Nichols was one of them.

Polly, who had probably taken a few glasses that evening, did not go willingly into the cells. She swore, put up a fight, and "was very disorderly" at the police station. The following morning she was made to account for herself before Mr. Bridges, the magistrate. As the prisoners were marched into the courtroom, a journalist from the *Evening Standard* remarked that they "presented a woeful aspect, being dirty and very ragged." The police judged "Nichols" to be "the worst woman in the square."[4] It was described how she and a group of other women had made a business of begging beneath the terrace that separated the National Gallery from Trafalgar Square. These women waited for "respectable people" to appear, at which point they would "take off their shawls and shake themselves as if they were cold, in order to invite sympathy."[5] As a ruse, this appears to have been successful, or at least profitable enough to buy Polly a drink and a bed at a lodging house, should she wish it. Begging had kept her safely out of the workhouse, though, as she explained it to the judge, she had been reluctant to go to the casual ward "because they were kept there in the morning, and so lost any work they had to go to."[6] This was a doubtful excuse, and the magistrate would have known it. As Polly Nichols had been tramping since May of that year, it's unlikely she had any regular work at all.

It would have been with a heavy and dejected heart that Polly, on November 15, 1886, returned to Lambeth Workhouse. The security she had enjoyed with Thomas Drew had been pulled from under her feet, and she found herself once more in a position similar to what she had known after she parted with William Nichols. However, in this case her future was even less certain as she had lost the entitlement to receive a maintenance from her estranged husband. Into the admissions ledger beside her name was written "no home, calling: nil." Following her brother's death and her rift with her father, she must have felt an acute sense of isolation.

Fortunately for Polly, on this occasion her sojourn at the workhouse was not lengthy. Most workhouses operated schemes designed to prepare girls and young women for jobs in domestic service. Not only did this provide an opportunity for girls who might otherwise have ended up in a life of vice to acquire skills and a source of income, but it also helped to mitigate workhouse expenses; the fewer the inmates, the lower the cost to the local ratepayer. Lambeth Workhouse appears to have extended this practice to include the placement of older women into service. The rationale would have been a similar one, in that it offered women who would otherwise be stuck in a workhouse cycle of poverty, the opportunity to begin their lives anew. As most middle-aged women would have several decades of experience in cooking, cleaning, mending, and looking after children, their skills were easily transferable. They knew how to clean a grate, scrub a floor, nurse a sick infant, and prepare meals. There were plenty of employers willing to overlook the blemished background of a workhouse inmate in order to make use of the free or low-cost labor. To have been selected for such a scheme, Polly would have had to have demonstrated good character from the outset, proving herself worthy for this opportunity through her diligence, compliance, and docility. As there was no alcohol to be had in the workhouse, this was unlikely to have proven too difficult. On December 16, Polly was duly "discharged to service," as the register reads, though where she was employed is unknown.[7]

Regrettably, this placement was not to become a permanent one. Servants and masters were not always compatible and the unspecified circumstance that cost her the position by the following spring may not have been down to a failing on her part. Whatever the situation, it appears that in May 1887, Polly could not bear the prospect of yet another sojourn in the workhouse and instead decided to take her chances tramping.

A tramp, or vagrant, had a life that combined different roles: part iterant worker, part beggar, and sometimes, depending upon circumstances, part criminal or prostitute. Unfortunately, the Vagrancy Laws did not attempt to distinguish between these "professional" identities; a beggar or a criminal or a prostitute — anyone who lived on the street — was viewed similarly and simply categorized as a nuisance. However, a tramp's life and means of self-support varied markedly from person to person and was often determined by age, gender, the presence of an infirmity, or any number of circumstances. A tramp took work where he or she could get it: selling various items on the street, taking laboring jobs such as loading and unloading goods at markets and at the docks, or doing odd bits of childcare or cleaning for working-class households. Life was lived hand-to-mouth, and the quest for work, food, and shelter was constant, sending men and women "tramping" from one end of town to the other, from lodging house to workhouse to public house and back again. While some tramps argued that this lifestyle provided them with freedom and that they enjoyed sleeping wherever they chose, the majority were pushed into this existence through want and a desire to avoid a lengthy and oppressive stay inside a workhouse. However, most were not averse to making use of the workhouse casual ward when it suited them.

The concept of the casual ward, or "the spike," as it was frequently called, was devised in 1837 when the government required that Poor Law authorities provide temporary overnight shelter for anyone destitute and in urgent need of accommodation.* Like the workhouse itself, the casual ward, often located in a wing of the workhouse, was not designed for comfort. The objective was always to discourage vagrancy, while offering the most basic assistance. Vagrants would be given a nauseating meal of skilly and bread and could spend the night in one of the single-sex dormitories, in exchange for several hours of work the following day. By the end of the century, anyone who entered a casual ward was made to spend two nights on the grubby beds in exchange for a full day's labor in between, picking oakum, undertaking cleaning jobs, or breaking stones. If the superintendent believed an inmate wasn't working hard enough for his or her keep, the inmate could be detained. Both the casual ward and the workhouse were havens for bullies.

The spike was no less miserable than the workhouse proper; the only thing that made a stay there bearable was its brevity. Nevertheless, demand for accommodation was constant. In the late afternoon, outside the casual ward door a line would begin to form. Admission usually began between five and six o'clock, and there was no guarantee that beds would be available for all comers, especially in the winter. Not unlike those entering the workhouse, inmates at the casual ward, having secured a place, were fed their skilly and then required to strip off their filthy street clothes. These were not washed, but rather "stoved" at a high temperature, to kill the lice and fleas. In exchange for their clothes, the inmates were given nightshirts; they changed into them after bathing in the blackened waters of the communal tubs. The American author Jack London, who passed a night in the spike while writing his exposé *People of the Abyss*, was horrified to observe that twenty-two inmates washed in the same water before using "tow-

---

* See Peter Higginbotham, *The Workhouse Encyclopedia* (London, 2012), p. 254. The etymology of the word *spike* as a term for the casual ward is debatable. Peter Higginbotham offers a number of possibilities, including reference to the spiked implement that was used for picking oakum, the spike on which one's admission ticket to the workhouse was placed upon entry, or the word *spiniken,* the tramps' name for the workhouse.

els wet from the bodies of other men." London noticed that one of these men had a back covered in "a mass of blood," the result of "vermin attacks."

The combination of vermin, the uncomfortable straw-filled mattresses in narrow berths, and the air of menace within the dormitories made a decent night's sleep difficult to come by. The social investigator J. H. Stallard, who passed a night in a women's dormitory, claimed her stay was spent "in a state of constant misery the whole night through." She remarked that she was "covered with vermin" and ". . . could neither sit nor lie." In order to "get a breath of fresh air" in the close, unventilated room, she was forced to move "as near to the door as I could get" in the hope that some breeze might "come in through the narrow opening."[8] Although the inmates were locked in at seven o'clock and expected to get some rest, Stallard describes the general agitation that prevailed. Discomfort and disturbance punctuated the entire night; women were sick from the food, others came in drunk, children cried, fights broke out. Some just sat up chatting and "singing lewd songs" by the light of the single gas jet. Whether or not they had managed to catch some slumber, they were roused at six in the morning to begin their work. There was more skilly and stale bread, and then a second hellish night before release at nine the next morning.

One problem with spending the night at the casual ward was that it often hampered opportunities to find work the following day. Most laboring jobs began before 9 a.m., and those truly in pursuit of work may have had a long walk to get to a place of potential employment. If there was no work to be had and no money to be found for food or shelter on that next day, a vagrant would be forced to begin the cycle once more and join the line at another casual ward. The law prohibited vagabonds from returning to the same spike within a thirty-day period, so most tramped in a circuit among neighboring facilities, often using different names to evade the regulations. A tramp lived in an almost perpetual state of hunger, exhaustion, and discomfort: cold, rain-soaked, itching from bites, sore-footed from miles of walking in worn-out shoes, to say nothing of the psychological torment. Life was led hour by hour in search of an opportunity to earn or beg a few coins. If a tramp could find a day or even a few hours of employment, he or she might secure enough money for a night or so in a cheap lodging house. This was, of course, if the funds were not drunk away in a fit of despair. In the middle of the nineteenth century it was estimated that "seventy thousand persons in London . . . rise every morning without the slightest knowledge as to where they shall lay their heads at night."[9] Whether they passed an evening in a casual ward, a lodging house, or, as was frequently the case, beneath the stars, these tramps were what we today would recognize as London's homeless population, and Polly was among their number.

In piecing together the narratives of those who fell victim to Jack the Ripper, it is remarkable that both the police and the press appear to have ignored the fact that a significant number of outcast women who slept in lodging houses also slept rough on a regular basis. A lodging-house bed, like a casual ward bed, was used in rotation with nights spent curled up in doorways. This pattern was an inevitable part of tramping. But as William Booth, the founder of the Salvation Army, asserted, this omission may not have been intentional; the well-to-do classes simply did not appreciate precisely what it meant to be homeless. "To very many, even of those who live in London, it may be news that there are so many hundreds who sleep out of doors every night," he wrote in *In Darkest England and the Way Out,* one of the era's most influential explorations of poverty:

> There are comparatively few people stirring after midnight, and when we are snugly tucked into our own beds we are apt to forget the multitude outside in the rain and the storm who are shivering the long hours through on the hard stone seats in the open or under the arches of a railway. These homeless, hungry people are, however, there, but being broken-spirited folk for the most part they seldom make their voices audible in the ears of their neighbours.[10]

Rough sleepers may have felt invisible to "respectable society," but they filled London in their numbers. In 1887 the estimate of those sleeping in Trafalgar Square varied between "more than two hundred" and "six hundred" each night. William Booth recorded 270 on the

Thames Embankment and 98 in Covent Garden Market during one night in 1890.[11] At least as many were believed to shelter in Hyde Park. However, these locations were only the most conspicuous haunts. Each of the capital's neighborhoods was riddled with others. The area around Christ Church, Spitalfields, was another favorite, in addition to those "little nooks and corners of resort in many sheltered yards, vans, etc., all over London."[12]

While the experience of homelessness in Victorian London was one of wretched misery for all who were forced to endure it, women like Polly, who found themselves without shelter, might also expect to become victims of sexual violence. As women who lived without male protection or a roof over their heads were considered outcasts, and outcasts were regarded as defective women, so it followed that outcasts were also morally corrupt and sexually impure. It was generally accepted by all levels of society, without question, that such women would do anything for food and a bed. Because they were desperate, they were there to be used. In some cases, their permission needn't even be solicited.

Mary Higgs, a minister's wife who went undercover as a female tramp to study the effects of poverty, was horrified to find that in her ragged dress she was continually verbally assaulted by men. "I had never realised before that a lady's dress, or even that of a respectable working-woman, was a protection," she wrote. "The bold, free look of a man at a destitute woman must be felt to be realised." When staying at a casual ward she learned that the lecherous male porter had a key to her dormitory. When she complained about this, she was told that at another workhouse "the portress left the care of the female tramps to a man almost entirely," and it was accepted that "he did what he liked with them." On another occasion, when sleeping outdoors, she was approached by a man who "began to talk in a familiar and most disagreeable manner. He asked me where my husband was, and insinuated that I had been leading an immoral life" before suggesting that Higgs spend the night with him in exchange for a share of his breakfast. After five days of such treatment from the men she encountered, Higgs concluded, "I should not care to be a solitary woman tramping the roads." At the time, Higgs was traveling with a female companion, but she found herself being warned by other women that if she tramped for any length of time, it would be necessary "to take up with a fellow."[13] Many women did, and therefore accepted the sexual advances of another vagrant in order to seal a relationship. Their "free" behavior was then used as further proof to reinforce the belief held by the police and the press that "all vagrant women were prostitutes."

When J. H. Stallard visited a number of female casual wards, she heard stories similar to those told to Mary Higgs. In her account, Stallard related the story of "Cranky Sal," a "grey-haired woman" whose face had been disfigured by a stroke. One day she noticed that Sally had acquired a black eye. When Stallard inquired how she got it, Cranky Sal claimed it was "because I would not let a man do as he liked with me." She explained that she had been on the New Cut in Lambeth when a "decently dressed" man offered to buy her a pennyworth of whelks and a two-penny pie. "Then we strolled along, and stopping at a doorway he offered me a shilling. He said that would get a lodging for the night . . . and he asked me if I was going to take his money, and I said Oh no! I don't do business like that, and he gave me a violent blow." When Sally approached a policeman for help, he laughed at her and joked "that the man must have a strong stomach to fancy such as me." She met with a similar response from another officer, "who . . . refused to listen, and pushed her from the pavement into the middle of the street." Stallard was moved by Sal's plight and asked how she managed to survive on the streets. "It is hard to tell you," she replied, seemingly uncertain as to how she managed to cope. "I do not do anything really bad. You know what I mean; I beg and pick up what I can, and go about anywhere for a bit of food or a night's lodging. Sometimes I make do on what they give me at these places here; sometimes I get a few pence given me."[14]

The selling of sex was not the sole means available to the female vagrant for acquiring sustenance and shelter, nor was it central to her ability to survive. Even if she did resort to it, "casual prostitution" among older women, who did not possess the physical allure of their younger counterparts, frequently did not involve penetrative intercourse, but rather manual stimulation or a grope up the skirt. Much of the era's alarmist writing about impoverished and homeless women focused on the young who turned to prostitution without taking into account that older women faced a slightly different set of circumstances. For a woman no longer in her youth, there were other options. When work could not be had, begging, even among other beggars, could yield the pennies, and the cup of tea or piece of bread, needed to survive another day. As social commentators marveled, charity was "frequently derived from the lowest orders"; the most lethargic old female vagrants were tended to by "the energetic, prosperous mendicant" who "is called upon to give to those who are his inferiors in his profession."[15] The journalist George Sims remarked, "Friendly leads, whip-rounds, and benefits are nowhere so common as among the labouring classes whose earnings are precarious . . . the street-hawker or the dock labourer flings his sixpence into the hat extended for a poor cove he has never seen in his life without a second thought." Among the homeless who frequented the lodging houses, these charitable practices were a way of life. Sims noted that if a man came into such a place "who has not the four pence to pay for his bed" and "his woes appear real, round goes the hat in a minute, and the other lodgers pay for his night's rest." Food too was divided among poorer lodgers: "a man, seeing a neighbour without anything, will hand him his teapot, and say, 'Here you are, mate' and offer him the leaves for a second brew."[16] Although not everyone was fortunate enough to have their bed and tea bought every night, this tradition of lending assistance was an invaluable aid to a tramp.

Polly's experience of tramping would not have differed from that of other women. Initially, life on the street would have been shocking and distressing, and then gradually accepted with resignation. It is no wonder that by the time she was arrested in Trafalgar Square, in 1887, after nearly six months of vagrancy, the formerly respectable, well-behaved tenant of the Peabody Buildings had evolved into a disorderly, foul-mouthed menace.

Following her hearing on October 25, Polly was "released on her own recognisances," but was instructed to go into the workhouse or face arrest.[17] On this occasion, she complied and went directly to the nearest one, on Endell Street in Covent Garden. From here she was transferred to the Strand Union Workhouse in Edmonton, where she remained until December, when, evidently, she could bear her stay there no longer and discharged herself.

Invariably, when she traded the regimentation of institutional life for tramping, Polly was soon reminded of its hardships, especially in midwinter. On December 19 she turned up once more at the gates of Lambeth Union Workhouse, but it seems there was some question as to whether she still belonged to the parish where she once lived. After passing Christmas inside the workhouse, the one day of the year when inmates were fed a proper dinner of roast beef and plum pudding, Polly was sent on her way. Now uncertain as to what part of London she might legally call her home, Polly began to wander north of the river, toward Holborn. She passed several nights in the casual ward at Clerkenwell and managed to scrape together the pennies for three nights at a lodging house in Fulwood's Rents, a dingy court off Chancery Lane, in the area she had known so well as a child. When she had run through what small amount of money she possessed, she handed herself over to Holborn Union Workhouse. Tramping in the cold and damp of January had taken its toll, and Polly soon fell ill, at which point she was transferred to the infirmary in Archway.[18]

While Polly was under Holborn Union's care, the guardians, in accordance with the Poor Law, had to determine if she actually belonged there, or if some other Poor Law Union should be footing her bill in its own workhouse. After Polly had recovered, she was interviewed on February 13, 1888. It was then decided that she should be sent back to Lambeth, to the workhouse that had only just turned her out.[19] On April 16, she was dispatched like a human parcel to Renfrew Road Workhouse. Shortly after her arrival there, Polly stood before the matron, Mrs. Fielder, who eighteen months earlier had placed her in service. One might imagine some sighing and scowling from both sides. Lambeth Union did not want Polly and was prepared to offer her another placement in domestic service, hoping for a better outcome this time.

Mrs. Sarah Cowdry of 16 Rosehill Road in Wandsworth, South London, had made it known to the Lambeth guardians that she and her husband would be willing to take a woman from the workhouse into their home as a servant. As observant Baptists, the Cowdrys wished not only to lend assistance to those less fortunate, but also to lead lives of moral rectitude, and to serve as examples to those receiving their charity. As chief clerk of works to the Metropolitan Police, Samuel Cowdry had undoubtedly acquired a certain understanding of the city's social ills, and, perhaps in response, he and his wife had committed to a life of abstinence from alcohol.

On the morning of May 12, Polly Nichols arrived at the Cowdrys' comfortable middle-class home with nothing more than the clothes on her back. As the only servant in a household occupied by one couple in their early sixties and an unmarried niece in her twenties, Polly's duties would not have been especially demanding. She would be expected to clean the rooms and cook the meals, but also could enjoy her own attic room and her own bed, which must have seemed a luxury after months of tramping or suffering in the workhouse. As Polly had no attire befitting her station as a housemaid, Mrs. Cowdry would have provided her with at least one, if not two changes of clothes, along with a decent bonnet and shoes, a nightgown, caps, pinafores, a shawl, a pair of gloves, undergarments, and a variety of other accouterments, such as a hairbrush, combs, and pins. No middle-class mistress wanted her maid to appear ragged before her visitors.

During her first week at "Ingleside," as the Cowdrys called their home, Sarah probably suggested that Polly write to her family and inform them of her whereabouts. Her mistress brought her paper and a pen, and Polly, perhaps for the first time in two years, gathered the courage to address her father:

I just write to say you will be glad to know that I am settled in my new place and going alright up to now. My people went out yesterday and have not returned so I am left in charge. It is a grand place with trees and gardens back and front. All has been newly done up. They are teetotallers and very religious so I ought to get on. They are very nice people and I have not much to do. I do hope you are all right and the boy [Polly's elder son, who was then living with his grandfather] has work. So goodbye for the present.

Yours Truly,

Polly

Answer soon please and let me know how you are.[20]

What ensued over the next two months at the house in Wandsworth is unknown. In the beautiful warm days of summer, Polly might have considered her life a paradise compared to what she had known on the streets and in the casual wards. She had access to the Cowdrys' peaceful garden; she wore clean clothes and had vermin-free hair. There would have been three meals a day; dinners that included meat, fruit, sweets, and other foods she may not have tasted since she parted with her family. She had a real bed, an employer who wished to help her, and no fear of drunken attacks in the middle of the night or abuse from the staff of the casual ward.

It is also possible that she was marched to chapel regularly, pressed into saying her prayers and studying her Bible, and made to feel ashamed of who she was and how she had led her life. And even if her employer was unstinting in her kindness and forgiveness, Polly may not have allowed herself to feel worthy of such comfort. Additionally, at the Cowdrys' house Polly had no company other than her master and mistress and their niece, Miss Mancher, who would not be inclined to chat with her or share jokes and secrets. With no other staff for companions, Polly may have found that her days and nights were long and empty. She had too many hours in which to pine for all she had lost.

Then, of course, there was also the matter of drink and whether at that point in her life it was possible for her to live without it.

On July 12, Sarah Cowdry sent word on a postcard to Renfrew Road Workhouse that Polly Nichols had absconded with clothing and goods worth three pounds and ten shillings. Polly had evidently packed up the belongings that Mrs. Cowdry had provided for her — the dresses, the bonnet, the shoes, the pinafores, and everything else — and taken her leave.

It is doubtful that she had any plan in mind as she crept out the servant's entrance at Ingleside. In her former itinerant existence, Polly would have grown accustomed to catering to her immediate needs. Returning to the workhouse would not have been on her agenda. With a variety of goods at her disposal she would have gone first to a pawnshop or a dealer of used clothing to turn a few of Mrs. Cowdry's charitable gifts into ready cash. Although she would not have received full value for these items, she would have enough money for food and board at lodging houses for at least a couple of weeks. Her next stop was likely a public house.

With a pocketful of change, it's not surprising that Polly becomes untraceable from the middle of July until the first of August, on which date she spent a night at Grey's Inn Casual Ward, along her tramping route to Whitechapel.* Here she knew there was a wealth of cheap lodging houses, which would allow her to spin out her hoard of coins for as long as possible. Of all the establishments she could have selected, Polly decided to take a bed at Wilmott's Lodging House at 18 Thrawl Street. Unlike many other such businesses in the area, Wilmott's catered to female lodgers only; for a solitary woman, this was the safest accommodation available. At Wilmott's, which housed up to seventy women, Polly shared what has been described as "a surprisingly clean" room with three others. This included an older woman named Ellen Holland, with whom Polly also occasionally split the price of a double bed.

Ellen, who came to know Polly over the three weeks she lived at Wilmott's, was evidently the only person there who formed anything like a friendship with the lonely woman. Ellen described her roommate as "melancholy" and said "she kept herself to herself," as if "some trouble was weighing upon her mind."[21] The two women shared no acquaintances in common, and Ellen knew Polly to have no male companions, "only a female with whom she ate and drank for a few days," as

---

* Before entering a casual ward, tramps often hid or buried their belongings and cash in secret locations, to return for them upon release. This was done to avoid losing valuables, which might be confiscated.

was usual practice among vagrant women.[22] Holland also did not deny that Polly drank and that she had seen her the "worse for it" a couple of times.

Polly Nichols's last movements are largely known through the testimony that Ellen Holland offered at the coroner's inquest into her friend's death. Unfortunately, as there are no official transcripts of this hearing and since all documentation of the inquest has been lost, the only accounts that exist to paint a picture of events are those that appear in contemporary newspaper reports. Naturally, these rapidly scribbled summaries taken down by journalists in the courtroom are riddled with errors and inconsistencies. When written up as newsworthy stories, they were further shaped and embellished to suit the needs of the specific paper — sometimes to heighten sensation, sometimes to chop down a tale to fit the available column inches. Syndicated pieces were then sent out to smaller newspapers across the country. Journalists there, including some who had never even traveled to London or visited Whitechapel, cannibalized these stories, fabricating quotations and even interviews. Misinformation took root in the public consciousness as readily as it does today.

According to Ellen Holland, Polly remained at Wilmott's until roughly August 24, when it seems her funds were running short. It was common practice for a deputy keeper of a lodging house to extend credit for a night or so to those who were regulars; but Polly, who was not especially well known, did not receive this kindness. She was turned out. Once more, Polly was back on the street, tramping and reduced to acquiring a few coins and lodging where she could. Holland believed she had spent some time around Boundary Street, in Shoreditch, and a few nights at another lodging house called the White House in Whitechapel, on the notoriously wretched Flower and Dean Street.[23] Until about 12:30 a.m. on August 31, Polly had been drinking in the Frying Pan, a pub on the corner of Thrawl Street. She was quite intoxicated when she left and, in spite of having drunk away her doss money, thought she might try to secure a bed at Wilmott's, which she preferred to other lodging houses. The deputy lodging-house keeper was, however, not in the habit of handing out beds to penniless drunks and so sent Polly on her way. As she left, she attempted to hide her disappointment with a laugh and a sharp comment, saying that she would "soon get her doss money."[24]

Shortly before 2:30 a.m., Ellen Holland, returning from watching a large fire at Shadwell Dry Dock, encountered her former roommate on Osborn Street, heading toward the Whitechapel Road. Polly was not in a good way. She staggered and couldn't walk straight. When Ellen stopped her, Polly slumped against a wall. Greatly concerned for her friend, Ellen kept her chatting "for about 7 or 8 minutes," during which she attempted to convince Polly to return to Wilmott's with her. However, Polly's incident with the deputy keeper earlier that evening must have firmly convinced her that she would not be permitted to stay there that night. Polly bemoaned the fact that she had no money and appeared anxious that she had to "make up the amount for her lodgings," though, as she could barely walk, any such undertaking did not seem likely.[25] "I have had my lodging money three times today and I have spent it," she said to Ellen, with drunken remorse, but for Polly this predicament could hardly have been a new one.[26] The prospect of not having a bed for the night may not have been welcome but it was by no means a situation to which she was unaccustomed.

Ellen Holland repeated this story to the police and then told it again at the coroner's inquest, where journalists were in attendance to hear all of the details. However, before they had even listened to the full account, both the authorities and the press were certain of one thing: Polly Nichols was obviously out soliciting that night, because she, like every other woman, regardless of her age, who moved between the lodging houses, the casual wards, and the bed she made in a dingy corner of an alley, was a prostitute. Working from this assumption, the police and the press would form their theories about the killer. Initially, two possibilities were forwarded: the first was that a "high-rip gang," or group who extorted money from prostitutes, had committed the murder; the second, which later gained more traction, posited a lone "prostitute killer." Whichever scenario a person might favor, everyone was certain, without so much as a single shred of actual evidence to reinforce their convictions, that Polly Nichols was a prostitute.

These assumptions subsequently had a hand in crafting the direction of the entire investigation, the coroner's inquest, and the way that the story was reported in the newspapers, even though virtually everything in the testimonies of the three witnesses who knew Polly most intimately — Ellen Holland, Edward Walker, and William Nichols — runs counter to the preconception that she was engaged in prostitution. At times the coroner's inquest became a moral investigation of Polly Nichols herself, as if the hearing was held in part to determine whether her behavior warranted her fate.

When Polly last spoke to Ellen Holland on that night of August 31, she made it clear that she disliked her new accommodation at the White House. When Ellen asked her where she was staying, Polly claimed "she was living in another house together with a lot of men and women." This was also variously reported as "a house where men and women were allowed to sleep."[27] The comment was made in contrast to the lodgings available at Wilmott's, which were single sex and which she preferred. In reference to the White House, Polly stated that "she didn't like to go there" and that "there were too many men and women." She wanted to return to Wilmott's and promised Holland that it wouldn't "be long before she was back."[28]

At the inquest, the coroner several times posed questions to Ellen about her friend's moral character, in the hope she would make an incriminating statement about Polly's assumed profession. At each juncture, she made it perfectly plain that Polly was not what the officials insinuated. When Ellen was asked if she knew what her former roommate did for a living, Holland claimed she did not know. She answered similarly when pressed as to whether Polly stayed out late at night.

"Did you consider that she was very cleanly in her habits?" he inquired.

"Oh, yes; she was a very clean woman," she replied.

The coroner took the opportunity once more to question Ellen as to her comment that Polly intended to find the money for her lodgings. "I suppose you formed an opinion of what that meant," he interjected.

"No," Ellen Holland stated adamantly. She reiterated that Polly was intent on returning to the single-sex lodging house.[29]

So absolute were Ellen's statements that a number of newspapers, including the *Manchester Guardian,* paraphrased the information she gave during her examination simply by stating, "the witness said she did not think the deceased was leading a fast [meaning immoral] life; in fact she [Nichols] seemed very afraid of it."[30]

It is hardly surprising that those most intent on presenting Polly's character as insalubrious were the newspapers. Whether through sloppy note taking, the mishearing of testimony, or deliberate embellishment, journalists frequently twisted statements into those that cast a shadow over Polly's moral character. When the coroner asked Edward Walker about his daughter's behavior when she lived with him, in the wake of the breakdown of her marriage, he inquired as to whether Polly "was fast." According to the *Morning Advertiser,* the *Evening Standard,* and the *Illustrated Police News,* his response was this: "No; I never heard of anything of that sort. She used to go with some young women and men that she knew, but I never heard of anything improper."[31] Yet the *Daily News,* in paraphrasing this statement, inserted something far more suggestive. "She did not stay out particularly late at night," Walker is claimed to have said, while also purporting to add, "The worst he had seen of her was her keeping company with females of a certain class."[32] Whether Walker actually said this is debatable, as there are at least two competing versions of his testimony. Similarly, the coroner's attempts to goad William Nichols into elaborating on his wife's character only succeeded in casting doubt over his own behavior in light of his marriage breakdown. When asked why he discontinued Polly's five-shilling maintenance payments, he claimed that in the two-year period since their estrangement she had been living with "another man or men."[33] This provided the newspapers with all the evidence they required to judge Polly for being an adulteress and a "fallen woman"; however, Nichols never once asserted that his wife was making a living as a prostitute.

When the story first broke, before anything substantial was known about Polly's life, almost every major newspaper in the country carried a piece stating, "It was gathered that the deceased had led the life of an 'unfortunate,'" in spite of also reporting that "nothing . . . was known of her."[34] In order to validate their assessment of her lifestyle, the papers set about slanting the slender facts available. Polly's comment to the deputy keeper at Wilmott's — "I'll soon get my doss money, see what a jolly bonnet I've got now" — included the detail that she then gestured to a hat that no one had apparently noticed before. Some reporters used this to insinuate that she used an illicit method to acquire money.[35] Whether Polly actually said this is questionable. And if she did, her meaning may have been quite innocent. Polly's "jolly bonnet" was likely the one she had acquired from the Cowdrys a month earlier and planned to pawn so she could return to a familiar bed at Wilmott's. However, the truth of this detail, like so many others surrounding her final hours and her death, remains unknown. Like Ellen Holland, whose name the journalists could not even bother to confirm or record correctly, Polly was just another impoverished, aging, worthless female resident of a Whitechapel lodging house.* There was nothing else the police, the coroner, the newspaper scribblers, or their readers needed to learn about her.

Ellen Holland remembered the clock on "Whitechapel church" striking half past two when she parted with her friend. She watched Polly, in her jolly straw bonnet edged with black velvet, sway off in the direction of Whitechapel Road and disappear gradually into the darkness.

At that hour, Polly would know that her hopes of begging money for her doss were slim. With her head spinning from drink and exhaustion, she wandered, stumbling through the network of East End streets. She steadied herself against walls and the sides of buildings, feeling her way through the night, groping for a place that might become a bed. Polly would have learned how to locate such a spot — somewhere with a step or a slightly recessed doorway. The cavities beneath stairs, the landings in communal buildings, the semiprivate yards that lay just beyond unlocked gates, were the better places to attempt slumber. As one relatively new to the neighborhood, she would not have known the locations of Whitechapel's secret sleeping corners, or even the name of the road onto which she had turned. Slight flickers of light from a window or a distant lamp would have guided her

---

* Ellen Holland was called Emily Holland, Jane Oram or Jane Oran, and Jane Hodden.

down Buck's Row. She passed beyond a set of flat-front brick cottages, which offered no convenient nooks or porches, until the curb dipped and the wall became a gate, set back slightly from the footpath. She may have pushed on it and found that it refused to give way, or she simply slid down, with her back against it, to rest. Her heavy head would have slumped, and her eyes eventually shut.

But for the postcard she wrote to her father in the final few months of her life, we have been left no clear glimpse into Polly Nichols's thoughts. Ellen Holland saw, in the woman who slept beside her, something deeply melancholic; a personality folding in on itself, private, alienated, and grieving. However, from these rough outlines, a faint but distinct pattern of a woman can be defined. There is enough here still from which to observe her experiences, a way to understand her not as a fictional character, but as a person. Polly had been born among printing shops and presses, against the very backdrop where some of the most famous Victorian stories were fabricated. In death she would become as legendary as the Artful Dodger, Fagin, or even Oliver Twist, the truth of her life as entangled with the imaginary as theirs. She had been brought into the world along the Street of Ink, and it is to there, riding on its column inches, its illustrated plates, its rumor and scandal, that she would return: a name in print.

On September 1, 1888, William Nichols prepared for the worst. Uncertain of what he was about to encounter, he felt he should dress appropriately and attired himself in mourning clothes: a long black coat, black trousers, a black tie, and a top hat. It was raining that day, and he must have felt physically sick as he stepped out the door and unfurled his umbrella, turning his back on his home on Coburg Road, where he lived with Rosetta and the children.

He was to meet Inspector Abberline at the mortuary and view the body of the woman who, it was supposed, was his wife. It had been three years since he'd seen her, and he had no inkling of where she had gone in that time, though he could have hardly anticipated such a shocking turn of events. The police inspector warned him that he might have some difficulty recognizing Polly, but hopefully he would be able to provide a positive identification. He then escorted Nichols through a rear door and into a yard, and across it stood a modest brick shed. The men stepped inside, and Nichols faced the plain pine coffin. He removed his hat and braced himself as the lid was pulled back.

Even with her injuries, with the stitched-up gash across her throat and the deep cuts along her body, William Nichols knew his wife. He recognized her small, delicate features and high cheekbones. Her gray eyes, though vacant now, were familiar to him, as was her brown hair, which since they had last met had become streaked with silver. This was indeed Polly, as he used to call her — the woman he had once dearly loved, and married. It was Polly, who had borne six of his children, who had comforted and coddled them, who had nursed him in times of illness, the woman with whom he had shared laughter and at least a handful of joys for sixteen years. It was Polly, who at eighteen had been his girlish bride, holding her father's arm as she walked down the aisle at St. Bride's. They had been happy, even if only for a short while.

Abberline noticed that the color had drained from Nichols's face. He was noticeably shaken by the sight and then broke down.

"I forgive you as you are." He addressed Polly as if she were merely sleeping and the brutish cuts on her body had not ended her life. "I forgive you on account of what you have been to me."[36]

It took William Nichols some time to compose himself. The coffin lid was moved back into place, and Abberline showed the grieving husband back across the yard and into the station.

PART II

ANNIE

September 1841

September 8, 1888

SOLDIERS AND SERVANTS

THE NEWSPAPERS DESCRIBED the rain as torrential. It poured in buckets. It drenched everything. It seeped through wool cloaks and coats; it cascaded from the brims of hats. This was chilling February rain, certain to bring on chest ailments and fevers to those who persisted in standing in it, yet none of the spectators' "spirits were in the least damped." They came in the thousands, pressing against the rails of Buckingham Palace, and lined the route to St. James. Most of those assembled were, as the *Morning Chronicle* wrote, "generally of the working classes." They "scrambled and pushed and squeezed" for a position allowing them to catch a glimpse of Queen Victoria and Prince Albert in their wedding attire.[1] Young men scaled trees, and police officers promptly yanked them down. On several occasions, the crowds threatened to move onto the parade route, but horse-mounted detachments of the Queen's Life Guard, their shining breastplates partially covered by their scarlet winter capes, held them back. Excitement surged as a procession of carriages appeared. Loud whoops and cheers could be heard, followed by cries of "God save the queen!" The crowd heaved forward, reaching out their hands to touch the vehicles and the horses, to spy the bright blue eyes of the royal bride. The troopers of the 2nd Queen's Life Guard advanced, cracking their whips above the heads of the masses, holding the line "with a mixture of firmness and good humour which won the approval of all present."

It was for this — the spectacle of such pageants, the pride of serving in the cavalry of one of the most prestigious regiments in the country, the thrill of sitting tall on a mount and wearing polished boots — that George Smith, just fifteen in 1834, had left his home in rural Lincolnshire and come to London. Three years earlier a recruiting sergeant had come to the nearby village of Fulbeck and enlisted his elder brother, Thomas, in the 2nd Regiment of the Life Guard. As a young boy, George could scarcely wait to join him. When he appeared at Regent's Park Barracks, he was still underage, but the regiment nevertheless accepted this enthusiastic recruit. They taught him to ride like a cavalry trooper and how to polish his breastplate and clean his helmet. He learned quickly the strict routines of army life — how to stand, march, salute, and discipline his body so that he never slouched or "loafed about." George and his brother were recruited because they were strong, healthy country lads of sturdy physique, perfect for sitting astride a mount. According to his army records, George stood at five feet, ten inches tall when he enlisted; he had a fair, clear complexion and brown eyes. The regimental barber cut his light-brown hair short, but because George was a trooper in the cavalry, he was permitted to cultivate a fine mustache.

Under the guidance of his regiment, George came of age. His position in the household cavalry secured him a front-row seat to history. He witnessed the passing of the Georgian era and the birth of the Victorian age: in 1837 he served at the funeral of King William IV and in 1838 at the coronation of the new queen. On February 10, 1840, he was there to participate in the ceremonies of state on the occasion of her marriage, guarding his monarch against the crowds.

On that day, when Londoners crowded into the streets and celebrated the marriage of their monarch, it is likely that a twenty-two-year-old servant called Ruth Chapman was among them. Little is known about this Sussex-born young woman, who, like so many others, left home to work in the capital. Her family at least thought it wise to baptize her at fifteen before sending her off into the wide world, with its manifold temptations. What good it did her is questionable;

by the time of the queen's nuptials she had already met and formed an attachment to a trooper of the 2nd Life Guards.

It is possible that she and George met somewhere near his barracks on Portman Street. A relation of Ruth's worked for a Sussex family who lived at nearby Clifton Place, where she too may have been employed. Hyde Park, a notorious venue of flirtation for soldiers and servants, lay just in between. According to Henry Mayhew, it was here that housemaids and nursemaids walking in the park to and from their place of work often first encountered "the all powerful red coat" and "succumbed to Scarlet Fever." Soldiers were by no means unaware of the impact their dashing uniforms and well-groomed military air could have on young women, and deployed these features to their advantage. As the army actively discouraged marriage among enlisted men, and low wages meant that the average private "could not afford to employ professional women to gratify his passions . . . he is only too glad to seize the opportunity of forming an intimacy with a woman who will appreciate him for his own sake, and cost him nothing but the trouble of taking her about occasionally."[2] More important, at least from the army's perspective, a monogamous relationship with a decent working-class girl "was unlikely to communicate some infectious disease" to a soldier and would keep him away from prostitutes.[3] Such arrangements may have served an ordinary enlistee well, but it placed the object of his affection in a difficult, and potentially ruinous, position. By January 1841, Ruth found herself in just such a situation.

The precise day on which Annie Eliza Smith was born in September 1841 is unclear. Because she was an illegitimate child, Ruth may have attempted to hide the facts of her birth. The conditions in which Annie arrived could not have been entirely happy for Ruth, who would have lost her employment as her pregnancy advanced and would have found herself dependent upon meager and unreliable handouts from George. In the eyes of society, and the army, Ruth had become a "dollymop": a soldier's woman. Though such a woman did not quite fall into the category of "professional," she was deemed a sort of "amateur prostitute." Fortunately, the army's position on dolly-mops was a pragmatic one, so long as only six out of every hundred enlisted men in a regiment were permitted to marry. In the field, such women would have been known as camp followers and allowed to earn their keep by taking in the regiment's laundry; when the cavalry remained in barracks, these women were often called upon to perform the same duties. One trooper's woman remarked that she made ends meet by doing "a little needlework in the day-time" as well as "some washing and mangling now and then to help it out." She lived in a room near the barracks, for which she paid a shilling a week.* Ruth's circumstances would have been similar.

For five months after Annie's birth, Ruth's position remained a precarious one, especially as she soon found herself pregnant with a second child. Regardless of George's affection for her, there remained the ever-present possibility that he might be posted abroad, a circumstance known to be the death knell of many romantic attachments between soldiers and the women they hadn't married. Had fate taken this turn, Ruth would have been left with no financial support, two children, and a soiled reputation. When placed in such a position, it was conventional for dolly-mops to remain loyal to the regiment and seek another protector within it, or from within the barracks. However, this remedy was not without consequences; in doing so they committed themselves to a career in prostitution. Fortunately, on February 20, 1842, two years after the commencement of their relationship, George received permission to marry his sweetheart. Whether it was George's expressed wish or the thoughtful intercession of his commanding officer, the date of his nuptials was backdated by two years on his military records. Anyone who inquired would learn that George and Ruth's wedding had taken place in the same month and year as that of Queen Victoria and Prince Albert.

From the day of the couple's first acquaintance through their subsequent years together, the army would completely define the lives of George, Ruth, and their children. Although marriage ensured that Mrs. Smith was now "on the strength," meaning that she was included

---

* Peter Burroughs, "An Unreformed Army? 1815–1868," in *The Oxford History of the British Army*, edited by David Chandler and Ian Beckett (Oxford University Press, 1994), p. 173. Cavalry soldiers were paid marginally better than ordinary foot soldiers and at midcentury earned one shilling and three pence per day.

as an official regimental wife, this did not necessarily make life more comfortable for her. The army provided Ruth and her children with half rations and permission to live within the barracks, but these arrangements were not pleasant, nor even healthy. Designated married quarters were not provided until the 1850s, and so newlyweds like George and Ruth had to make do with corners of the communal barracks room, screened off with sheets and blankets. Women dressed and undressed, lay in bed, washed, gave birth, and breastfed their babies surrounded by single men, who often strode about half-naked, swearing, jeering, and singing lewd songs. Sanitation was not much better. When a national inspection of barracks was made in 1857, the dwelling spaces were revealed to be in appalling condition. Many dormitories were set over the stables and ill-ventilated. Dampness and poor lighting were the norm, as were insufficient washing and latrine facilities. In some barracks large barrels were used as communal chamber pots; these same receptacles were emptied and then used for bathing. Kitchen facilities too were found wanting. Most contained no ovens, which had a significant impact on the diet and health of military men, who subsisted largely on boiled food.

There were, however, some benefits for families who "lived on the strength." Army savings banks were established to allow soldiers to put aside small sums, medicine from regimental supplies was made available to sick men and their families, while all ranks and their dependents were given access to the barracks' library. Most important, by 1848, families "on the strength" were allocated a small allowance for suitable accommodation outside the barracks; though the amount did not ensure many comforts, it did at least permit soldiers and their wives some privacy and a home of their own. This would have proved especially timely to the Smiths, whose number continued to expand over the decade. Shortly after Ruth and George's marriage in 1842, a brother, George William Thomas, joined Annie and her parents. He was followed by Emily Latitia in 1844, Eli in 1849, Miriam in 1851, and William in 1854, bringing the number of children to six.* Annie and

---

* With the arrival of a second child and the solemnizing of their union in 1842, Ruth and George also decided to have Annie baptized, on April 23, at Christ Church, St. Pancras.

her siblings would enjoy one of the greatest benefits of "life on the strength": the regimental school.

More than twenty years before a British system of mandatory state schooling was implemented, in 1870, the sons and daughters of families on the strength were required to attend organized lessons funded by the army. This was meant to counteract the possible negative effects of growing up in and around the barracks, an environment thought to be "incompatible with decency." Many believed that children might acquire habits of "idleness and vice" there; girls in particular were to be shielded from "the more masculine habits of drinking and swearing." These schools were also meant to assure soldiers that the sovereign cared about the education and welfare of their children, and to help the children of enlisted men "acquire the means of making themselves useful and earning a livelihood."[4] Having been instilled with military ideals that included discipline and respect, most regiments regarded this school attendance as compulsory; families that hesitated to enroll their children were threatened with being struck off the strength. Of course, the regiment also expected soldiers to pay for this privilege. George would have been charged two pence a month for Annie to attend, and then one penny for each sibling who joined her.

The curriculum of the regimental schools was similar to that of civilian charity institutions. The schools were divided into those for small children and those for grown ones. The younger children were taught by a schoolmistress in the morning, while the elder children were instructed by the schoolmaster. Following lunch, the sexes were separated for more gender-specific occupational instruction. The boys remained with the master, and the girls joined the schoolmistress. Considering the instructional standards of the first half of the Victorian era, these children received a fairly rigorous education. The small ones were taught spelling, reading, and singing, a curriculum that would expand to include lessons in writing, diction, grammar, English history, geography, arithmetic, and algebra. Under such a regimen, Annie would have received an education far superior to that of most of her working-class peers, both male and female. As a girl, she would also benefit from afternoon lessons in "industry" — specifically, in every type of needlework, from embroidery to making clothes, crocheting, and knitting. Girls thus acquired skills that would render them useful to the regiment, in mending and making garments, and also assist them in finding paid work when their schooling was complete. The only complication in this arrangement was that army life was mobile and necessitated frequent moves between barracks and postings, which regularly interrupted the children's instruction.

Although George and his family never had to endure the hardships of a foreign posting, neither were they able to grow too comfortable in their domestic surroundings. Regiments were rotated between barracks, often with little notice. Moving to and organizing new lodgings near barracks on Portman Street, Hyde Park, and Regent's Park in London involved inconvenient relocations a few miles in one direction or the other; the larger upheaval of traveling to a posting in Windsor, more than twenty miles outside the city, required great effort and expense. Over the course of George's service with his regiment, from the 1840s through the early 1860s, the family lived at no fewer than twelve addresses between London and Windsor.

One curious aspect of growing up as the child of a soldier in a socially prestigious regiment involved straddling two disparate worlds. The cavalry, with its aristocratic officers and its proximity to the royal family, brought opportunities to glimpse, from afar, a realm of status, privilege, and wealth. Annie's girlhood was spent between Knightsbridge, with its elegant stucco-fronted villas, and Windsor, in the shadow of the royal family's residence. The sight of landaus, filled with ladies in expensive silk bonnets and titled gentlemen whose uniforms clanked with medals, would have seemed ordinary, as would a glimpse of Queen Victoria or a royal prince trotting on horseback through Windsor Great Park. When Ruth and her children stepped out from the door of one of their temporary homes, they walked along clean, broad, well-lit streets, comparatively free from signs of want. They inhaled the fresh air of Hyde Park alongside the perfectly attired, parasol-twirling members of high society. From a young age, Annie would have been taught to take pride in her father's position and to adopt his love of queen and country as her own. The regiment's values of honor and dignity would have been inculcated in her as well. How Annie stood and spoke and comported herself, while not making her appear privileged, would have demonstrated that she understood the rules of appropriate conduct and was aware of her place within her surroundings. These skills and discernment would remain with her into adulthood, so that she always gave the impression of having come from a good family.

Yet Annie also experienced life as a child of the working class. Despite the privileges of her father's position, his salary was meager. While the family lived in Windsor, they rented lodgings on Keppel Terrace, a road whose houses had been constructed and decorated "at considerable expense," in order to appeal to "small, genteel families." Each three-story property, with its "Portland stone mantels," "rich cornicing," and "fine views over the River Thames," was comprised of "two parlours, three bedrooms and servants' quarters" in which three army families lived, while sharing a kitchen and lavatory facilities.[5] The quality of some of their housing in Knightsbridge was at times even worse. Hidden between Knightsbridge's "fine mansions and respectable abodes," and no more than a moment's walk from its exclusive shops, existed a small pocket of "insalubriousness" across the road from Hyde Park Barracks. "From Knightsbridge Green all along the High Road stood a succession of music halls, taverns, beer-stores, oyster saloons, & cheap tobacconists" deemed "a disgrace to any portion of London."[6] Here also was situated some of the only housing that the families of enlisted men could afford. When possible, the Smiths lived at a distance from these establishments. In 1844, they took a small cottage on Rutland Terrace near the Brompton Road, but as the century progressed, rents in the better areas increased and pushed regimental families into the densely populated streets between two of the most notorious music halls: the Sun and the Trevor Arms. Raphael Street ran east to west, just on the fringe of this carnival of iniquity, and although its housing stock had been completed only in the past couple of years, its homes had already been carved up and portioned out to multiple families on lower incomes. In 1854, the Smiths were living at number 15 with at least two other families; each occupied two rooms.

In the late spring of that year, just when the weather had turned milder, the London newspapers began to write of an alarming rise in the number of cases of scarlatina, or scarlet fever, recorded by the London Fever Hospital. Soon outbreaks were reported in Islington,

Knightsbridge, and Chelsea, though journalists attempted to offer some reassurance to the wealthier part of the population by confirming that: "the disease is principally among the labouring classes." On May 3 the *Daily News* wrote that a coachman who lived near the very wealthiest of society in Eaton Mews South had watched as "malignant scarlatina carried off all five of his children in nine days." The paper warned readers that the outbreak "was very bad in this district." Tragic stories of what was now declared an epidemic continued through the summer. "Scarlatina increases weekly," wrote the *Morning Post* on July 27; "the . . . disease has visited some families with severity, and . . . an instance is reported in which three children died of it in the same family within 6 days." In early June, the London Fever Hospital hit a crisis point, when "upwards of 100 patients" were admitted for scarlet fever alone. The situation was exacerbated by the arrival of a second epidemic: typhus.

Whereas scarlet fever, a flu-like streptococcal illness characterized by a red rash, predominantly affected children, typhus attacked both young and old alike. Commonly known as "camp fever" or "gaol fever," the disease was communicated through the bites of fleas and lice. These insects were present in the clothes, blankets, and bedding shared among people in close quarters. Like those afflicted with scarlet fever, typhus sufferers also experienced a high fever as well as a rash, which spread across the body. Eventually, in fatal cases, the infection moved to the brain.

In mid-May, both epidemics arrived at Raphael Street. An infant named John Fussell Palmer, not quite eighteen months old, was the first to die of scarlet fever. How rapidly the disease crept through the porous plaster walls and crowded rooms along the street is unknown, but shortly after the Palmer child fell ill, sickness came to settle in the Smiths' home. Annie would have helped care for two-and-a-half-year-old Miriam when their mother was busy with her newborn, William. Little Miriam would have been toddling about the family rooms, giggling and prattling, turning over chairs and getting underfoot. A fever and sore throat, flu-like aches, and much crying suddenly replaced these activities. When the rash appeared, there was no doubt as to what had befallen her. She suffered until May 28, and was buried quickly on the following day. While Ruth and George were nursing their youngest girl, William too was afflicted by the rash and fever, and five days later, he died at the age of five months, on June 2. After carrying away the two youngest, seven days later, scarlet fever took its next victim, Eli, at the age of five.

It cannot be imagined what George and Ruth felt when their eldest son, George Thomas, who had just turned twelve, fell ill. Like the others, he had a fever, which raged for two weeks, and a rash spread across his body. He lay in his sickbed, his condition worsening, while the family buried his brother Eli. Because families of enlisted men were not permitted to call upon the services of the regiment's physician, the Smiths were forced to summon a doctor whose fees they could hardly afford. George Thomas was diagnosed with typhus. He struggled with it for three weeks before expiring on June 15.

Over the span of only three weeks, death had claimed four of the Smiths' six children. The enormity of this tragedy is almost inconceivable to modern sensibilities, particularly as their lives might have been spared had they lived in an era of antibiotics. However, George and Ruth were powerless in the face of incurable illness. The death of children was simply an unfortunate but not uncommon aspect of life, though this fact did not make the experience easier for the parents or the surviving siblings. Now only two of the Smiths' children remained: Annie and Emily. Long after the event, this calamity continued to cast a heavy shadow over the family.

Somehow Ruth and George found it in their hearts to move forward. Two years later, in 1856, a daughter, Georgina, was born in Windsor. She was followed by another Miriam: Miriam Ruth, in 1858. In the midst of this, Annie grew into a teenage girl with dark, wavy brown hair and an intense blue-eyed stare. At about the time that her mother's arms were once again filled with a newborn, Annie would have been nearing her fifteenth birthday. Traditionally this was considered the age when a girl's education was complete and she would be expected to start earning a full-time wage. For a large number of teenage girls, this meant entering domestic service. This transition was almost a rite of passage: a young woman took on the burden of supporting her younger siblings and made the sacrifice of leaving her family home. Although removing herself from her parents' protection did pose potential moral dangers, domestic service had advantages over other options, such as factory work, because a young woman could gain skills that would prove useful in her future married life. As a result, between 1851 and 1891, nearly 43 percent of British women between the ages of fifteen and twenty entered this occupation. Ruth Smith herself had been in service. When Annie came of age, Ruth had Emily at home to assist with the younger children, thereby freeing Annie to begin to make contributions to the family income.

By 1861 Annie Smith was working as a housemaid for William Henry Lewer; whether this was her first job in domestic service is unknown. A successful architect, Lewer lived at numbers 2 and 3 Duke Street in Westminster, a part of London that a number of designers and engineers called home. Several doors down, at numbers 17–18, lived Isambard Kingdom Brunel, the great creator of railways, bridges, and tunnels, and his family. As long-term residents of Duke Street, the Lewers and Brunels, who shared professional interests, would have been acquainted socially. It is likely that Annie and her fellow housemaid, Eleanor Brown, as well as the Lewers' housekeeper, Mary Ford, would have recognized the family, or even had the privilege of waiting upon them in their masters' drawing room.

In 1861, Annie was the junior of three women who tended to sixty-seven-year-old William Lewer and his bachelor brother, Edward, a retired stockbroker. Although all three would have begun their working day at 5 or 6 a.m., Annie's responsibilities would have been the most arduous. Sometimes described as "maids-of-all-work," servants in small households were expected to perform every task, from the miserable chore of washing dishes three times a day, to hauling buckets of coal up flights of stairs, making the beds, and lighting the fires in the grates. At the Lewers' home, Mrs. Ford, the housekeeper, may have doubled as the cook; it's likely that Annie would assist in the preparation of meals and in serving them as well. Even though she served only two older gentlemen, Annie's list of jobs would rarely allow her a spare moment. When she wasn't dusting, or clearing out fireplaces, she was scrubbing the floors, beating rugs, drawing water for baths, polishing boots, or mending clothes. The Lewers may have sent their dirty linens to one of London's many commercial laundries, but if they didn't, the strenuous work of washing, rinsing, wringing, and ironing would have fallen to Annie as well. For their hours of toil, housemaids were remunerated poorly. Mrs. Beeton, in her *Book of Household Management*, published in 1861, suggested that a maid-of-all-work should receive annual pay of nine to fourteen pounds; if the employer supplied the maid with an allowance to purchase her own tea, sugar, and small beer, this figure was reduced to seven and a half to eleven pounds.* Employers believed these small sums were justified because they were providing the young woman's room and board. In the Lewer household, where apparently space was plentiful, Annie and Mrs. Ford had their own rooms above the architect's office at number 2 Duke Street, while Eleanor slept in the attic at number 3. For Annie, who had spent her life sharing two or at most three rooms with her entire family, the privacy she enjoyed in William Lewer's servants' quarters must have seemed strange and wonderful.

When Annie began life as a live-in domestic, she would expect to see very little of her family. For a housemaid, time off was granted at the discretion of her employer, and most servants could expect no more than a day or even a half day away from their duties each month. An hour or so on Sunday for attending church was also permissible. These restrictions, however, would have made it difficult for Annie to travel to and from Windsor, where the Smiths were based until 1861.

For roughly twenty-one years, the army had beaten the march that the Smith family followed. For both Ruth and George, the regiment, and the families and officers who comprised it, formed the defining framework of their lives. This closed, clanlike community, who migrated together between barracks, who had shared housing and meals, whose children had been schooled together and grown up as if they were cousins, who had consoled one another, and lent each other

---

* Servants and the working classes consumed low-alcohol beer, or small beer, rather than water, because London's water supply was considered potentially hazardous. Servants in some urban households were also expected to buy their own refreshments from the local pubs and shops.

money, would leave an indelible stamp on each of the Smiths' sense of identity. This was especially so for George, who as he entered his forties would be forced to contemplate retirement and his future prospects. The 2nd Regiment of the Life Guards had been a family to him as much as his wife and children. So closely were the two intertwined that he chose to name his youngest son in recognition of those under whom he had served. On February 25, 1861, Fountaine Hamilton Smith was born at 6 Middle Row North, a short distance from Raphael Street, where George and Ruth had parted with three sons and a daughter in 1854. Perhaps, in that same year, George experienced some relief from this tragedy when John Glencairn Carter Hamilton (later 1st Baron Hamilton of Dalzell) became one of his captains. Whatever support Hamilton provided, whether financial, emotional, or spiritual, George never forgot his kindness. Neither was he able to forget the bond he had forged with another of his commanders, Captain Fountaine Hogge Allen, whose death, in November 1857, must have affected him profoundly. It is likely that Fountaine's birth signified to George the approaching end of his career, and inspired in him a desire to commemorate those men and experiences that had shaped his person.

As a loyal servant of the regiment, who had earned four distinguishing marks for good conduct, George was judged a suitable candidate to become a valet to his commanding officers. According to army regulations, cavalry officers who were not already attended by a civilian were permitted to employ a "soldier servant" from within the regiment to maintain their military kit and uniforms, care for their physical appearance, and manage the administrative details of daily life.

In 1856, Roger William Henry Palmer, a hero of the Crimean War who had participated in the charge of the Light Brigade, returned to Britain and exchanged his commission in the 11th Hussars for one in the 2nd Life Guards. When selecting a valet from among the men in his new regiment, Palmer spotted the necessary qualities for a "gentleman's gentleman" in Trooper Smith.[7]

Within the hierarchy of servants, a gentleman's valet had a prestigious role. Significant trust was invested in him. No other servant was permitted such intimate insight into an employer, from his physical weaknesses to his thoughts and personal secrets. To be selected

for such a position, George would have been judged to possess "po-
lite manners, modest demeanour, and respectful reserve," along with
"good sense, good temper, some self-denial, and consideration for
the feelings of others."[8] A valet had many tasks to perform. According to Mrs. Beeton, that arbiter of social custom, valets were required
to tend to their masters by "dressing them, accompanying them in all
their journeys" as well as acting as "the confidents and agents of their
most unguarded moments." More specifically, a valet took on "brushing his master's clothes, cleaning his top boots, his shooting, walking and dress boots; carrying up the water for his master's bath, putting out his things for dressing, assisting him in dressing, and packing
and unpacking his clothes when travelling . . ."[9] Although Mrs. Beeton
points out that many gentlemen preferred to shave themselves, a valet
had to be prepared to perform this task too, as well as regularly trim his
master's beard and mustache.

The benefits of George's association with Palmer would be wide-
ranging. Already a military hero when his path crossed with George's,
Palmer would eventually succeed to his family's Irish baronetcy. Being
a valet allowed George to remain within his regiment but excused him
from parades and barracks responsibilities, including the universally
disliked guard duty. It entitled him to live in the officers' mess, where
he received better food, and sometimes wine as well. When Palmer
was elected as a member of Parliament, George's duties took him
away from army life altogether and into the exclusive realm of country
houses, shooting parties, and the government. Because Palmer spent
much of his time as a commissioned officer traveling between his family estates in County Mayo, George got to see Ireland and the opulent
interiors of its castles and manors. Then, in 1862, George Smith, the
son of a Lincolnshire shoemaker, went to Paris.

The year before, George had begun to serve as valet for another
officer in his regiment: Captain Thomas Naylor Leyland. So much
had Leyland come to value his "soldier-servant" that when he chose
to marry and exchange his commission for one in the Denbighshire
Yeomanry, he asked George to leave the 2nd Life Guards and accompany him.[10] This opportunity would have required a good deal of de-
liberation, but it arrived at a time when reason demanded that George

take it. Leyland was offering him a paid position, which would place George among the butler and cook within the top rank of his household servants. He could expect to receive £25–£50 per year, in addition to his army pension of 1 shilling and 1½ pence per day. As a middle-aged man from the working classes, George could hardly do better than this for his family.

On March 19, 1862, less than a month before his forty-third birthday, Trooper George Smith became Mr. Smith. He bid farewell to his associates, the barracks, and the regiment that had made him, and set off to accompany Thomas Naylor Leyland to Paris, where Leyland had arranged to marry his fiancée, Mary Ann Scarisbrick, at the British embassy before embarking on a honeymoon in France.

From about the end of 1861, it appears that Ruth and George decided to settle the family more permanently in Knightsbridge, near Leyland's palatial, art-filled mansion, Hyde Park House. This was conveniently situated in the area that Ruth knew best, near the Hyde Park Barracks and within a short walk from the home of George's brother, Thomas, who had also retired from the regiment and returned to the family occupation of shoemaking. Much like Annie, George likely saw little of his family while occupied in domestic service, and this estrangement from his wife and children, and from his former regiment, began to bear down on him. A valet, when not tending to his master, had time to himself, to read, to think, and without the distractions of family or regimental life, there were many subjects George did not wish to ponder. Undoubtedly, the deaths of four of his children were among them.

In 1863, Captain Leyland had agreed to act as steward at the Denbighshire Yeomanry Cavalry Races in Wrexham, to be held on June 13. This large, convivial social gathering would include a grand dinner for the officers and their ladies. The evening before, members of the regiment and their guests arrived in town and retired to their lodgings. While his master resided in officers' quarters, George shared a room at a pub, the Elephant and Castle, with another member of Leyland's staff. As they extinguished the light that night, George appeared his usual self, and "quite cheerful." The next morning, between 7 and 8 a.m., the servant called out to George, to remind him of the time. "It's all right, I'm not asleep," he answered, though he made no attempt to get out of bed. Less than an hour later, when George had still not appeared, the landlady went upstairs and, much to her horror, discovered Leyland's valet "with his throat cut, in a shocking manner, with a razor lying by him covered with blood." George was dead by the time he was found, on the floor, "with only his shirt and drawers on."[11]

That day, which had been intended as an occasion of sporting amusement, immediately soured into one of shock and dismay. When informed of the horrible news, Thomas Naylor Leyland rushed to the scene and "was much affected" by what he beheld. However, so that the races would not have to be abandoned, the coroners quickly assembled that afternoon and presented a verdict of "suicide by cutting his throat with a razor while labouring under temporary insanity."[12] There was also the suggestion that George had been drinking, a problem to which he had succumbed quite seriously since leaving the army.

Notwithstanding the unfortunate turn of events, Leyland still appeared on the turf that afternoon to watch the horses run, though it cannot be imagined that he derived much pleasure from it.

He later paid the expenses of George's funeral.

∞∞∞

There is no record of what occurred when Ruth and her daughters received the news. Fountaine, who was only two, would never know his father. The pension to which George had been entitled expired with his death; in the mid-nineteenth century the law did not permit a widow to make a claim on behalf of a deceased husband. Overnight, the family was bereft of an income, other than the money that Annie sent home or that her sister, Emily, may have earned. For the Smiths, this dire situation could have landed them in the workhouse.

Curiously, this did not happen. By the following year, Ruth had returned to an address where the family had once lived, in 1851: 29 Montpelier Place, situated in the respectable lower-middle-class Knightsbridge neighborhood that they had come to know as home.* With

---

* This address at Montpelier Place was around the corner from Thomas Smith and his wife, who lived at 36 Montpelier Row. George and Ruth do not appear on the 1851 census, but the

three floors, including a basement kitchen and larder, as well as a first-floor parlor, which hinted at middle-class pretensions, this was certainly the most comfortable house the family had occupied. It is unlikely that Ruth could have afforded the rent on such a property without assistance. After George's death, Leyland would have paid what was owed of his valet's quarterly wage to his wife, and, given the tragic circumstances, he may have made a donation to the widow as well, a gesture not uncommon among employers at this time. Ruth invested the money she received wisely and, following the lead of many of her neighbors, took the lease on an adequately sized home and let out rooms to lodgers. Because the house was equipped with a full kitchen and scullery below stairs, she could make some extra income by taking in laundry.

Due to its affordability and its location near the mansions of Knightsbridge, Montpelier Place and the surrounding streets were a haven for those in domestic service. Housemaids, butlers, valets, and footmen filled the census returns for the area from the 1860s through the 70s. Additionally, the street's position close to several mews (or groups of buildings that include private stables) meant that more than ten addresses on Montpelier Place alone were occupied by coachmen and grooms. Among them was a young man named John Chapman.

Little is known about the man who appeared one day at the door of 29 Montpelier Place and inquired about lodgings. Although he and Ruth shared the same surname, their families apparently had no connection; still, John's name may have endeared him to his soon-to-be-landlady at their first meeting. Born in 1844, John came from a family of "horse-keepers" in Newmarket, Suffolk. This center of racing and horse breeding would have given Chapman an immersive education in the needs and care of these animals. He and four of his brothers started out as stable assistants and grooms, brushing, feeding, and exercising horses, before eventually working their way through the ranks to become coach drivers. By the second half of the 1860s, John had

---

birth certificate of Miriam in 1851 gives their address as 29 Montpelier Place, confirming that the family had lived here earlier.

come to London to pursue his trade, probably in the employment of a family.

It might be that Annie met her mother's lodger in the kitchen of the family home, on a rare day away from her workplace. Or perhaps Annie was residing at home when John came into her life. Either way, something blossomed between them, though it is impossible to say what, exactly. Annie, at age twenty-seven, was not yet married, a situation not unusual for a woman who had spent her "eligible years" in domestic service. But at this age she knew that to refuse an opportunity to marry might mean passing the rest of her days as a spinster, a person universally regarded with pity. With the exception of Fountaine, who was still a boy, the Smiths were now a family of women, headed by a widow. The addition of a man, who might earn a steady livelihood and act as paterfamilias, would have been most welcome. This would have been Annie's great moment — a chance to make a success of her life, to become everything society intended for her. No longer just a helpmeet to her family, she could become the mistress of her own home and, most important, a wife and a mother.

MRS. CHAPMAN

LIKE MANY VICTORIAN newlyweds, Mr. and Mrs. John Chapman made an appointment to have their photograph taken, dressed in their Sunday finest. John removed his hat when they arrived at the Brompton Road studio, and the couple were shown to a corner, where a suitable backdrop had been unfurled behind some furniture. Either they or the photographer had chosen the pleasant outdoor scene: a set of garden steps leading to a church in the distance. The canvas was flanked by drapery, to make it look as if the sitters were posing before a large picture window. Annie was placed at the center, upon a chair, while John was directed to stand beside her and lean, with casual authority, against a wood-and-plaster plinth. Since this photograph was to commemorate the start of a new marriage, the photographer rested a Bible on Annie's lap. As a wife and would-be mother, she was to be the family guardian of all that was sacred in the state of matrimony: fidelity, fecundity, compassion, meekness, servility, and cleanliness of body and soul.

When the photographer removed the camera's lens cap and exposed the negative to the light, he caught Annie and John as they were in May 1869. Mrs. Chapman was no stranger to the fashions worn along the sidewalks of Knightsbridge and the tree-lined promenades of Hyde Park. She sits back in the chair, the shape of her corset visible beneath her dress. Her gown, in a checked pattern, with small black buttons along the front of her bodice and dark piping around her cuffs and shoulders, is draped about her tapered bell-shaped hoop skirt, very much à la mode in 1868–69. Although the Chapmans were not wealthy, Annie's dress does not lack ornamentation. In addition to her wedding ring, she wears little gold-hoop earrings and a large ornate brooch at her throat, while a dark belt with a prominent gilt clasp cinches her waist. John, in his frock coat, one leg crossed and an arm leaning with easy confidence on the plinth, displays the gold chain and fobs of that essential piece of coachman's equipment: his pocket watch. Although neither Annie nor John would be considered conventionally handsome by the standards of their era, both convey an air of assurance. Beneath a broad forehead, framed by fashionably braided dark hair, Annie's large blue eyes stare intently at the camera. John matches her expression with one of pride and a stern, down-turned Victorian mouth.

The Chapmans' image was recorded in a daguerreotype, an early form of photography widely available by the middle of the nineteenth century. The less prestigious studios, which catered to the better-off working classes, offered customers a very plain image, without furniture or backdrops. The Chapmans might have chosen to celebrate their union cheaply and simply at such a studio. For five shillings, they would receive a set of three cartes-de-visite, small photographs (three and a half by four inches) pasted on card. But John and Annie aspired to something better. They wished to own a photograph that expressed their hopes for a prosperous future, and they were willing to pay for it. The picture they ordered was a cabinet photograph, a larger size intended for framing and typically set on a mantel or a side table in a middle-class parlor.

The couple had been married on May 1 of that year at All Saints Church on Ennismore Gardens in Knightsbridge, where the Smith family had attended services since Annie was a girl. It is likely the couple and the wedding party walked from Montpelier Place, Annie proudly parading through the neighborhood on her bridal day. Emily signed as Annie's witness, and John was attended by his colleague, a fellow coachman called George White, with whom the newlyweds are believed to have shared a house at 1 Brooks Mews North, shortly after they were married.[1]

Annie, the daughter of a gentleman's valet, had done well to marry a gentleman's coachman. John Chapman was not a hackney-cab driver, the sort known to loaf about in pubs with a glass of brandy, speak in strings of swear words, and spend the night asleep in the back of his cab; nor was John a hassled omnibus driver, who hauled common working people east to west, or north to south. A private coachman was employed by a wealthy family as the head or second driver of his master's or mistress's vehicles. The primary coachman had charge of the larger, more prestigious carriages, such as the barouche, which required two horses, whereas the second coachman would drive vehicles drawn by a single horse. Like Annie's father, her husband had a role that placed him near the top of the servants' hierarchy. Unlike most other domestics attached to a household, the coachman was granted a certain degree of independence. If married, he and his family were expected to live in the mews, adjacent to or above the stables, where he could keep watch over the groom's activities, maintain the vehicles, and care for the horses. Although he might opt to dine with the upper servants in the housekeeper's room, the coachman more regularly took his meals alongside his wife, in their own home. In London, where some extensive residences had their own mews and stabling, a coachman might live rent-free; in other cases he would be granted an allowance permitting him to choose his own lodgings, provided they were nearby.

In the 1860s, a coachman like John could expect to earn between thirty-five and eighty pounds per year, depending upon the social standing of his employer. This sum did not include tips, which would further pad his wages. Employers also typically provided their coachmen with at least one or two sets of stable dress for working and one livery (a uniform), which included two pairs of boots and two hats (because hats tended to blow away in inclement weather). These benefits — a reliable income, possibly a rent-free home, and very few clothing expenses — would allow John's family a slightly better quality of life than many others of their social class. Money could be set aside and aspirations ignited.

Socially, much like the family of the gentleman's valet, the private, London-based coachman and his dependents occupied an awkward no-man's-land within the territory of the working classes. Described as "one of the most important and comfortable" of servants, the coachman was said to preside "over a little establishment of his own; his horses and coach, as well as the stables, are all tended by 'help.'" This allowed him to look "forth from his elevated position with an aspect of stolid gravity."[2] These privileges of the private coachman were sometimes known to give his family, especially his wife, delusions of grandeur. The journalist and social reformer Henry Mayhew comments that the typical coachman boasted that his position meant that his spouse did not have to work; coachmen could "keep [their] wives too respectable for that." Some families were well enough resourced to hire a maid of their own, or even to send their daughters to boarding school. However, these trappings of middle-class life rubbed against reality. Coachmen generally lived in the narrow mews, strung with laundry lines and smelling of stables. Nonetheless, these humble homes, usually with three or four rooms, one of them designed as a respectable parlor, were located in some of the country's most aristocratic districts.

This was especially true for John and Annie. During the first eight years of their marriage, John worked for a family in Onslow Square; an employer who lived near Jermyn Street, in St. James; and "for a nobleman on Bond Street."* Their little houses sat in the shadow of imperial London, a short stroll from the imposing gentlemen's clubs of Pall Mall and the gates of Buckingham Palace. Annie's daily walks would have taken her past the twinkling gaslit shop windows of Piccadilly and Bond Street and through the Burlington Arcade, with its colorful displays of the latest hats, shoes, walking sticks, glassware, jewelry,

---

* The Chapmans lived for at least three years at 17 South Bruton Mews, off Berkeley Square (near to Bond Street), as well as at 69 Onslow Mews, behind Onslow Square, in Belgravia, and at 4 Wells Street, off Jermyn Street in Piccadilly. Neither the Chapmans nor the address, 17 South Bruton Mews, appears on the rate books for the period they lived there, which suggests that the property may have belonged to part of a larger holding, which paid rates separately. This would support the suggestion that John was employed by a nobleman — as of yet to be identified.

lace, watches, cigars, flowers, and wine. These busy thoroughfares rattled with the conveyances of statesmen and society beauties, en route
to Westminster or the rooms of the newly built Criterion for tea. It is
likely that Annie was more than just a spectator of these pleasures, but
partook of them as well. John's salary allowed a few special purchases:
gloves, a nice hat, a book from Hatchards, a peek at the wonders of the
Egyptian Hall or the Royal Academy at Burlington House.

While life in London held many benefits for a private coachman,
John's work could come and go like the tide. Employers who engaged
staff while they dwelt in the capital were often there only temporarily,
for a few years or a season or two. An ideal situation would be one of
more permanence, with a landed family whose main residence lay outside London. Given the series of tragedies to have befallen the Smiths,
it is likely that Annie and John remained in London on account of
her reluctance to part with her mother and siblings. As John was the
only adult male in the family, he too may have come under pressure
to superintend the interests of Ruth, Emily, Georgina, Miriam, and
young Fountaine, who had recently won a place as a boarding pupil
at the Grey Coat School in Westminster. Even after their marriage,
the couple returned regularly for visits and slightly longer sojourns at
29 Montpelier Place. In 1870, rather than summon Ruth to assist her
in the birth of her first child, Annie returned to the sanctuary of her
mother's home in anticipation of the first pangs of labor. On June 25,
she delivered a little girl, whom she named Emily Ruth, for the two
women with whom she shared the closest bonds. By 1873, this child
had been joined by a sister, Annie Georgina.

Much as she had done on the occasion of her marriage, Annie would
later insist on having photographs taken of her little girls. At the end
of 1878, Annie dressed eight-year-old Emily Ruth in her best clothes: a
tartan dress, with a large bow at the neck and a set of buttons running
down the front. She put her in a pair of striped stockings and boots,
and tied a ribbon at the top of the girl's shoulder-length brown hair.
As a final touch, a large necklace of girlish beads was strung about her
neck before her mother took her down the Brompton Road to the
studio of Wood & Co. The photographer, an expert in coaxing even
the worst-behaved children into position, got the wan, delicate-look-

ing Emily to lean her elbow against a writing table, as if posing in a schoolroom. Three years later, this exercise was performed again with Annie Georgina. During a visit to Ruth, Annie dressed her younger daughter in the same handed-down frock and beads that her sister had worn and once more went down the Brompton Road, this time to the Sutch Brothers studio. Annie showed the photographer Emily Ruth's picture and instructed him to pose the slightly more robust-looking Annie Georgina in precisely the same manner, though against a different backdrop. Placed side by side in a frame, the daughters, captured at the same age, in the same clothing, gazed toward each other.

The timing of the first of these pictures was significant, in that it marked a change in the Chapmans' fortunes. It is likely that a copy of Emily Ruth's photo was intended for her grandmother, for by the beginning of 1879, John had accepted the position of head coachman to Francis Tress Barry, a gentleman of considerable wealth with a country estate in the county of Berkshire. The Chapmans could not have hoped for a more promising opportunity.

Like many nineteenth-century industrialists, Francis Tress Barry had come from a relatively ordinary upper-middle-class family. Born in 1825, he completed his schooling at sixteen and directly entered business. After establishing himself as a merchant in northern Spain, Barry began to explore the commercial possibilities in the copper mines of Portugal. It was here that he made his fortune, eventually becoming the head of his own successful mining firm, Mason and Barry. The honors and sinecures needed in order to rise in society soon followed. In 1872 he was made the consul general for the Republic of Ecuador, and in 1876 he was created Baron de Barry of Portugal. However, acquiring similar recognition in Britain demanded a good deal more patience and strategy. It was not until 1890 that he was elected an MP for Windsor, and nine years later was granted a baronetcy by Queen Victoria.

Barry was a savvy entrepreneur, and his purchase of the estate of St. Leonard's Hill in 1872 was obviously designed to place himself and his family under the nose of the queen. The 627-acre estate in Clewer, a village at the periphery of Windsor, was said to "yield one of the noblest views of the castle from its eastern lawn." Additionally, it boasted more than "230 acres of old park and forest," home to "gigantic oaks, stately beech, elm, fir and Californian redwood." The property also came with an impressive pedigree. Its manor house had been built in the eighteenth century for Maria, Countess Waldegrave, and later came into the possession of the Earls Harcourt. When Barry acquired it, he intended to create an elegant and impressive stately home in the most modern fashion. His vision was placed in the hands of the architect Charles Henry Howell, who set about constructing an industrialist's palace in the modish French chateau style. While Howell maintained some of the original eighteenth-century rooms, he rebuilt much of the house and added many unique late Victorian features. When guests entered the Mexican onyx–lined central hall of St. Leonard's Hill House, they were greeted by frescoes depicting scenes from Greek mythology and by an imposing staircase. There were grand reception rooms: a dining room, large and small drawing rooms, and, through a set of mahogany doors, a winter garden. Upstairs were six suites of bedrooms, and because Japanese decor had become the rage, Barry had one created in this style. On the ground floor, he could entertain lavishly, impressing his guests with a billiard room, a smoking room, a card room, and a library. As Barry wished for St. Leonard's Hill to have only the most modern conveniences, an early central heating system was installed, as well as conventional fireplaces, gas lighting, hot running water, toilets, and two hydraulic service elevators. Such a residence could not have been managed without a full complement of employees, and so Howell created a downstairs service area large enough to accommodate a staff of thirty servants.

John Chapman had been hired not only to drive Francis Tress Barry's coach, but also to maintain and supervise the running of his stables, which, like his employer's home, was a considerable affair. The stable block was built in a style similar to the mansion's and could house no fewer than thirty horses, along with several vehicles. Upon assuming his position, John became the master of two grooms, four stablemen, and a second coachman. The handling of the stable's accounts, the ordering of feed, supplies, and equipment, also fell into his charge. As Barry was one of the wealthiest and most prominent landowners in the area, John's duty was to represent him from atop his employer's highly polished carriage, in a tall hat and shining boots, and with a clean-shaven face. To most villagers and inhabitants of Windsor, Barry would only ever be known by his passing coach, and his coachman had to ensure his master left an impeccable impression.

John's prestigious position at St. Leonard's Hill entitled him and his family to live in the coachman's house, across the yard from the stables. For Annie, accustomed to life in London's mews, this was a significant improvement. The coachman's cottage was a house on an entirely different scale. It included a sitting room or formal parlor, and a living room, where the family would dine and spend most of their time, as well as a kitchen, a scullery, a wash house, a larder, and three bedrooms.[3] The family photographs in their neat frames would now have a proper room in which to be displayed.

If Annie aspired to officially enter the middle class, then their arrival at St. Leonard's Hill was a significant step forward. With a reasonably sized home and a comfortable income, Mrs. Chapman would hire a charwoman or a day maid to assist her with the more laborious homemaking tasks. Once the Chapmans had settled in, they sought to place nine-year-old Emily Ruth in "a highly respectable" young ladies' school in Windsor.[4] Annie and her children (when they were not in school) had the use of Francis Tress Barry's parkland and forests in which to wander and amuse themselves, and should the coachman's wife wish to visit the shops in Windsor, she could use one of the estate's fly carriages to convey her into town.

Annie was proud of having successfully scaled a rung on the social ladder; on occasion, she could be boastful. The way she described her husband's work reveals something of this attitude. In the spring of 1881, while John remained at St. Leonard's Hill, Annie brought her children to visit 29 Montpelier Place. Her sojourn at her mother's house happened to coincide with that year's census. When John, still at his job in Berkshire, was asked to provide his "rank, profession or occupation," he did not hesitate to describe himself as a "coachman, domestic servant." Mrs. Chapman, when the same question was posed to her, stated she was "the wife of a stud groom." It is possible that John's responsibilities had been extended to include the purchase and breeding of racing stock for Barry, yet Annie's way of describing herself may point to more grandiose ambitions. The landed gentry venerated stud grooms, the servants who managed a gentleman's racehorses. Due to his knowledge of equine flesh and ability to create prizewinners, the stud groom was regarded as a type of racing oracle. He had his master's ear and his respect, allowing a slight breach in the strict divide between social classes. A stud groom might be invited to carouse with gentlemen, taken to races, and asked to dine with his master. In this, he was something more than a coachman ever could be: a confidant of those in the upper ranks of society.

Francis Tress Barry well understood that the nearer a man placed himself to the social class above him, the better the chance of maneuvering himself into it. Since the completion of St. Leonard's Hill in 1878, Barry had made a concerted effort to announce his arrival by hosting dinners and gatherings. He took his place among the established landowners of Clewer — Sir Daniel Gooch, Sir Theodore Henry Brinckman, and Edmund Benson Foster. As it happened, Barry's conviviality may not have been the cause of his eventual entry into royal and aristocratic circles. He most likely won the friendship of Edward, Prince of Wales, and Princess Alexandra because of the location of St. Leonard's Hill. It was just four miles from Ascot Racecourse.

On June 15, 1881, Barry obligingly gave his house over to the royal party for Ascot week. Among those hosted at St. Leonard's Hill were the Duke of Cambridge, the Earl and Countess Spencer, the Countess Lonsdale, the Earls of Fife and Clonmell, Rear Admiral the Honourable H. Carr Glyn and his wife, and a number of the Prince of Wales's wealthy associates who enjoyed the racetrack and his fast living. Two visits to the races in Semi-State were planned for Tuesday and Thursday, to be followed by a series of private entertainments, including a picnic and boating party at nearby Virginia Water, and a modest ball at St. Leonard's Hill for "some of the parties in the neighbourhood" on the second-to-last night.[5] The preparation for this weeklong house party would have been months in the planning, and while John Chapman would be occupied with juggling the carriages and horses of the royal guests, Annie would have been able to watch the spectacle from afar.

On each trip to Ascot, the royal procession set out from the mansion in five open-topped landaus, led by "Her Majesty's bay and grey horses sent from the Royal mews at Windsor."[6] Flanked by outriders and postilions in livery, they proceeded down the drive and through Windsor Forest, as all the estate looked on at the excitement. The sight of their return in the afternoon would be no less thrilling: the ladies in frilled, feathered, and flowered bonnets and veils, Princess Alexandra's unmistakable curls, the Prince of Wales with his hat and triangular beard, looking fat and bored. Later in the evening, the party might be seen walking along Francis Barry's grounds, trailing bustled skirts and shadows. The carriages would come and go throughout this week, and later, on other occasions too. St. Leonard's Hill had done the trick for Barry, drawing him firmly into the prince's circle. The royals and their retinue would be back for further dinners, shooting parties, and races. The sounds of merrymaking — music and laughter — would blow down from the mansion to the coachman's cottage nearby; the cottage where John and Annie's children slumbered in their own bedrooms, the cottage with a sitting room, the cottage that had brought constancy and what should have been contentment. This might have been Annie's story in its entirety; it might have ended in quiet, middle-class comfort on a gentleman's estate. When it came time for John to retire, their saved-up pennies might have bought them a little house in Windsor. Their girls, whose schooling they could pay for, might have grown up to marry middle-class men, perhaps a shopkeeper, a clerk, or even a local lawyer. The courses of all of their lives may have ended quite differently had Annie Chapman not been an alcoholic.

DEMON DRINK

I N 1889, A letter from a confirmed teetotaler and committed Christian appeared in the *Pall Mall Gazette*.[1] Throughout the nineteenth century, newspapers were accustomed to receiving this type of correspondence from the many adherents of the temperance movement, who sought to restrict the sale and consumption of alcohol. However, this letter differed from those offering the usual condemnation and biblical quotes. It was written by a parishioner in Knightsbridge by the name of Miriam Smith.

"Just before I was six years old, my father cut his throat, leaving my mother with five children, three girls older, and one [child] younger than myself," the missive began. Miriam Smith then went on to provide details of how she and her sisters came to sign the abstinence pledge, promising to forgo the use of "fermented spirits." All but the eldest sister had committed herself to this path. "We tried to persuade the one given to drink to give it up. She was married and in a good position. Over and over again she signed the pledge and tried to keep it. Over and over again she was tempted and fell."

Annie's struggle had been lifelong. Miriam suggested that her sister had inherited "the curse" of alcoholism from their father, and that her problem began "when she was quite young." How young, precisely, she did not say, but it is likely that Annie's discovery of the pacifying effects of the bottle may have corresponded with the loss of her siblings and her placement in service shortly thereafter. As London's water was largely contaminated, in its place, low-alcohol beer was usually provided to laborers. In fact, alcohol was ubiquitous, and almost unavoidable, in daily life. Any middle-class house, aside from those that had adopted abstinence, would have brandy, sherry, sweet wine, or some form of spirit on hand to imbibe as a "tonic" for anything from a headache to a cold, a fever, a toothache, or to rub on the gums of teething children. Spirits and medicine were considered almost interchangeable; a hot brandy and water was taken to aid sleep, ward off the chill, and dispel malaise. The principal ingredient in most shop-bought curatives for coughs, rheumatism, and nearly any complaint was alcohol. The "dose" and the "dram" might even taste and smell identical; medicines differed only in the addition of substances such as laudanum or cocaine, which could also be addictive.

Like many whose drinking becomes an issue, Annie, in the early years of her disease, when she was still working as a servant, may not have perceived that her alcohol consumption was becoming a problem. During the mid-nineteenth century, working-class amusements still revolved around the convivial drink and camaraderie to be found in the local pub, where servants often congregated during a spare hour or on their day off. Habitual drunkenness became an issue only when it impinged on an employee's ability to perform work. By the 1870s, however, addiction had been identified as a problem with moral implications. Drunkenness, especially in public, came to be seen as a marker of a person's degenerate character, "intemperate" nature, poor judgment, moral weakness, and idleness. Invariably, conspicuous inebriation became associated with the poor and the most uncouth of the working classes. Those among them who aspired to a middle-class identity, as Annie did, would attempt to conceal or deny any growing dependency. This was easily accomplished when one had a stock of medicinal brandy, cordials, or whiskey on hand in a cabinet, or a headache was an excuse for a trip to the pharmacy for a little bottle of spirit laced with laudanum. In a pinch, the baby's gripe water might be drunk, with no one being any the wiser. For a time, Annie would have been able to hide her addiction within the confines of her home, but her family would have known of it.

Annie's tendency to drink may have been precipitated by loneliness. One commentator remarked that this problem was especially noticeable "in young wives whose husbands are away all day." This was the paradox of upward mobility: a wife who doesn't have to work, who can afford a maid, and whose children are at school has to find some way of distracting herself. As a coachman, John might work very early and exceptionally late hours, leaving little time for sociability at home, if indeed he returned home. His work ferrying his master or mistress about likely took him on lengthy excursions, leaving Annie quite isolated, especially after the Chapmans moved to St. Leonard's Hill. It was suggested that middle-class women in such circumstances often acquired the habit of 'nipping,'" in order to ward off their melancholy spirits. By the last quarter of the nineteenth century, the appearance of "ladies saloon bars" meant that having a "wee nip" in public might also be veiled with respectability. Moralists complained that it was "now the regular thing for women to go in and have a drink when shopping," and it was not unusual to see a well-dressed woman joining her husband or son for a tipple. As London boasted of twenty thousand pubs by 1870, there would have been no shortage of opportunities for Annie to have taken "refreshment" either inside or outside her home.

It was perhaps Annie's drinking and a desire to remove her from the temptations of city life that played a role in John's decision to accept Francis Tress Barry's offer of a position at St. Leonard's Hill. However, so long as his wife desired drink, it would never be entirely beyond her reach. Far from her mother and sisters, Annie was likely to have felt a greater sense of isolation and boredom, which would have only increased her itch to self-medicate with alcohol. The public houses of Windsor were easily accessible during an excursion to the shops, as were the drinking establishments of the villages of Clewer and Dedworth, only a short stroll from home.

Keeping Annie away from drink was but one of the challenges the couple faced. Miriam Smith's letter to the newspaper revealed that over the course of her sister's marriage, she gave birth to eight chil-

dren, though "six of these have been victims to the curse [of alcohol]."
Annie's first child, Emily, appeared to be healthy as an infant, but by
the time she was eight, she was suffering from epileptic seizures. Emily's illness may not at the time have been associated with her mother's
addiction, but later such disorders were discovered to be linked to maternal drinking during pregnancy. On March 5, 1872, Annie gave birth
to a second daughter, Ellen Georgina, who lived no longer than a day.
The following year, Annie Georgina was born with what is now recognized as fetal alcohol syndrome. Its physical characteristics include
small, wide-set eyes, a thin upper lip, and a smooth ridge that runs below the nose to the top lip; these features are clearly distinguishable in
Annie Georgina's childhood photograph. Annie's two little girls were
briefly joined by another, Georgina, born on April 25, 1876, who lived
only until May 5. Shortly before the Chapmans left London, Annie
gave birth to George William Harry, in November 1877.[2] The infant
was born sickly and died eleven weeks later. Annie was soon pregnant
again and delivered Miriam Lily on the St. Leonard's Hill estate on July
16, 1879. This daughter survived a week less than her brother and died
in October. On November 21, 1880, John Alfred arrived. This boy, the
last of the Chapmans' children, suffered from paralysis.* As Miriam's
letter suggested, it was obvious to Annie's family, and perhaps to Annie
too, what lay at the heart of these tragedies.

Late-nineteenth-century science had already begun to uncover the
links between maternal alcohol consumption and its danger to children. As early as 1878, one medical journal asserted that substantial evidence had been gathered to prove that "drunkenness in the parent before and after birth has more effect on infant mortality than all other
causes."[3] The realization that her drinking was likely to have been behind the suffering of her children may have pushed Annie deeper into
despair at her perceived inability to control her impulses. By 1881, her
difficulties in remaining sober while caring for an infant with a disability may be the reason for her prolonged visit to her mother when John

---

* Miriam Smith's letter asserted that Annie gave birth eight times, though to date, it has been
possible to identify seven of the children she bore. The other child may not have been carried
to term or was a stillbirth, which didn't require registration.

Alfred was about four months old. It is believed that while in London, Annie sought to place her son in an appropriate hospital for children.

By the time of Annie's visit to 29 Montpelier Place in early spring, her sisters, Emily Latitia and Miriam, had set up shop as dressmakers in their own home at 128 Walton Street, which ran to the rear of the recently expanded Harrods department store. According to Miriam's account, she and her sisters had not only become Presbyterians but had also embraced teetotalism after "hearing a sermon on Christians and Total Abstinence." The complete rejection of alcohol resonated with those who found themselves balanced precariously on the edge of middle-class life. By eschewing drink, a hardworking man or woman could save money and build a better life for themself and their family. Annie's sisters not only adhered to this creed but prospered by it financially.

This determination to live in sobriety went hand-in-hand with the popular philosophy of "self-help." Its proponents held that a person's own choices and behavior were the cause of poverty and problems such as alcoholism; tough-mindedness and grit could overcome them. Signing the "abstinence pledge," in the presence of family or a member of the clergy, was viewed as a solemn promise to adhere to the principles of teetotalism. It included a commitment to restrict one's impulses, to moderate one's desires, and to make a conscious effort at moral improvement. Unfortunately, sincere effort did not always make for a successful outcome. In Miriam's letter she made it clear that Annie desperately did want to give up drink, but found it almost impossible. Her sisters had convinced her to commit several times to the pledge; they had prayed for her and with her in her difficulties, but could not get her to adhere to it permanently. During her visit in 1881, they likely witnessed how desperately she struggled, and the degree to which the disease had taken hold.

In the following year, Annie's battle with addiction came to a head. Toward the end of that November, her eldest daughter, twelve-year-old Emily Ruth, began to sicken. When the child's high temperature gave way to a spreading red rash, Annie would have recalled the signs and symptoms of scarlet fever, the disease that had devastated her family when she was a girl. The doctors came and went, and eventu-

ally informed Emily's mother that her child was afflicted with menin-
gitis, which bore similar traits and was no less life threatening. Annie
did not contend well with her daughter's raging illness and the painful
memories that certainly accompanied it. As the days passed and Emily's condition worsened, Annie drew support from her usual source,
the bottle and the stultifying haze its contents threw across her distress. When Emily died on November 26, her mother was not present at her bedside. Instead, Caroline Elsbury, the wife of a local farm
laborer, who may also have charred for the Chapman family, tended to
the girl in her dying moments.*

At some point prior to that autumn, Annie had begun to acquire
a reputation among the local police and the Windsor magistrate for
public drunkenness. She had been found wandering between the villages and along the roads from the St. Leonard's Hill estate. From all
accounts, the coachman's wife did not make for an ugly drunk, but
rather a sad, sullen, quiet one, weighed down by heartache. That final
week of November her pain would have been unbearable.

It is unknown for how long Annie had absented herself or where she
was eventually found; ensconced in a public house or swaying down
the road in Clewer in search of respite. Whatever the circumstances,
her behavior was enough to raise serious alarm among her family. On
November 30, the day that the Chapmans buried their daughter, Annie's sisters, Emily and Miriam, paid an urgent visit to the Spelthorne
Sanatorium, on the outskirts of London.

In 1879, growing public concern about the societal impact of alcoholism gave rise to the Habitual Drunkards Act. The law, which sought
to offer rehabilitation for alcoholics instead of punishment in prison,
was responsible for the establishment of asylums, or sanatoriums,
for the treatment of those "who by a means of habitual intemperate
drinking of intoxicating liquor is dangerous to . . . herself, or to others, or incapable of managing . . . herself, and . . . her affairs." Patients
were admitted to these "retreats" either voluntarily or "upon the application of their friends" and were required to spend at least a month,
but no more than two years, in treatment. Spelthorne Sanatorium in

---

* Caroline Elsbury is cited on the death certificate as having witnessed the death.

Feltham was one such institution, designed especially for the treatment of women, predominantly of the middle class.

An entry of December 9, 1882, in the Spelthorne Sanatorium logbook reads, "Mrs. Chapman arrived — brought by her sister from Windsor." As Miriam's account asserted, Annie agreed to enter this "home for the intemperate . . . of her own accord." This process involved writing a formal letter of application to the head of Spelthorne, which was then witnessed by a justice of the peace. As Francis Tress Barry, her own landlord, held that title in Berkshire, it is possible that he may also have had a hand in her admission for treatment.

It is likely that the Misses Smith had been told of Spelthorne before their sister was in urgent need of its support. Its founders, the Antrobus family, lived in Knightsbridge and drew their charitable cause to the attention of local clergy, who spread the word among parishioners.* As alcohol dependency was viewed in part as a weakness of the will, the rehabilitation offered at the sanatorium was largely spiritual in nature. However, in addition to daily attendance at chapel, the program also sought to correct the habits of mind and body. Spelthorne's setting, on four acres surrounded by yew trees and country lanes, was considered the sort of clean, uplifting, and health-promoting environment that also improved the spirit. Its facilities and dormitories, situated within "a fine old country house," were decorated with "gaily-striped counterpanes, suitable pictures and texts," and "plain yet shining furniture" intended to draw "the mind away from thoughts of debasing self-indulgence."[4] The institution's "patients" (used in place of the typical institutional term "inmates" so as not to "wound the pride") were encouraged to walk and amuse themselves on the grounds when not cultivating the two kitchen gardens or working in the laundry — washing, drying, and ironing their own and their fellow patients' clothes. Any form of idleness was discouraged, as it was thought to open the

---

* In 1884, after the death of "Miss Antrobus," Spelthorne was taken over by the order of St. Mary the Virgin in Wantage, an Anglican convent. Interestingly, this order also had links with the Anglican Sisters of Mercy in Clewer, an organization concerned with the rehabilitation of "fallen" and troubled women. The order had a large presence in Clewer during Annie's residence at St. Leonard's Hill, and it is possible that the sisters there offered some assistance or advice in dealing with her behavior.

door to cravings. Instead, the women were allowed to read and encouraged to produce crochet and needlework, which was displayed during inspections by board members and donors. When women had demonstrated a suitable level of progress, they were reintroduced slowly to the outside world and its temptations. This usually involved escorted walks through the local area or even shopping excursions to nearby Hounslow. Inmates also received regular treats, such as "musical evenings" or group outings to London, presumably to stave off melancholy and despair, which married patients were especially prone to.

Annie committed herself to a yearlong program of treatment. According to the logbooks, her time at Spelthorne was relatively quiet. Her name isn't recorded among the occasional troublemakers, the women who found giving up alcohol nearly impossible, who tore their clothing, destroyed furniture, or lashed out in violence. Annie was permitted visitors as well. On December 30, shortly after she arrived at the sanatorium, the logbook recorded that "Mrs Chapman's husband called to see her." John, who must have worried incessantly about his wife, had begged leave from his obligations to the Barrys during the height of the Christmas social calendar to ensure that she had settled in well. It was he who was paying the expense of her treatment, at a cost of twelve pence per week.

Shortly before she was discharged, in November 1883, it appears that Annie was permitted to make a short visit home, perhaps to assess her readiness to resume her old life. Evidently she passed this simple test sufficiently and returned to Spelthorne on November 14 to complete the final month of her program. She was officially released on December 20, in the company of one of the nursing sisters, Laura Squire, who, it is recorded, "took Mrs Chapman to Windsor to join her husband."

That Christmas and the New Year period would have been a joyful (and dry) one among the Chapman family, now four in number. As Miriam wrote, her sister "came out a changed woman — a sober wife and mother, and things went on very happily."

The story that Annie's sister then goes on to relate sounds almost apocryphal: like a cautionary tale from a teetotaler's handbook. Several months after Annie's reunion with her family, John was stricken with "a severe cold." As "his duty compelled him to go out," he "took a glass of hot whiskey" to fortify himself against the poor weather. With a bottle under the roof of her own house, it was remarkable that Annie managed to resist temptation for as long as she had. John "had been careful enough not to have it in her presence." But on this occasion he "drank it and came to kiss her before departing. In that kiss the fumes of alcohol were transmitted and all the cravings came back."

According to Miriam, that kiss quite literally brought about the death of everything Annie had fought to achieve.

Annie must have turned over every room in search of that bottle. It did not matter in the end whether she found it. "She went out" and "in less than an hour was a drunken mad woman."

Annie's failure, after more than a year of progress, completely devastated her. "She never tried again," lamented her sister. Annie said to her, in words redolent with the profound suffering of the chronic alcoholic, "it was of no use, no one knew the fearful struggle . . . unless I can keep out of sight and smell, I can never be free."

John had arrived at this realization as well. His wife's return to her old habits found her once more wandering stupefied through the St. Leonard's Hill estate. In the past, the Barrys had been lenient concerning the problems of their head coachman and his wife. It is likely that Annie's residency at Spelthorne came about due to a gentle ultimatum issued by the family. Now that the Barrys moved in society's highest circles, they could not risk the embarrassment of harboring a notorious and unpredictable inebriate on their grounds. Spelthorne was intended to cure Annie, and the failure of this plan was the last straw. Francis Barry made it known to his coachman that he would not indulge Mrs. Chapman any longer. John had two choices: remove Annie from his home or face dismissal.[5]

Although John had served his master since 1879, it is unlikely he would have received the sort of reference necessary to acquire another job as well remunerated or prestigious. As the father of two children, one severely disabled, it was necessary that he consider their long-term welfare.

The decision to separate appears to have been amicable, but it was not without heartbreak for both parties. John's devotion to his wife, in spite of her affliction, demonstrates nothing short of genuine love. It would have been out of character for him to simply cut adrift the mother of his children and, in her fragile state, set her loose into the world. Just as placing Annie at Spelthorne had involved her entire family, they would have a role in deciding what was to become of her now. When John made arrangements to pay Annie a maintenance of ten shillings a week, it was almost certainly with a view to having her return to her mother's home. Back at 29 Montpelier Place, Ruth and Annie's siblings could watch over her. Ten shillings a week, some of which would have assisted Ruth in supporting her daughter, would have gone a long way toward buying some comfort and a few of the middle-class luxuries — perfumed soaps, inexpensive jewelry — to which Annie had grown accustomed. She would be better off among her devoted sisters, John would have reasoned, and perhaps might even stand a chance of recovering. With the support of her beloved family, Annie might just be all right.

DARK ANNIE

Although John's scheme had been well-intentioned, it lasted little longer than it took for Annie to arrive in London. Whether it was a matter of weeks or days, Annie would have found it impossible to have lived under the auspices of her family. Neither her mother nor her sisters would have tolerated her drinking. The shame of her affliction, the shame of her inability to cure herself, and now, the shame of having failed as a mother and a wife, would have made a relationship with them almost impossible for her to bear. Miriam wrote that her sister told them "she would always keep out of our way" but that "she must and would have the drink." Ultimately, Annie, like so many addicts, chose to live without those she loved rather than live without the substance she craved.

In previous attempts to recount the events of Annie Chapman's life, one of the greatest oversights has always been a failure to examine how someone who had lived on a country estate in Berkshire and resided in Knightsbridge ended up in Whitechapel. This alteration in circumstance could not happen overnight; both geographically and socially, it is not a natural trajectory. Even for a person based in Knightsbridge, in the west of the capital, a sudden slip into financial hardship would not necessitate a relocation to the slums of Whitechapel in the east. The East End did not have a monopoly on cheap lodgings; they, along with destitution and criminality, could be found in large and small pockets throughout London. If Annie had found life insufferable at her mother's house, she needn't have traveled any farther than the streets across from Knightsbridge barracks to find a four-penny-a-night lodging house or a room for five shillings a week. Had she wished to avoid her family altogether, she might have strayed farther afield to the nearby down-at-heel neighborhoods of Chelsea, Fulham, or Battersea, or ventured to the center of London, to Marylebone, Holborn, Paddington, St. Giles, or even Clerkenwell or Westminster; lodgings might also be found south of the river in Lambeth, Southwark, or Bermondsey. There was no obvious reason why Annie, who had spent most of her life between Knightsbridge and the West End of London, would have had any cause or inclination to move to a part of town with which she had no familiarity — unless, of course, she knew of or accompanied someone there.

In the late nineteenth century, Notting Hill, just across Hyde Park and to the west, became notorious for its shabby working-class housing and deprivation. While many of its streets are marked in black on Charles Booth's poverty map and are condemned in the notebooks of Booth's social researchers as "hopelessly degraded," others are simply described as being occupied by the working poor; residents whose windows were covered with "dirty curtains" and whose children wore "threadbare clothes."[1] Notting Hill's proximity to the area of the city Annie knew best, while also lying beyond the immediate reach of her family, would have made the location a likely place for her to have settled. Here, she might maintain herself quietly, collecting her weekly allowance from the post office, while living in a single room and pursuing her drinking undisturbed. As an addict in a new community, it would not have been long before Annie discovered fellow travelers among her neighbors, especially in the local beer houses and pubs. It is likely that one such establishment was the place where she became acquainted with a man whom her friends would come to call "Jack Sievey." It seems that "Sievey," or "Sievy," acquired his name on account of his profession as a maker of wire or iron sieves. Little more is known about him, except that he had a connection with Notting Hill and that he and Annie eventually became a pair, almost certainly on account of their shared love of drink.

It is difficult to fathom the emotional despair to which Annie must have succumbed when agreeing to part with her husband and children, and after turning her back on her mother and siblings. As one whose family subscribed to religious teachings and who strove to maintain respectability, Annie would have perceived her fall as an unredeemable one. According to the era's definition of womanhood, she had failed. She had proven her inability to mother her children, to maintain a home for her husband, or to care for anyone, even herself. The female drunkard was considered an abomination, one who allowed "their most brutal and repulsive penchants to come to the surface," one who "abandons herself to sensuality, and who . . . becomes unsexed in her manners."[2] Perversely, recognition of her own disgrace kept the "female inebriate" drinking "in order to drown her shame." Although her transgressions were not of a sexual nature, Victorian society conflated the "broken woman" with the "fallen woman." The woman who had lost her marriage and her home through her moral weakness was viewed with no less abhorrence than the woman who had engaged in extramarital sex. A woman who was "drunk and disorderly," who embarrassed herself in public, who demonstrated no regard for her appearance, was considered as much of a degenerate as a prostitute. They became one and the same; outcast women. Just as was the case with Polly Nichols, Annie's precarious position as a lone woman demanded that she find a male partner, despite the fact that she was still legally married. Whether or not she actually wished to throw in her lot with another man, her circumstances compelled her into what society would consider a state of adultery. However, this was a vicious circle. Annie was already considered morally ruined, so entering into a common-law relationship with Jack Sievey, which in legal terms rendered her an adulteress, no longer mattered.

Annie's ties to Jack Sievey provide a possible explanation for her appearance in Whitechapel during the second half of 1884, where it is likely he went in search of work. Since her arrival in that part of town, all of what remained of Annie's identity — the daughter of a guardsman, the wife of a gentleman's coachman, the mother of two children, the woman who strolled through Mayfair and Hyde Park, who sat proudly for her photograph in gold hoop earrings and a brooch — was left behind in West London. Annie was only ever known as Sievey's wife; Annie Sievey or Mrs. Sievey, and on occasion, as "Dark Annie," on account of her wavy brown hair, now streaked with gray. Annie did not speak much of her past, so that even her new friends, including the kind and loyal Amelia Palmer, the wife of a former foreman at the docks, were told only scant facts. When asked about her children, Annie gave mocking answers, saying that she had a son who was unwell and "in hospital" and a daughter "who had joined the circus" or "lived abroad in France." She told no one but Amelia the truth — that she was separated from her husband, who lived in Windsor, and that she had a mother and sisters with whom "she was not on friendly terms." Amelia remarked that in spite of this, her friend remained "a very respectable woman" whom she "never heard use bad language." Amelia also described Annie as "straightforward" and "a very clever and industrious little body" when she was sober.[3]

According to Amelia Palmer, the two friends met when Annie and Jack Sievey lived in and around Dorset Street. Although Dorset Street would not be crowned "the worst street in London" until the 1890s, its reputation for degradation was already well established. Even in the previous decade, it was composed almost exclusively of the cheapest, filthiest lodging houses and moldering, verminous "furnished rooms." Journalists and social reformers who visited there remarked that it was thronged with criminals. Even Charles Booth, who had walked nearly every byway of the capital, expressed near disbelief at what he witnessed there: "The worst street I have seen so far, thieves, prostitutes, bullies, all common lodging houses." The local police inspector, who escorted him, echoed his sentiments: "in his opinion [this is] the worst street in respect of poverty, misery, vice, of the whole of London. A cesspool into which had sunk the foulest & most degraded." Booth remarked that even Notting Hill or Notting Dale (as the poorest part was known) "is not so bad as this. Notting Dalers he said were very poor, shiftless & shifting; always on the move, poor tramps who might stay a month in the Dale and then move on doing the round of the London casual wards & ending up again in the Dale." Dorset Street, the inspector said, was different; it "might be stirred but its filth will always sink again in the same spot."[4]

When Annie and her "new husband" came to live there, most of Dorset Street was owned by two landlords — John McCarthy and William Crossingham — each equally ruthless and unprincipled when it came to managing their crumbling, vice-teeming properties. "Mr. and Mrs. Sievey" were known to stay at lodging houses on the street, primarily number 30, where Amelia and her husband also lived, but when the pair had managed to reserve some money, they would rent a furnished room instead. While these rooms offered more privacy than a communal lodging house, many believed their condition to be "infinitely worse." For ten pence a night, tenants might have a poorly ventilated room or one with broken windows, rotting wooden floors, damp walls, and ceilings with holes. Hot water was out of the question, and a stinking, malfunctioning toilet might be found at the top of the stairs or in the yard behind. The minimal furnishings, according to a journalist from the *Daily Mail,* consisted of "the oldest furniture to be found in the worst second-hand dealers in the slums. The fittings . . . are not worth more than a few shillings."[5] Annie's new situation was a far cry from her parlor and living room at St. Leonard's Hill. The recognition of this would have required still more drink to dull this memory and the emotions it aroused. Tragically, unlike most of the women residing nearby, Annie needn't have lived in such reduced circumstances, on "the worst street in London." Jack Sievey would have brought in an income and, failing that, they could always rely on ten shillings a week, Annie's maintenance. This sum might have paid for a better room elsewhere, as well as for food and coal. Instead it paid for alcohol — at least until December 1886.

In that month, quite without warning, the weekly payments suddenly stopped. According to Amelia Palmer, Annie was so alarmed by this that she sought out her "brother or sister-in-law," who, Amelia believed, "lived somewhere near Oxford Street in Whitechapel" in order to learn the cause.* John, she was informed, had fallen gravely ill. This news shook her so deeply that she determined she must see her husband and set off on foot to Windsor, in the midst of winter. She covered just over twenty-five miles in two days, trekking through West London and out beyond Brentford into the frozen countryside along the Bath Road. When it grew dark, she sought shelter at the casual ward at Colnbrook. Treading this road, alone with her thoughts, Annie must have turned over her every deed and each wrong turn in her mind. She had ample time to fret over her upcoming encounter and to worry about her children, even to feel heartsick at the thought of returning to Windsor and revisiting her past. All the while, she would fear arriving too late.

Staying the night at the casual ward set her back at least a morning, as she would be required to pick her share of oakum in exchange for her bed.† Upon her departure, she faced another five miles to New Windsor, the area she had known as a girl, off what was then called the Spital Road.‡ Before Annie had set out, she had learned of John's retirement, due to ill health, six months earlier. She had been told by relations that he no longer lived on Francis Tress Barry's estate, but rather he had taken a house on Grove Road, where he lived with the children for a time. Uncertain of his precise address, Annie stopped at the Merry Wives of Windsor, a pub on the corner of the street, and inquired after her husband. The publican distinctly recalled the visit from what he described as "a wretched looking woman having the appearance of a tramp." Annie told him that she had "walked down from London" because she had "been told that her husband, who had discontinued

---

* Amelia Palmer was not always reliable in recalling details about Annie's family, and it's likely that her in-laws did not live on or near Oxford Street in Whitechapel, but rather on or near New Oxford Street in Holborn. John Chapman's brother Alfred and his wife, Hannah, were the only members of his family who lived in London, and according to the 1871 and 1881 censuses, they seemed to be settled at addresses in Holborn. When the police made inquiries on and near Oxford Street in Whitechapel, they were unable to find anyone who knew or was related to John Chapman.
† Some casual wards loosely applied the two-night rule, and the facility at Colnbrook was believed to be one of them.
‡ This is now St. Leonard's Road, New Windsor.

sending her ten shillings a week, was ill." She then hardened her expression and claimed "she had come to Windsor to ascertain if the report was true and not merely an excuse for not sending her the money as usual."[6] The publican pointed her in direction of John's house — 1 Richmond Villas, Grove Road — and "did not see her again."

What next occurred is unknown. Presumably, Annie arrived prior to John's death, on Christmas Day, though she did not linger long enough to witness his passing. At the time, he was being nursed by Sally Westell, an elderly friend from the nearby almshouses.[7] The reunion between husband and wife must have been a bitter one indeed. Annie's addiction and the collapse of their marriage had felled John completely. Annie's sister Miriam described his appearance shortly before his premature death at age forty-five: "a white-haired, broken hearted man." Whether Miriam knew it or not, John too had apparently taken to drinking. According to his death certificate, his demise was on account of "cirrhosis of the liver-ascites and dropsy."[*]

John's death devastated Annie. Whatever mercenary reasons she had cited for marching to Windsor and back, her interest in seeing her husband was more than purely financial. When she returned to Dorset Street, she cried as she recounted the details of her ordeal to Amelia.[8] Annie would never be the same. "After the death of her husband," her friend recalled, "she seemed to give way altogether." Whether it was on account of losing the extra ten shillings or because Annie had grown morose and mournful, Jack Sievey decided he was done with John Chapman's widow. In early 1887, he left her to return to Notting Hill. Now, without a husband or a common-law protector, Annie found herself entirely unsupported. Few women found it easy to survive in the slums without a male companion; it was therefore imperative that she find one.

For a time, it seems she took up with a hard-drinking peddler of chapbooks called "Harry the Hawker," who also inhabited the lodg-

---

[*] Though John did drink, it is questionable whether his decline was due to this habit or another cause, such as hepatitis or a genetic condition. If he did drink excessively, it had not impaired his ability to work, and his extremely vigilant sister-in-law failed to spot any hint of dependency.

ing houses of Dorset Street, but this relationship did not last long. As Amelia described it, Annie was not happy and was increasingly unwell physically; her life had become "a pitiful case" marked by "drink and despondency . . . hunger and sickness."[9] Certainly by 1887 she had begun to suffer from what appears to have been tuberculosis, which, according to George Bagster Phillips, the divisional surgeon of police, had been longstanding and had begun to affect the brain tissue.* Although ill, Annie assiduously attempted to earn an income. Amelia reported that "She used to do crochet work, make antimacassars, and sell matches and flowers." Saturdays were spent "selling anything she had" at Stratford Market, a hub for small traders who came from all over the surrounding countryside and the East End. In the late summer of 1888, despite her deteriorating health, Annie still insisted that she would join the annual migration into the fields of Kent to go hop picking, if her sister would send her some boots.

Not surprisingly, it was during this unfortunate period of her friend's life that Amelia Palmer worried most about her. Curiously, Amelia claimed that she "was in the habit of writing letters for her friend" to "her mother and sister," who, she seemed to recall, "lived near Brompton hospital."† This statement raises a number of questions as to why Annie, who was able to read and write, would permit this. Was she at times too unwell to write, and in need of money, or was she simply too ashamed to do the asking? In her account of events, Miriam asserted that Annie would never disclose her address to her family, undoubt-

---

* Phillips was brief about the nature of Annie's illness because it played no role in her death. His entire (paraphrased) statement was that she displayed a "Disease of the lungs (which) was long standing, and there was disease of the membranes of the brain." Recently, a number of authors have, without any evidence, stated that Annie suffered from syphilis, because of this mention of damage to the brain. The type of damage that Phillips reported is known to occur in cases of tuberculosis, as the bacteria spread to various parts of the body. If Annie had been exposed to syphilis, signs of brain degeneration, or the neurosyphilis that occurs in the tertiary phase of the illness, would not have appeared for at least ten to thirty years after the initial exposure. There is no evidence whatsoever to support the claim that Annie engaged in prostitution as a teen or through her married years, or that she was ever exposed to syphilis.

† The Brompton Hospital, in Chelsea, treated those with respiratory illness, specifically tuberculosis. It catered to people of all classes, from the rich to the very poor. It's possible that Annie went there for treatment and Amelia recalled this association.

edly on account of shame and the fear that they might attempt to thwart her drinking. Nevertheless, although she remained estranged from them, Annie found it impossible to isolate herself from members of her family altogether. Miriam wrote that, on occasion, "she used to come to us at home . . . we gave her clothes and tried in every way to win her back, for she was a mere beggar."

The Smiths were heartbroken at the path Annie had chosen, and do not seem to have refused her small amounts of financial assistance when she requested it. However, her younger brother, Fountaine, may have offered her slightly more than this. In his rather confused testimony at the coroner's inquest, Annie's sibling seemed to indicate that he had met with her on two occasions: once, on the Commercial Road and also, in an apparently unplanned encounter, in Westminster. In one instance, Fountaine stated he lent her two shillings, while in another that he gave her this money. That which the newspapers did not report is that, like Annie, her brother was also an alcoholic, though one who had, at least temporarily, held down a job as a manager in a printer's warehouse. In truth, Fountaine may have seen more of his sister than he was willing to indicate, either to the public or to his family. As someone who was equally fond of the bottle, her brother would have been a softer touch and good for standing her a drink or two. Neither would chastise the other for their weaknesses, and in a family of teetotalers, Fountaine's behavior would have been subject to as much scrutiny as Annie's. The five pence that Annie procured from "her relatives" on September 7, 1888, likely came from Fountaine, who lived nearby, in Clerkenwell (directly opposite St. Bartholomew's Hospital), rather than from her sisters in Knightsbridge.

By 1888, Annie had also begun to benefit from a steadier relationship with Edward Stanley, a "florid-faced" forty-five-year-old "man of a respectable appearance," who worked for a local brewery.[10] Although Ted, or "the Pensioner," as he was commonly called, claimed that he had known Annie for two years, their part-time cohabitation had started only that summer. By then, Annie had become a regular at 35 Dorset Street, a lodging house known as Crossingham's, where she and Ted would pass the weekends together. According to Timothy

Donovan, the deputy keeper there, Annie used to wait for Ted at the corner of Brushfield Street on Saturday, when the couple would go to the pub. He usually remained with Annie until Monday morning, during which time he did what was expected of any Victorian man in the company of a woman — he footed their expenses, which included the cost of Annie's lodging until at least Tuesday morning. At the lodging house, Annie and "the Pensioner" were recognized as a couple. Stanley even made it clear to Tim Donovan that he understood his relationship with Annie to be exclusive and, as a jealous partner, asked the lodging-house keeper to prevent her from becoming involved with anyone else. Interestingly, in the time that she knew "the Pensioner," it was claimed that Annie had purchased some brass rings, which she wore on her left hand. Only Ted confidently stated that they were two in number — "a wedding ring and a keeper" (an engagement ring), which he claimed was "of a fancy pattern."[11] These rings were not a gift from Ted, yet apparently Annie wore them to affect an air of marital respectability, regardless of her true circumstances.

Although Annie was by the standards of the nineteenth century considered both a "broken woman" and a "fallen woman," she was not a prostitute, and should not have been characterized as one by police or journalists. According to orders issued by the police commissioner, Charles Warren, on July 19, 1887, roughly a year before Polly Nichols's murder, "the Police are [not] justified in calling any woman a common prostitute, unless she so describes herself, or has been convicted as such . . ." The order went on to state that although a police constable "may be perfectly convinced in his own mind that she is such," he should "not assume that any particular woman is a common prostitute" unless there are witnesses and proof to attest to this.[12] As in the case of Polly Nichols, no reliable evidence exists to suggest that Annie Chapman either worked as a prostitute or identified herself with the trade. Contrary to romanticized images of the Ripper's victims, she never "walked the streets" in a low-cut bodice and rouged cheeks, casting provocative glances beneath the gas lamps. She never belonged to a brothel nor had a pimp. Neither is there any evidence that she was arrested or even cautioned for her behavior. Following "enquiries made amongst women in the same class . . . at public houses in the locality," the police could find not a single witness who could confirm that she had been among the ranks of those who sold sex.[13] Those who worked in the trade were generally well known, not only to one another but frequently to the police, as well as to their neighbors and local publicans. In impoverished areas like Whitechapel, where little stigma was attached to the sale of sex, a woman's friends, family, and associates were not bashful about openly identifying her as a prostitute when she genuinely was one.

As the police were still of an opinion that the Whitechapel murders were committed by either a "high rip" extortion gang or a lone prostitute-killer (believed, early in the investigations, to be John Pizer, known as "Leather Apron"), it was essential that the victims be identified with the sex trade. Evidently paying no heed to Charles Warren's order of July 19, the police of the H Division simply wrote the word "prostitute" in the space designating a victim's occupation on forms documenting Annie's murder. Just as they had with Polly Nichols's case, the authorities began their inquiry from a fixed position: that Annie *must* have been a prostitute, a stance that from thereon guided the direction of their investigation, as well as the attitudes and interrogations of the coroner's court.

The newspapers were not inclined to question this assumption either. As this murder occurred in the middle of the inquest into Polly Nichols's death, the press seized the opportunity to link them. These two similar killings, committed within weeks of each other, whipped the papers into a frenzy of excitement. The number of journalists in Whitechapel swelled. Murders sold newspapers, and the editors spun out the stories for as long as possible. The papers wanted to capture the sense of "moral panic"; they wanted interviews, site visits, opinion pieces, and detailed coverage of the Chapman inquest. The result was a panicked pandemonium of writing far more extensive than that inspired by the Nichols case. A chaos of contradictory statements derived from hearsay, badly transcribed notes, and testimony reframed to fit particular journalistic angles emerged in the newspapers. Yet again, as with Polly Nichols's case, the official transcripts of what was actually said at the coroner's inquest, as well as most of the police documentation, does not survive; we lack a definitive set of records. As a result, virtually all that is known about Annie Chapman's life in Whitechapel is drawn from this morass of confused "facts" reported in newspapers.

Statements from the coroner's court testimony of Amelia Palmer, Tim Donovan, and the night manager at Crossingham's, John Evans (those most familiar with Annie and her habits), vary markedly from publication to publication. Placed side by side, one account often directly contradicts another. On September 9, the *Guardian* writes that Palmer stated, "As a regular means of livelihood she [Annie] had not been in the habit of frequenting the streets, but had made antimacassars for sale. Sometimes she would buy flowers or matches with which to pick up a living." This claim was repeated in a number of syndicated northern newspapers, including the *Hull Daily News* and the *Eastern Morning News*. By contrast, on the eleventh, the *Star,* which tended to take the most sensationalist angle, has Amelia claiming, "I am afraid the deceased used to earn her living partly on the streets." Other newspapers, including the *Telegraph,* cite Amelia's testimony more ambiguously, and refer only to the fact that Annie "was out late at night at times." Some publications even omitted a reference to her mode of life altogether. As a definitive version of this statement does not exist, Amelia's actual words can't be confirmed and therefore can't be used to support a claim that Annie prostituted herself.

Reports from Donovan's and Evans's testimonies contain similar vagaries. According to the *Morning Advertiser* of September 11, John Evans said, "I have known that the deceased was out at nights, but I have known only one man with whom she was associated," and Tim Donovan asserted that "I could not say whether the deceased walked the streets." Donovan was most likely telling the truth; it's unlikely that he had taken much notice of or interest in the daily activities of one among his many lodgers until circumstances forced him.

Even when it's possible to pick through the journalistic inconsistencies for information that accords with a historical understanding of how impoverished women lived, Donovan's carefully crafted testimony does not provide much compelling evidence to suggest that

Annie made her living by the sex trade.* According to several publications, Donovan was asked about Annie's associations with men, as was another witness, Eliza Cooper, who was known to have an antagonistic relationship with Annie and had recently come to blows with her over a borrowed bar of soap. Moreover, Annie had once been connected with Cooper's current partner, Harry the Hawker. Both the deputy keeper and Eliza asserted that as far as they knew, Annie had been connected with only two men, Harry and Ted Stanley. However, Cooper later claimed to have seen Annie "with several other men," though she added that "[Annie] only brought them casually to the lodging house."[14] If this were the case, then according to Tim Donovan, these men didn't get very far. In his testimony Donovan explained that Ted Stanley had instructed him "not to let the bed" if Annie came to Crossingham's with another man. The deputy keeper maintained that he kept to his word and in his defense cited that "As a rule [Annie] occupied a double bed by herself."[15] Neither of the two witnesses were questioned about this discrepancy between their stories, nor asked whether Annie was ever successful in obtaining entry in spite of Donovan's alleged bar, nor what she did in the event she was denied access. Neither is the character of Annie's relationship to these other men known, or whether they were as "casual" as Annie's rival in love suggested that they were. Even Charles Warren's police order had recognized the difficulties in distinguishing a prostitute and her behavior from that of other poor, working-class women. This was, and remains especially the case, when the context of a woman's actions, as well as her own voice, are missing from the equation.

The Victorian newspapers ignored such fine distinctions. Stories were crafted on top of assumptions, and the biggest assumption of all was that Annie Chapman was a prostitute. As the *Star* confidently declared, "We are able to see the kind of existence that women of CHAPMAN'S unfortunate class are compelled to live . . . Probably she did not rise until the shades of night enabled her to ply her hideous trade,

---

* In the past, notwithstanding the wealth of contradictory newspaper summaries of witness statements, those who have written about the murder of Annie Chapman have always selected the versions that support the presumption that all the victims were prostitutes.

and she then seems to have spent her time in passing from liquor shop to liquor shop with the fitting companions, male and female, of such orgies."[16] The *Star*, and other publications, failed to view Annie as an individual, but rather saw her as a cipher within a large "unfortunate class," a category that lumped together all impoverished women, regardless of age or particular circumstances. As the *Daily Mail* pointed out, "No criminal centre is wholly criminal, and to represent even the lodging houses of Dorset Street as wholly inhabited by the utterly depraved would be wrong."[17] Though the *Star* suggested as much, Annie did not sleep all day in order to rise when "the shades of night enabled her to ply her hideous trade." She sewed and crocheted, intent on earning money through what Amelia Palmer referred to as her own industry. Such depictions of her also did not take into account the state of her health. Annie was seriously, if not terminally, ill with tuberculosis. In addition to tablets, two bottles of medicine and what appear to have been letters of prescription given to her during a visit to St. Bartholomew's Hospital were recovered from among her belongings after her death. This, as much as her desire to spend the night with Ted Stanley, would explain her insistence on having an eight-penny double bed. Not only were these "doubles" surrounded by a wooden partition, which afforded a rare degree of privacy, but as Elizabeth Allen, a fellow lodger at Crossingham's, commented, "an eight penny bed" carried "with it greater advantages than those accorded by a four penny . . . doss. The lodgers having the cheaper bed . . . were expected to turn out earlier in the morning." Toward the end of her life, Annie would have valued an extra hour in bed before being put out on the street at midmorning, feverish, aching, and racked by coughing fits.

In the last few months of her life, as her health deteriorated, Annie became increasingly dependent on Ted Stanley to fund the cost of her lodgings. When he stayed with her on the weekend of September 1, he gave Annie enough money to pay for her bed until Tuesday, as he usually did. On that afternoon, Amelia Palmer spotted her friend "looking very pale" and walking slowly by Christ Church, Spitalfields. Annie confessed that she was feeling ill and thought she might go to the infirmary. Completely penniless, she "had not even had a cup of tea that day." Amelia gave her two pence and instructed her not to buy rum with it. She next saw Annie on that Friday, the seventh, lingering on Dorset Street, looking just as unwell. Amelia asked her if she would be going to Stratford to sell her crochet work. "I am too ill to do anything," Annie answered wearily. When Amelia returned to the spot ten minutes later, she was quite alarmed to see that her friend had not moved. Annie hadn't a penny and was too sick to earn the sum she so urgently needed for a bed. "It's no use in my giving way," she said to Amelia, recognizing the gravity of her situation. "I must pull myself together and go and get some money or I shall have no lodgings."[18]

One of the mysteries that the journalists covering Annie's story seemed unable to solve was the issue of where precisely she had gone during that last week. Timothy Donovan confirmed that when she left 35 Dorset Street on that Tuesday afternoon, he did not see her again until Friday. It is believed that Annie went to the infirmary at St. Bartholomew's Hospital, but as her name does not appear on the in-patients register, it is likely she was examined by a doctor and sent away. Similarly, her name is absent from extant admissions records at the casual wards; even if she did go to such a place, this would account for only two nights. On the whole, this is not inconsistent with Annie's past behavior; there is no evidence that she ever stayed in a London casual ward or workhouse. This was almost certainly because such a sojourn would entail going without a drink. According to a study conducted by the 1904 Vagrancy Committee, those truly addicted to alcohol preferred sleeping rough to the restrictions they would face by placing themselves in the care of institutions.[19]

As Annie never sought shelter from her siblings, and no one among Whitechapel's lodging-house keepers or residents came forward to claim that she regularly slept anywhere other than Crossingham's, it is unlikely that she did. Yet, at the same time, Elizabeth Allen asserted that Annie only ever had money enough to stay "3 or 4 nights a week" at 35 Dorset Street, the period that she spent with Ted Stanley. Logically, this would imply that Annie had no bed at least three nights out of every week.

It is unrealistic to suppose that an impoverished, sickly addict, whose primary concern was finding money for drink, would have had a regular bed every night. According to the social commentator Howard Goldsmid, Whitechapel, like the Embankment, Hyde Park, and London Bridge, was "night after night, thronged with dossers, who have no money for a night's shelter." He witnessed many who slept "crouched in a doorway, or huddled in a heap upon the pavement." "Dozens of homeless creatures, male and female," whom he described as "hungry, ragged men and women," congregated near Christ Church, Spitalfields, where they might be found "hanging onto the railings, or crouching down by the walls," while others half-leaned and half-lay on the low rail-topped wall that surrounded the buildings. Goldsmid commented that most of these people had been turned out of their usual lodging houses on Thrawl Street, Flower and Dean Street, and Dorset Street because they couldn't produce their doss money. "When you enter the kitchen of a doss-'ouse, it would be a mistake to suppose that all the people you meet there are going to spend the night under its roof," he wrote.

> Many of them are reg'lar 'uns, who, in consideration of their constant patronage are permitted to spend the evening, or a portion of it, before the blazing coke fire, for though the deputy will give no trust, he knows better than to offend a regular lodger. As the evening wears on, however, these poor wretches become restless and moody. They pace the floor with their hands in their otherwise empty pockets, glancing towards the door at each fresh arrival to see if a "pal" has come in from whom it may be possible to borrow the halfpence necessary to complete their doss money. At last, their final hope being gone, they shuffle out into the streets and prepare to spend the night with only the sky for a canopy.[20]

On the night of September 7, Annie Chapman was faced with just this scenario. According to Timothy Donovan, Annie reappeared at Crossingham's that afternoon, and after explaining that she was unwell and had been to the infirmary, asked if she could sit downstairs in the kitchen. Donovan granted her request, but in the early evening (about the time when she encountered Amelia) she went out again. By around midnight, Annie was seen back in the kitchen, asking a fellow lodger, William Stevens, to fetch her a pint of beer from a nearby pub. In doing so, she seemed to indicate that she had "been to her relations" and managed to beg five pence. That money, which might have paid for a bed, was quickly converted into drink. After she finished her pint with Stevens, she set off to the Britannia, a pub on the corner of Dorset Street and Commercial Street. Having taken her fill, Annie returned once more to Crossingham's kitchen and ate some potatoes. By then it was about 1:45 a.m., the time when Donovan began to clear the kitchen of those who did not have the pennies for their doss. He asked the night watchman, John Evans, to go downstairs and do the collecting. Annie came up short but went to Donovan's office to plead for her usual bed, number 29.

Interestingly, a point that never emerged in the press but that Tim Donovan revealed to the police was that Annie had specifically "asked him to trust her" for that night's doss money. This "he declined to do."[21] Had this incident become common knowledge, it's likely that Donovan would have faced an even worse public backlash for his role in Annie's demise.* "You can find money for your beer, and you can't find money for your bed," the deputy keeper is said to have spoken in response to her request. Annie, not quite willing to admit defeat, or perhaps in a show of pride, responded with a sigh: "Keep my bed for me. I shan't be long."

Ill and drunk, she went downstairs and "stood in the door for two or three minutes," considering her options. Like the impecunious lodger described by Goldsmid, she too would have been contemplating from whom among her "pals" it might have been "possible to borrow the halfpence necessary to complete [her] doss money." More likely, Annie was mentally preparing "to spend the night with only the sky for a canopy." She then set off down Brushfield Street, toward Christ Church, Spitalfields, where the homeless regularly bedded down.

Her thoughts as she stepped out onto Dorset Street, as the light from Crossingham's dimmed at her back, can never be known. What route she wove through the black streets and to whom she spoke along

---

* Donovan was accused by some of the newspapers for having a hand in Annie's death because he turned her out onto the street rather than extending her credit for her bed.

the way will never be confirmed. All that is certain is her final destination.

Twenty-nine Hanbury Street was typical of most dwellings in the area. At least a hundred years old and three stories high, it consisted of eight decaying rooms, inhabited by seventeen people. As rooms were rented out individually, no one paid much attention to the communal spaces — the passages, stairway, landings, or the yard behind, which formed part of the property. Neither the gate to the yard nor the door to the building was locked, and an assortment of people came and went through this public, though concealed, space at all times of the day and night. According to the police and the residents, the location was well known among the streetwise inhabitants of the area. Occasionally, "the yard was used for immoral purposes" by "strangers" and was just as regularly occupied by rough sleepers.*

Over the past two years, Annie, like any of Goldsmid's dossers, would have become acquainted with the best corners, the most inconspicuous doorways, and the least traversed passages in which to lay her head. The yard adjacent to 29 Hanbury Street was not a place Annie stumbled upon accidentally in the early morning hours of September 8, but rather a familiar space sought for its solitude. She would have known about the gap between the house's steps and the fence. It was an ideal spot in which to curl up with her back against the wall, and she would have been relieved to find it vacant.

Of the many tragedies that befell Annie Chapman in the final years of her life, perhaps one of the most poignant was that she needn't have been on the streets on that night, or on any other. Ill and feverish, she needn't have searched the squalid corners for a spot to sleep. Instead, she might have lain in a bed in her mother's house or in her sisters' care, on the other side of London. She might have been treated for tuberculosis; she might have been comforted by the embraces of her children or the loving assurances of her family. Annie needn't have suffered. At every turn there had been a hand reaching to pull her from the abyss, but the counter-tug of addiction was more forceful, and the

---

* Shortly after Annie's death, a man was found sleeping rough in the very place where she was killed.

grip of shame just as strong. It was this that pulled her under, that had extinguished her hope and then her life many years earlier. What her murderer claimed on that night was simply all that remained of what drink had left behind.

─── ✦ ───

Sometime around September 8 or 9, the Smith siblings — Emily, Georgina, Miriam, and Fountaine — received the dreadful news. Whether a police constable paid them a visit or they read the story in the newspaper, the realization that their sister had been the victim of a brutal murder would have devastated them completely. Emily, Georgina, and Miriam could not bear to tell their elderly mother that the child she had lost to alcohol had been killed in such a gruesome and dehumanizing way. They smothered their grief as they held the hands of Annie's two children, who would never know the fate that befell their mother. The pain and humiliation Annie's sisters suffered as story after story appeared in the papers, calling her a prostitute and describing her degraded life, cannot be imagined. For three devout women, the shame of this and the need to keep silent about their suffering would have been almost more than they could withstand.

As the man of the family, the worst tasks — the public ones — fell to Fountaine, who, in addition to his sorrow, carried in his heart his own private turmoil. He, like Annie, and like their father, was also an alcoholic. Perhaps, without his family's knowledge, he had seen Annie only recently, handed her a few coins, and shared a few drinks. It was Fountaine who went to identify the torn, bedraggled body of his elder sister and later stood before the coroner. His distress on this occasion was so great that he was hardly able to make his voice audible.

Fountaine Smith was not a man built of strong stuff. He buckled under this misfortune, and as he fell, he grabbed for the one thing he knew would provide immediate, if fleeting, relief: the bottle. Within a month of the harrowing ordeal of his sister's death, Fountaine suffered a breakdown. After stealing money from his employer to buy drink, he lost his job as a warehouse manager. Friends intervened and found him another position, but Fountaine's misery followed him here too. One day, unable to cope, he filled himself with alcohol and his pockets with his employer's money, abandoned his wife and two children, and disappeared.

A week later, the family received a letter from Gloucester; Fountaine had walked into a police station and surrendered. "Oh, my darling wife, it is all the cursed drink," he wrote at the bottom of his confession; "for God's sake don't let the children touch it."

Annie's brother was taken back to London and tried at Marlborough Street Magistrates Court, where he was found guilty and sentenced to three months' hard labor at Millbank Prison. Upon his release, Fountaine resolved to start his life over again and took his wife and children across the Atlantic to settle in the dust and heat of Texas.

PART III

ELISABETH

November 27, 1843

September 30, 1888

THE GIRL FROM TORSLANDA

THE CANDLES SPREAD a warm yellow light through the wood-paneled rooms of the farmhouse. They and the hearth fire worked together to cast out the darkness of a Swedish late November, a time when the skies shift swiftly between shades of gray and the black of night. In one room of the four that belonged to Gustaf Ericsson, his wife, Beata, lay on her back, laboring with their second child. Three years earlier, she had brought a daughter, Anna Christina, into the world. On this occasion, the farmer would have hoped for a son to assist him in managing the livestock and bringing in the harvests. He had no such luck; on November 27, 1843, little Elisabeth's newborn cries filled the couple's bedroom.

The Ericssons were more fortunate than many who tended the land in Torslanda, an area that lay roughly sixteen kilometers to the west of the city of Gothenburg. Although Elisabeth had been born during a period of drought, which had begun in the early 1840s, the family remained relatively prosperous. Not only could Gustaf Ericsson afford to cultivate fields of grain, flax, and potatoes, but he also owned a barn, several cows, pigs, chickens, and a horse. The clapboard house in which Elisabeth, her elder sister, and eventually her two younger brothers, Lars (born in 1848) and Svante (born in 1851), were to share was considered spacious, with a large kitchen in which the household took their meals, a sitting room, and at least three bedrooms arranged on the ground and upper floors.

As a farmer's daughter, Elisabeth would have been initiated into the routines of agricultural life as soon as she was steady enough on her feet to carry pails and gather eggs. When older, she would have assisted with the basic chores of milking, tending the chickens and pigs, making butter, and, as was traditional in Swedish households, learning how to distill aquavit, the alcoholic liquor offered at mealtimes. In the winter months, the mornings would begin many hours before dawn, when she, her sister, or her mother would rise in what felt like the middle of night, and light the fires and lamps. In the summer, the men and women in the fields would work long into evening, beneath an almost never-ending twilight. Where previously, farmers' wives would have toiled alongside their husbands in the fields, by the middle of the nineteenth century, the availability of cheap labor meant that the more demanding tasks could be performed by hired help, freeing Beata and her daughters to tend primarily to affairs within the home. Notwithstanding this privilege, daily rural life was fairly egalitarian. Little distinction was made between master and servant; "they all sat at the same table and ate off the same plate," reminisced a farmhand of the era, who also recalled that everyone in a household "did the same jobs, and the daughters of the farmer shared the bed with the maids."[1]

In the small settlement of Stora Tumlehed, they also prayed together. Sundays in this conservative Lutheran community were reserved for church and close study of the Bible. As the head of the household, Elisabeth's father would be expected to shepherd not only his family but also his hired help in their daily religious duties. Prayers would have punctuated the day: prayers before meals, prayers before bed, and prayers upon waking, offering thanks to the Lord for seeing his sheep safely through the long night.

It is unlikely that Elisabeth ever imagined she might depart from the constant rhythm of farm life: the turning of the seasons, the cutting of the fields, the freezing of the earth, the thaw of the ice, the sowing of seeds. As a girl, little was expected of her beyond a mastery of housekeeping, childcare, and basic animal husbandry, all of which

she could learn from assisting her mother. Her minimal schooling reflected this. Rural parents often thought that anything but the most
basic education amounted to "superfluous knowledge," something
that distracted children from the business of agriculture. Though by
the mid-nineteenth century each parish was required to establish a
common school for local children, the learning offered there extended
little beyond reading and arithmetic, as well as writing lessons for the
boys.

Among Lutherans, the ability to read was considered of prime importance, as the study of the Bible and the understanding of catechism
lay at the center of all devotions. Elisabeth and her siblings would regularly make the nearly hour-long walk to the church in Torslanda to receive tutelage in scripture in order to prepare them for confirmation.
As children, they were taught the Small Catechism from Martin Lu-
ther's 1529 *Book of Concord,* which set out the tenets of the Lutheran
faith. Elisabeth's instruction included memorization of the Ten Commandments, the Apostles' Creed, the Lord's Prayer, the Sacrament of
Holy Baptism, the Office of the Keys and Confession, and the Sacrament of the Eucharist. However, as it was also necessary that all members of the faith possess a thorough comprehension of God's word, her
education would have included an analysis of scripture and a regular
drilling by the parish priest and her father as to its meaning.

"What are the Ten Commandments?" the priest would ask.

"The Ten Commandments are the law of God," Elisabeth would be
expected to answer.

"How did God give His Law?"

"When God created people, He wrote the Law on their hearts.
Later He arranged the Law in Ten Commandments, wrote it on two
tablets of stone, and made it known through Moses" was the anticipated response. Such statements were then bolstered with relevant
quotations from scripture.

"What is the sixth commandment?" Elisabeth was asked on numerous occasions.

"One shall not commit adultery."

"What does this mean?"

"We should fear and love God so that we lead a sexually pure and decent life in what we say and do, and husband and wife love and honor each other. Carnal relations are reserved for matrimony and that we should not give in to base lusts," she would have been taught to respond.

By these means, Elisabeth was prepared to assume her role as a committed member of the faith. At the age of fifteen, on August 14, 1859, she stood before the congregation in the ancient cottagelike church at Torslanda and was confirmed. In doing this, Elisabeth demonstrated that she was prepared to enter the adult world, armed with a strong knowledge of the word of God, to face the trials and temptations that might await her.

Just over a year later, and a month before her seventeenth birthday, Elisabeth Gustafsdotter set out for Gothenburg to seek employment as a servant. In 1857, Anna Christina had undertaken the half-day walk to the city for the same purpose. In Sweden, as in other European countries, it was traditional for young women to gain experience of domestic life beyond the confines of their homes and communities. For many, the years prior to marriage spent in the kitchens, the nurseries, or scrubbing floors under the auspices of other women functioned as a type of apprenticeship before they assumed command of their own households. This period of labor also offered girls the opportunity to earn dowries, money that would assist in purchasing the clothing, linens, and other items required for married life and childbearing. For young women like Elisabeth and her sister, who came from rural communities, a move to the city also broadened their prospects of meeting an appropriate husband. Though the daughters of land-owning or land-leasing farmers were raised alongside agricultural laborers and others of a lower social status, marriage between the classes was actively discouraged. In an urban center, filled with the sons of craftsmen and shopkeepers, there was a greater possibility of finding a suitable spouse.

In this regard, Anna Christina was especially fortunate. Not only was she able to secure a place working in the home of Bernhard Olsson, a shoemaker, but also, after seven years of service, in 1864 she married her master. This situation was not uncommon when employer and servant were of a similar class.[2] In many cases, elder sisters already established in service were able to assist younger ones in obtaining positions, sometimes within the same household. By these means, it is likely that Anna Christina had some influence in obtaining work for Elisabeth in Gothenburg. According to her residency records, Elisabeth was living in Majorna, a working-class suburb of Gothenburg, by October 5, 1860; four months later, in February, her name appears officially on the census as a maidservant to the family of Lars Fredrik Olsson.[3]

Like Anna Christina's employer, Olsson and his family were not wealthy, but rather were members of the more comfortable segment of the lower middle class. His employment as a *månadskarl* implied that he performed the role of a caretaker, possibly for the block of apartments in which the family lived on Allmänna Vägen, a hill above the port.* Olsson's fortunes appear to have been on the rise, and by the 1870s, he had purchased further property in Majorna.

The social line dividing Elisabeth from her employer would have been a relatively thin one, but as the Olssons' prospects were improving, they would have been keen to demonstrate their resources to their neighbors and associates. As female labor in Sweden was extremely cheap and the Servant Act made it compulsory for those who did not have an income through land to find employment in service, families with even meager means were able to hire girls to work in their homes. Lars Fredrik and his wife, Johanna, were able to afford two: Elisabeth and Lena Carlsson, who would have shared a bed in a loft above the family's rooms. Indeed, how much work might have been found to occupy two women, as well as their mistress, in maintaining a handful of rooms and caring for the couple's three- and four-year-old sons is questionable. Nineteenth-century Swedish commentators such as Henrik Cornell often remarked that lower-middle-class families frequently employed more servants than there were tasks to occupy them. Cor-

---

* The now antiquated term *månadskarl* had two distinct meanings: literally it means "a worker who is hired on a monthly basis," but in western Sweden it was also used to describe a caretaker or manager.

nell, reflecting back on his childhood, recalled a middle-class wife who busied her bored, underemployed maids by making them carry wet linen through the rooms in order to catch the dust before it settled.[4]

Swedish law was fairly explicit about the relationship between a master and mistress and their employee. While the employer may have had an obligation to house, feed, clothe, and tend to a servant while ill, in return, a servant was expected to offer complete obedience. "Unfounded discontent over the food" or "treating a fire or the master's property in a careless way" constituted grounds for dismissal, as was the "visiting of inns or other places where alcoholic beverages were served."[5] Once such agreements were struck, they were considered binding, and a servant was required to work out her term of employment unless both parties agreed to dissolve the contract.

Why precisely Elisabeth's term of employment with the Olssons was dissolved in early February 1864 is likely to remain a mystery. Census records indicate that on the second of that month, she moved no more than a short walk along the cobbled streets of brightly painted clapboard buildings to the neighboring district of Domkyrko.[6] When the clerk who added her name to the register asked her occupation, she told him that she was a servant, but the address where she was employed was not recorded, and neither was the name of her master or mistress. It is possible that this was simply an omission, an oversight on the part of the clerk, or perhaps it points to something else: that Elisabeth herself was uncertain of her future and into whose hands she was placing it.

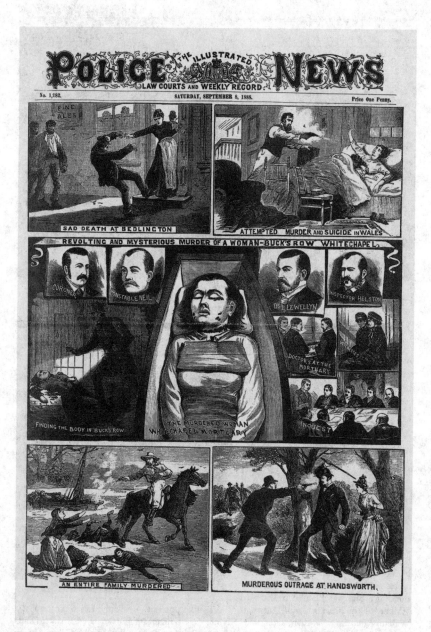

Front page of the *Illustrated Police News*, Saturday, September 8, 1888, depicting the murder of Polly Nichols. *Lordprice Collection / Alamy Stock Photo*

Peabody Buildings, Stamford Street, Lambeth. The Nicholses were among some of the first families to be approved as tenants for the charity-operated Peabody Buildings, which boasted of many "mod cons." They moved into number 3, D block, on July 31, 1876. *Peabody, London*

Rosetta Walls was a neighbor of the Nichols family while they lived in D block at the Stamford Street Peabody Buildings. She was blamed by Edward Walker for the breakdown of Polly and William's marriage. William later married Rosetta after Polly's death.

With permission of Andy and Sue Parlour (Ten Bells Publishing Ltd.)

A family portrait, probably taken around the time that William Nichols married Rosetta Walls in April 1894. Back, left to right: George Percy Nichols (Polly's second surviving son) and William Nichols. Front, left to right: Mary Ann Cushway (George's wife) and Rosetta Walls.

With permission of Andy and Sue Parlour (Ten Bells Publishing Ltd.)

The Smith family home, Montpelier Place, Knightsbridge, London. The Smith family is recorded as having first lived at 29 Montpelier Place in 1851. The house then became the family's permanent address around 1863–4, after the death of George Smith. *Courtesy of the author*

John and Annie Chapman, photographed at a studio on the Brompton Road, Knightsbridge, around the time of their wedding in May 1869. *Private collection*

Emily Ruth Chapman, the eldest daughter of Annie and John, circa 1878. Emily is about eight years old. *Private collection*

Annie Georgina Chapman, Annie and John's second daughter, circa 1881, wearing her sister's dress. Annie Georgina displays a number of the facial features associated with fetal alcohol syndrome. *Private collection*

Sir Francis Tress Barry employed John Chapman as his head coachman from the late 1870s. A wealthy businessman who made his fortune in the mining industry, Barry purchased the St. Leonard's Hill estate in Clewer, near Windsor, where the Chapman family lived. He was later granted a baronetcy and became an MP for Windsor. *"Black & White" Parliamentary Album, 1895*

St. Leonard's Hill House. Francis Tress Barry purchased the St. Leonard's Hill estate in 1872 and hired Charles Henry Howell to build him a "modern" Victorian manor house in the French chateau style. *Courtesy of the author*

Front page of the *Illustrated Police News,* Saturday, September 22, 1888, depicting the events of Annie Chapman's murder. *Lordprice Collection / Alamy Stock Photo*

The farmhouse where Elisabeth Stride was born, Stora Tumlehed, Sweden.
© Stefan Rantzow. Reprinted with permission.

Portrait illustration of Elisabeth
Stride from the *Illustrated Police
News*, October 6, 1888. Although
Elisabeth is recognized as being
among the "canonical five" vic-
tims, many continue to question
whether she was truly a victim of
Jack the Ripper.
Lordprice Collection / Alamy Stock Photo

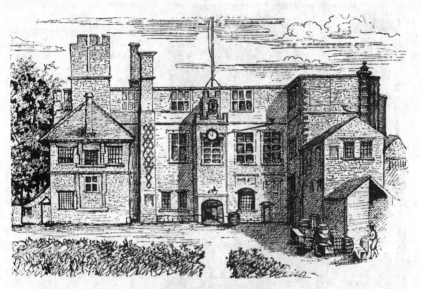

Engraving of the Old Hall Works, Wolverhampton. The Old Hall, or Turton's Hall, had been built by the Leveson family in the sixteenth century. By the eighteenth century it had fallen into disrepair, and by the end of that century it had been turned into a tin factory.
Wolverhampton Archives and Local Studies

Drawing of Kate Eddowes from the *Penny Illustrated Paper*, October 13, 1888. It is unknown if this image was copied from a photograph of Kate or is an artistic interpretation of her appearance.
Popperfoto / Getty Images

A LOST WOMAN
MARY KELLY
IN MILLER'S COURT

Mary Kelly, "A Lost Woman." In the wake of her death, Mary Jane Kelly's enigmatic life was subject to much speculation and romanticizing. As the youngest, most beautiful, and most overtly sexual of the five women, her life remains the most investigated. *Private Collection / Bridgeman Images*

13 Miller's Court was the last address shared by Mary Jane Kelly and her partner, Joseph Barnett. Kelly was murdered in her bed in the early hours of November 9. It is believed that the killer may have gained access by reaching through a broken windowpane to unlatch the door. *Mary Evans Picture Library / The Image Works*

ALLMÄN KVINNA 97

IN THE NINETEENTH century no household could operate efficiently without female labor, yet bringing unknown young women into a home was a risky business. Most employers knew the dangers of hiring girls from outside the city. Still, there was a preference for them; the pink-cheeked daughters of yeomen, who smelled like grass and goats, who had not yet learned how to dissemble or steal, who had been raised in close-knit communities where the parson presided over everyone's business. Urban girls, having been exposed to avarice and licentiousness, and who had witnessed the worldly ways of their betters, were considered more corruptible. While city girls might appear untrustworthy, their country sisters seemed innocent and vulnerable. Living in alien surroundings, in the households of complete strangers, they were prone to homesickness and loneliness. Their inexperience of metropolitan life rendered them perfect victims for the unscrupulous. Although it was a master's or mistress's responsibility to keep them from harm, frequently, the injury they suffered came from within the very place where they were employed.

Servants were not allowed to enter beer houses or spend a night outside of their master's home without permission; they had virtually no opportunity to form relationships with members of the opposite sex outside their household or immediate community. Their interactions with servants from the homes of their employer's friends and family, or with other workers, such as grocers, butchers, bakers, and those making deliveries, were brief (though often flirtatious and familiar). Their encounters with the men of the house were, by contrast, frequent. Young women, like Elisabeth, who lived cheek by jowl with the family who employed her could be as much a temptation to the male members of the household as they were to her. For men of all ages, sexual liaisons with a servant, who would have intimate knowledge of his habits, who may have made his bed, washed his clothes, and filled his baths, were considered commonplace occurrences. Whether or not she encouraged the advances of the master or his son, his brother, his cousin, his friend, or his father, there were plenty of opportunities to find oneself alone, to be coerced, overpowered, or to give in to mutual desire.

Service was believed to be the making of a young working-class woman's character, yet a sexual entanglement with a man beneath her master's roof tended to be the undoing of it. Such relationships were regularly cited as being among the factors that drew women into lives of prostitution: "the housemaid of a pharmacist or a surgeon might be seduced by her master's assistant; a lodging-house maid by a student, a commercial traveler or officer; . . . a hotel servant by a regular guest; a young clerk might seduce his parents' servant-girl," and so forth.[1] Often, the young woman's lover would promise to look after her, and many made good on their word, establishing her as his mistress in lodgings, perhaps a single room or an entire house, depending upon his resources. Some lived alongside their paramour, together posing as a married couple; others visited only on occasion. Some relationships continued for many years, or even a lifetime, but many more fell apart within weeks or months. While the nineteenth-century double standard enabled men to walk away from such attachments, it often devastated the lives of the women, who were left to bear the crying and gurgling consequences.

Elisabeth has taken to her grave the name of the man who altered the course of her life with his lust. It will be never be known whether her first encounter with him was consensual or forced, where it occurred, and under what circumstances. All that is certain is that through April 1865, she continued to describe herself as a servant, though her name cannot be found in the Gothenburg censuses. A likely explanation is that she did not remain long in her new position as maid before taking up lodgings with or paid for by a lover. In such cases, the regular practice was to conceal the true nature of the relationship by assuming a lover's surname, becoming, for however short a period, his wife, for propriety's sake.

In Gothenburg, maintaining a semblance of respectability while living in sin was done not merely to convince the landlord and the neighbors of one's good character, but also to hide from the law and the suspicions of the police. Until 1864, extramarital sex and illegitimate pregnancy had been punishable by law. Additionally, in 1859 a law regulating prostitution in the city had been introduced to quell the spread of venereal disease, specifically syphilis. The new legislation was a threat to any woman living in a potentially compromising situation.

In this large port city, with a growing population of over 100,000 and foreign ships dropping anchor daily along the Göta River, the authorities were greatly concerned about how easily this debilitating illness could be communicated through the civilian population and spread through the military. Sweden took its cue from other European nations, such as France and Germany; when faced with a similar threat, they instituted a series of strict laws designed to regulate the sex trade and ensure that the women who practiced within it were not carriers of disease. Britain too saw the benefits of introducing such measures in its port towns, and in 1864 passed the first of its Contagious Diseases Acts.

While the methods of enforcing regulation varied between countries, the concept that they all shared in common was that women in the sex trade should shoulder the blame for the transmission of syphilis. It was believed that if the state could control the morally corrupt "fallen woman," the instrument of the disease's spread, then the problem could be isolated. The male carrier was exempt from any such regulation. In Gothenburg, as in Stockholm, Paris, Hamburg, Berlin, and other cities throughout Europe, women in the sex trade were required to register their names and addresses with the police and submit to regular gynecological examinations to ensure they were free of disease. However, determining who exactly should be placed on this roll was down entirely to the whim of the prostitution police patrolling various neighborhoods. Many women who were forced to enlist themselves were not selling sex, but were suspected of what the police described as "lecherous living."[2] According to the historian Yvonne Svanström, Gothenburg's system employed two separate lists, one consisting of the names of acknowledged prostitutes and the other comprising pregnant single women, women frequently seen alone with men, or out at night, and those living as a man's mistress.

The police and Elisabeth's neighbors may have had suspicions about her for some time, but by March 1865, they became fairly certain that she was guilty of "lecherous living." She was then six months pregnant and could no longer hide her condition. Whoever had got her into that condition was no longer present to shield her from the consequences. To where he had gone and with what means of livelihood he had provided her while she carried his child will remain a mystery. At the end of March, when the wind was still sharp with ice, Elisabeth was ordered to appear at the first of what would become regular examinations of her genitalia by a surgeon at the police inspection house.

On her first visit, her name, Elisabeth Gustafsdotter of Torslanda, was inscribed on the official ledger as "Allmän Kvinna" (Public Woman) number 97.[3] Elizabeth was required to provide certification of her birth and information about her past, such as where she had previously worked and where she lived. She was deliberately silent on these matters, stating only that she had been born the daughter of farmers and that she had come from the country to town, where she had worked as a servant. When asked about her religious education, she stated (incorrectly) that she had been confirmed at age seventeen.* The official recording her details then looked up at the young woman and assessed her appearance. He noted that she had "blue eyes" and "brown hair." Her nose he described as "straight" and her face as "oval" — elongated rather than round. With the exception of her swelling,

---

* It is likely that the person transcribing her answers confused her response with the age at which she had come to Gothenburg.

maternal belly, he surmised that the twenty-one-year-old woman had not been living a life of gluttony. She was five foot two inches tall, with a "slender" build.[4]

The police would have explained to her the rules that would now govern her daily life. She had to attend the inspection house twice a week, on Tuesdays and Fridays, or face arrest and a fine or three nights in prison on rations of bread and water. She was not permitted outdoors after 11 p.m. She was to "conduct a quiet and silent life"; she was prohibited from loitering in the windows or doorway of her home and "calling out to passers by"; she was required to "dress in a decent way when appearing in public" and "not to call attention to herself." All these stipulations implied that Elisabeth, or any registered woman, was, without a doubt, a prostitute who solicited openly. The humiliation that women must have experienced at being lectured in such a way, especially if they did not associate themselves with the sex trade, or if their crimes were not public ones, but a rape or a private indiscretion with a lover, must have been overwhelming. Regardless of the fact that her name appeared on what was colloquially referred to as "the register of shame," Elisabeth continued to describe herself, in her documentation that spring, not as a prostitute but as a servant.

The routine of inspection was designed as much to chasten the city's "public women" as it was to screen them. To avoid offending the sensibilities of Gothenburg's respectable citizens passing along Östra Hamngatan, all suspected and known "public women" entered the police building through a concealed passage at the back. Once inside, they were required to strip naked and line up. Sometimes, if the wait was a long one, they were ordered to stand in the outdoor courtyard, shivering in the cold, as the uniformed officers stood watch over them.

For a young woman who had been raised in a religious community and drilled in her catechism, the indignity of this experience would have been shocking. However, as Elisabeth was pregnant with an illegitimate child, it is likely that she, like so many women of her era, would have internalized the punishment as a justifiable one. Society and the church would have her believe she had sinned against her parents, her community, herself, and God. Her sense of disgrace is reflected in her reticence to reveal, in her registration document, further details of her circumstances. When asked about her parents, she did not hesitate to pronounce them both dead. While this was true of her mother, who had died of tuberculosis in August 1864, Elisabeth's father was still very much alive, but the shame of her predicament would have kept her from returning to him.[5] Anna Christina too, who had married in May of that year, seems to have severed all ties with her sister, whom she may very well have regarded as lost to the family.

Since having her name placed on the police register in March 1865, Elisabeth would have been subjected to this routine no more than a handful of times before it was discovered, on April 4, that she had developed condyloma, or genital warts. The medical examiner recognized the meaning of this immediately: Allmän Kvinna 97 was presenting the symptoms of syphilis. She was committed immediately, under police escort, to the Kurhuset, or "cure house" — the venereal disease hospital.

By the time Elisabeth was placed on the police roll, her syphilis had already entered its secondary phase. The first presentation of the disease would have occurred roughly ten to ninety days after exposure and included the appearance of a telltale chancre, or painless sore on the genitals, which would subside within three to six weeks. After this, Elisabeth would have begun to experience flu-like symptoms; a fever, swollen glands, a sore throat, and then the eruption of a rash on her back, hands, and soles of her feet. In this stage, victims also suffer from wart-like growths and lesions on the genitals. This secondary phase may last for no more than several months or may continue to plague the sufferer for well over a year.

Although it is impossible to determine from whom Elisabeth contracted syphilis, the stage of the illness indicates that the father of her child may have transmitted it to her. The sexually inexperienced, who would not have known to look for symptoms of the disease on their partners, were more likely than those established in the sex trade to become infected.

According to Elisabeth's records, she was kept in the Kurhuset until May 13.[6] Far from being a sanctuary to which sufferers could retreat for a cure, Gothenburg's venereal disease hospital had a reputation for treating patients as prisoners. Because patients were committed there by order of the law, the attendants and nurses were allowed to use force and coercion to keep them locked in until they were pronounced cured. The comfort of those recovering was not a vital concern. In 1855, the Kurhuset housed 133 women in its syphilis ward, many of whom shared beds due to overcrowding. During those times when the numbers of patients exceeded capacity, the inmates were simply made to sleep on the floor.

By the 1860s, two types of treatment for syphilis were advocated by the medical establishment. The first, and more traditional, involved the ingestion of mercury as well as the topical application of this liquid metal to chancres and lesions. The second, more modern theory favored other metals and chemicals — gold, silver, copper, bromine, iodine, and nitric acid — to be taken internally or applied in ointments. Both approaches were hazardous to patients' health. Of these two methods, Gothenburg's Kurhuset appears to have favored non-mercurial cures. Elisabeth, during her stay, was treated internally with hydroiodic acid, the main components of which are iodine and hydrogen; her genital warts would have been dehydrated with a cream or cut off. After receiving this cure for seventeen days, Elisabeth went into premature labor. On April 21, while under lock and key at the Kurhuset, she gave birth to a stillborn seven-month-old girl.* She did not cite the father's name on the birth certificate.

The trauma of Elisabeth's experience between the end of March, when her name was placed on "the register of shame," and May 13, when she was discharged from the Kurhuset, cannot be overestimated. To have been publicly denounced as a whore, to have suffered the indignity of police examinations, to have discovered that she carried a potentially deadly and disfiguring disease, to have been incarcerated like a prisoner and subjected to excruciating medical procedures, to have suffered a miscarriage in a hostile environment and then to have been released onto the street with no relations to whom she could turn must surely have scarred her.

One of the consequences of a system that treated women suspected

---

* *Göteborgsposten*, 25 September 1888. Also: SE/0258G/GSA 1384-1/D1. Elisabeth's miscarriage may have been a result of the treatment she received or the disease itself.

of "lecherous living" no differently than it treated known prostitutes was to condemn them both to the same fate. Once a woman appeared on the police register, she could not procure respectable work. To earn a living, her only recourse was to enter the profession she had been wrongly accused of practicing. It is not known precisely how Elisabeth came to join the ranks of the women who sold sex on Pilgatan, Gothenburg's infamous "street of many nymphs," but by October 1865, she was citing it as her address.[7] As streetwalking and open solicitation were prohibited by the police, Elisabeth had to ply her trade indoors, either at one of the area's several "coffeehouses," which masqueraded as legitimate establishments, or from within a brothel, though a madam might hesitate to hire a woman who had undergone treatment for syphilis. Trawling the coffeehouses between Pilgatan and Husargatan and learning the unwritten rules governing relationships among the various women, their clients, and the owners of coffeehouses and brothels would have presented Elisabeth with a steep learning curve. Violence, or at least the threat of it, would be a daily concern. At this time Elisabeth's name does not appear on the census roll for Haga, the working-class district in which she claimed to live; she likely used an alias when she brought men back to her lodgings. The place she called home was probably one of a large number of small cubicle-like rooms known as *luderkupor* (whore closets) situated in the attic of many houses in the area. Specifically designed to be hired out to prostitutes, these spaces allowed the women to meet discreetly with clients and earn a meager living.

The incurability of the disease from which Elisabeth suffered was but one of many misfortunes to befall her and, undoubtedly, a good number of the men with whom she had sex. As the pathology of syphilis was not fully understood, it was erroneously believed that the afflicted were not contagious while there were no immediate signs of the disease. In spite of the determined efforts of the medical profession to cure patients, a successful treatment for this terrible illness was not available until 1910 with the introduction of Salvarsan, and later with antibiotics. It is therefore not surprising that by August 30, Elisabeth was once more manifesting symptoms of the disease. She was returned to the Kurhuset, where she remained until September 23. On this occasion, a lesion on her pubis was treated with applications of silver nitrate. No sooner was she discharged than twenty-three days later she was admitted again on October 17, for another lesion, this time on her clitoris. Elisabeth underwent a repeat treatment with silver nitrate and again was declared "cured," on November 1. Ensuing police examinations conducted on the third, the seventh, and the tenth attested that she was now "healthy," though in truth she would never be.[8] At some point after this date, Elisabeth's syphilis entered its latent phase. Although her symptoms would disappear and she would no longer be contagious, eventually, many years later, the disease would return for its destructive, and terminal, tertiary stage.

While the legal system took very little pity on those who found themselves caught in a vicious cycle of prostitution and disease, attitudes among some segments of the population were more sympathetic. Like many European nations, mid-nineteenth-century Sweden and its Nordic neighbors witnessed a groundswell of interest in the "rescue" of "fallen women." This work, largely undertaken through the church by middle- and upper-class women, aimed to rehabilitate those who might otherwise be lost to God. At this time it was widely believed that personal choice, and not circumstance, motivated women to take up prostitution. Having strayed off the path, a fallen woman could also decide to return to it. Her character could be reformed; it was possible to turn "a public woman into a private woman" by bringing her back into the domestic sphere, the proper place for good Lutheran women. Rehabilitation involved retraining as a housemaid or a laundress and learning how to clean, iron, cook, tend children and the sick, sew, and create traditional handicrafts. The Lutheran Deaconesses, a group at the vanguard of this work, opened reformatory shelters and laundries and regularly made recruitment visits to red-light districts and venereal disease hospitals as part of their mission.

It is likely that this is how Elisabeth was discovered by Maria Ingrid Wiesner. Maria, the wife of a German musician who had been employed by the Gothenburg Orchestra at the city's recently built New

Theatre, was not a wealthy woman. However, like the families of fellow musicians living in the clapboard block of apartments at 27 Husargatan, the Wiesners were accustomed to keeping a maidservant, a sign of social status. The decision to hire a fallen young woman who had been a patient at the Kurhuset may have come about as much as a result of the couple's financial position as it did from a sense of Christian duty. Months earlier, the orchestra had been disbanded due to lack of funding, and rather than return with his Swedish wife to his native Bohemia, Carl Wenzel Wiesner chose to remain in Gothenburg and make a living as an oboist. At this time the Wiesners were without a maid, and as Maria was shortly expecting her first child, the assistance would be welcome, especially as women from the police register might be hired on a bed-and-board basis alone.

On November 10, following Elisabeth's regular health examination, Maria, in her bonnet and winter cloak, would have been waiting for her outside the inspection house to escort her to her new life. This offer of work, of a home, and a hand held out in sympathy was an exceptional stroke of good fortune. According to the law, such an offer of work was the only way, outside marriage, for a woman to have her name struck from the police register. It was a rare opportunity to restart her life and restore her reputation. What it was precisely that made Maria Wiesner choose Elisabeth from among the many faces at the Kurhuset will remain unknown, but it is possible that something in Allmän Kvinna 97's tragic story moved her. Perhaps it was because they were of a similar age and both came from villages in the west of Sweden. Perhaps Maria, who had been married for two years, was in need of a companion as well as a servant. Perhaps too, she saw in Elisabeth a religious devotion and a genuine desire to alter her fate.

To have a servant's name stricken from "the register of shame," an employer had to write a letter of surety to the police, vouching for the future character and conduct of the former public woman. On November 13, three days after Elisabeth had followed Maria to the Wiesners' first-floor apartment, her employer wrote, "The servant-maid Elisabeth Gustafsson was engaged in my service on November 10 and I am responsible for her good conduct as long as she stays in my service."* On the subsequent day, Elisabeth was required to undergo one final health inspection. The doctor pronounced that her cure had been a success, and Allmän Kvinna 97 was no more.

It can only be hoped that Elisabeth's time with the Wiesners was happy. As 27 Husargatan was owned by an army sergeant who had played the trumpet in the orchestra with Carl Wiesner, the apartments appear to have been let to a number of his associates. Beside the owner, Johan Fredrik Bergendahl, the Wiesners shared the building with another army trumpet-player, Frans Oscar Malm, and an army widow and her children. This year, as winter closed in and returned its heavy, cold darkness to the city, Elisabeth found herself amid candlelight, a hearth fire, and music.

In the nineteenth century, it was music and art that drew all the disparate strands of society together. Although those who produced entertainment tended to hail from the working or "artisan" class, those who participated in and sponsored cultural endeavors were frequently some of the wealthiest and most influential members of the community. Artists, like their well-endowed patrons, traveled internationally; they mixed with a variety of people of all nationalities and could gain access to the ears of those in power. It is likely that it was through music that Elisabeth was given her next opportunity.

The commercial expansion of Gothenburg, which began in the eighteenth century, continued at a rapid pace through the nineteenth. The city's large port and access to raw materials, such as timber and ore, attracted a significant amount of foreign investment from the British, who saw grand possibilities for making their fortunes. Families such as the Dicksons, the Keillers, and the Wilsons started shipping empires. David Carnegie opened an investment bank, a sugar refinery, and a brewery. Gothenburg soon became a draw for British master brewers, as well as for Scottish and English engineers, who were contracted to design railways and sewage systems. The British

---

* SE/GLA/13187/P/10. At this time in Sweden, the traditional surname for women, based on a father's first name and the suffix "dotter," or daughter, was being gradually replaced with a single version of the family name, with a "son" suffix. Gustafsdotter became Gustafsson.

community exerted such a presence that Gothenburg soon acquired the nickname "Little London."

Gothenburg's "Little Londoners," who largely came from Scotland, were also some of the city's most generous philanthropists. James Jameson Dickson, his brother, and his father raised the money to fund the Gothenburg Orchestra and played a vital role in the lives of the musicians. The leader of the Gothenburg Orchestra and director of Gothenburg's military band, Josef Czapek, was Carl Wiesner's friend and had been his employer; Czapek also served as the organist at the English Church, the very heart of the British community. It was likely to have been through this network that the Wiesners were made aware of a position for a maidservant wishing to travel with a British family back to London.

It is possible that Maria and Elisabeth had discussed Elisabeth's feelings about Gothenburg. Although no longer on the police register or working as a prostitute, she only needed to step outside the door of the Wiesners' home onto Husargatan to see the faces of those who remembered what she had been. Each day, in the shops or at the market, she might encounter former clients, the owners of the coffeehouses, or women who shared her former profession. The police too would continue to watch her. So long as she remained in the city, Elisabeth could never escape her past, and so the possibility of beginning again in London, as a housemaid to an affluent family, must have seemed a gift from providence.

If fate had not already been generous, it bestowed on her one final offering. It is believed that while she lived with the Wiesners, Elisabeth received an inheritance of sixty-five crowns, said to be from the estate of her deceased mother.[9] However, as Swedish law stated that women under the age of twenty-five were not able to inherit money in their own right and that property belonged to a woman's husband after death, it is likely that this money indeed came from a different source.[10] It was not uncommon for a man parting from his mistress to offer her such a payment as recompense for any misfortune he had visited upon her. Wherever it came from, the relatively small sum would have helped Elisabeth purchase items necessary for her new life: clothing, shoes, hats, perhaps even a trunk for traveling.

In early February, the snow lay thick along the city streets. Gothenburg's canals were slicked over with ice. At the port, on February 7, 1866, dockworkers, sailors, and passengers were wrapped in wool and fur against the sharp cold. Elisabeth stood among them, preparing to board one of the London-bound ships whose funnels pushed toward the sky, pumping out warm clouds into the frozen air.

Five days earlier, she had filed her application for immigration to England and submitted a certificate of altered residence for the capital city. On the form she stated that she was traveling without her family. She had only recently turned twenty-two and would be the only Swede to immigrate to London that day.[11] She would not be traveling on one of the crowded immigrant ships that sailed to Hull, but in a certain degree of comfort with her new British employers. As she stood on deck or watched the peaks and domes of the city's skyline diminish through the windows, she could not have felt much remorse. Gothenburg had left a cruel mark upon her, one that would always remain, no matter where she called home.

THE IMMIGRANT

FEW MEN COMMANDED respect in Sheerness like William Stride. He was the sort of somber local figure at whom townspeople tipped their hats but were afraid to smile. Stride had done everything a laboring man could to improve his life and clamber into the ranks of the property-owning bourgeoisie. He had begun his career around 1800, doing work on the docks as a shipwright, but after decades of prudent saving and investment, he came to make his money in the development of land and the sale of houses. By the 1840s, he was living in one of his own buildings, on an entire street of homes that bore his name: Stride's Row. The man who had formerly repaired and constructed ships had become a commissioner of Sheerness Pier, and if anyone ventured to ask him what he attributed his success to, Stride would almost certainly have cited his devotion to God.

Shortly after his marriage in 1817, Stride converted to Methodism, a religion to which he adhered strictly throughout his life and which governed his every decision. In spite of his comparative wealth, Stride, his wife, Eleanor, and their nine children had an austere and abstemious existence. For most of it, the couple and their expanding family chose to inhabit one of the cottages on Stride's Row. According to the strictures of their faith, the Strides would have eschewed any of the outward signifiers of affluence: no expensive clothing, no jewelry, and nothing but the simplest furnishings. There would be no dancing, no theater, and no cards games; they upheld a weekly day of fasting. Most important, in this town of sailors and seaside amusement, the family shunned alcohol. In spite of the fact that he was abundantly able to do so, William Stride never employed a live-in servant, even after the death of his wife in 1858.

Into this environment of restraint and self-control, John Thomas Stride was born in 1821. As the second-eldest child, John was initiated into his father's profession and trained to become a carpenter. While the busy dockyards at Sheerness would have offered men of John's trade ample opportunities for work in the early part of his life, by the mid-nineteenth century, when iron came to replace wood in the construction of ships, employment would have become more difficult to secure. It is likely that this contributed to the reason why John, unmarried at the age of forty, continued to live at home, caring for his elderly father and keeping watch over his youngest brother, Daniel, who appears to have struggled with mental health issues. That year, in 1861, a difficult situation at home may have come to a head when John caught Daniel stealing six pounds, eleven shillings, and six pence from John's top drawer. William Stride would not have looked kindly on such behavior, and it is likely that it was his decision to denounce Daniel to the police. Daniel was arrested, imprisoned, and tried at the petty sessions in March, where John refused to prosecute him and instead secured his brother's release.[1] It was not long after this incident that the frustrated carpenter decided to leave Sheerness and seek work in London.

In the 1860s, any Londoner wishing to purchase a well-made set of dining chairs or a fashionably designed sideboard would pay a visit to one of over seventy furniture-making establishments situated around the northern part of Tottenham Court Road. The area, which spread from Marylebone Road eastward for over a mile to St. Pancras railway station, was filled with factories, warehouses, and shops where the scent of freshly cut mahogany and oak perfumed the air. By the time John Stride arrived in London, the city's "furniture district" was home to 5,252 employees who worked in every aspect of the trade, from upholstering to cabinetmaking to sales. Stride, with his box of carpenter's tools, would have been able to acquire work easily at one of the numerous workshops.

He also took lodgings within the area, in the home of Charles Leftwich, at 21 Munster Street, just off the Euston Road. Leftwich, who made his money as a lead merchant, a property rental agent, and an occasional inventor of plumbing devices, was a respectable middle-class family man whose finances were not beyond taking in a lodger to fill a spare room. John, a single, middle-aged Methodist who was accustomed to a quiet, teetotal life, was the ideal boarder. Nonetheless, the Leftwich family, tended to by two servants, likely maintained a socially discreet distance from John. Leaving for work as early as dawn and returning late, the carpenter would have taken his meals apart from the family — in his room, in the kitchen, or sometimes at Daniel Fryatt's coffeehouse at 6 Munster Street.

By the middle of the nineteenth century, the coffeehouse, often associated with the intellectual pursuits of the Georgian era, was experiencing a revival among all ranks of London's working men. Open from as early as 5 a.m. to as late as 10 p.m., these establishments offered simple meals of chops, kidneys, bread and butter, pickles, and eggs, along with cups of sugared coffee. The latest newspapers and periodicals were also available to read or to hear read aloud, but no alcohol was served. Coffeehouses became a retreat for those who had taken abstinence pledges or simply for men who wished to enjoy a convivial environment somewhere other than the pub. Factory workers and craftsmen who once drank porter in the mornings now stopped on their way to work to buy a penny roll and a cup of hot caffeine. Later in the day the busy atmosphere of the coffeehouse mellowed into something more restful for those on their way home from work. Patrons were encouraged to take their time amid the partitioned, dark-wood booths, enjoying a plate of pork chops, perusing the lightly stained periodicals. "In the evenings these places become reading rooms," wrote one observer. "They are convenient to thousands of persons who have not the comforts of domesticity at home. The good fire, the bright light, the supply of newspapers and magazines, and the cup of simple beverage, are obtainable for a few pence . . ."[2]

John Stride, without a wife or family and far from the familiar Kentish coast, must have passed many an hour in this pleasant environment, conversing with Fryatt and contemplating the possibility of opening a similar establishment. As a man in his forties, John would have no longer been able to ignore the physical strains of slaving over a carpenter's bench or in a furniture factory six days a week. Like his father, he recognized the worth of investing hard labor in a business that might generate a larger and more comfortable income, and might one day support a wife and children.

Like most skilled laborers, John had limited opportunities to meet women because of the length of his working day. Such socializing typically occurred at pubs, public parks, music halls, or church events. Coffeehouses, too, offered some possibilities.

Generally, women did not frequent these dark-wood rooms, which smelled of brewing coffee and fat and echoed with gruff male conversation. However, shop girls, servants, and those who worked for a daily wage often came in for coffee and a penny bun while on an errand for their mistress or for a lunch of soup, fruit, and tapioca pudding. This is most likely how John Stride came to meet a young housemaid from Sweden called Elisabeth Gustafsdotter.*

When she first arrived in London, in the winter of 1866, Elisabeth lived nowhere near the busy commercial surroundings of Tottenham Court Road, but in an elegant townhouse on the fringe of Hyde Park. At midcentury, few locations in the city were more synonymous with wealth and gentility than the streets encircling the beau monde's favorite spot for promenades. Although the identity of Elisabeth's employer remains a mystery, his social status is not. Elisabeth would have taken her place within a household of servants in the home of a prosperous, cosmopolitan family not unlike the Dicksons, who traveled regularly between Sweden, Britain, and continental Europe to superintend their shipping, iron, and timber empire. Such a prestigious position in domestic service came with high stakes. Now part of a hierarchy of staff, Elisabeth had to submit to the governance of a

---

* Elisabeth's name became Anglicized to Elizabeth when she moved to London, and it appears in English records as such from the time of her relocation.

housekeeper or a butler in a grand home spread over several floors, a stark change from serving a generous, lower-middle-class mistress in a handful of rooms. A position working for a gentleman came with a new set of rigid rules; clean hands, a straight back, and a silent tongue were essential. Elisabeth's eyes were never to meet those of her master or mistress. If, while crossing a hall or ascending a staircase, she encountered a member of the family, she was to turn her face to the wall. The demands of the job, the unfamiliar culture, and the new language would have presented many challenges to a young maidservant from Sweden.

When she accepted the offer of a job in London, Elisabeth also decided to settle permanently in Britain. Although it was not required that every Swede who moved to London register with the Swedish Church, it appears to have been an administrative formality for those who had applied for permanent residency in the UK. The journey from Hyde Park to the Swedish Church in Prince's Square in the East End of London would have been a time-consuming one for a servant allocated no more than a day off per month. By the time Elisabeth was able to make her way there, five months had elapsed since her arrival in Britain. Ultimately, her errand appears to have been carried out at the behest of her employer in the course of preparing for a move abroad. Elisabeth, who could not write, gave her name to the clerk of the church, who inscribed it on the register, along with a note stating her occupation and that she was single. At the same time, Elisabeth also expressed her intention to travel to Brest, in France, one of the centers of the shipping industry, and applied for a change of residency.[3] Whether she did indeed follow her employers to France is unknown; a line was later drawn through her application by another hand, perhaps before the intended departure or after a return to London.

The circumstances that led Elisabeth to leave her position in Hyde Park are unclear, but a strange inference made during the coroner's inquest in 1888 hints at a possible scandal, not unlike the one she may have been embroiled in at Gothenburg. Commentators have remarked that Elisabeth had been blessed with beautiful features. Chief Inspector Walter Dew observed wistfully that notwithstanding her trials and tribulations, "traces of prettiness remained in her face."[4] As a young woman in London, with an exotic foreign accent, a high forehead, and dark wavy hair, she would have caught the eye of many admirers. One of these, a policeman, courted her while she lived with her employers at Hyde Park, though due to the long hours she worked, it is not difficult to conceive how this relationship failed to blossom. However, it would appear that someone closer to home may have also had a claim on her affections.

More than twenty years later, Michael Kidney, a witness at the inquest into Elisabeth's death, was questioned about the details of his own romantic relationship with her. He implied that it was stormy but that he treated Elisabeth as he might a wife, regardless of the fact that she left him on several occasions.

"Do you know anyone else she has picked up with?" asked the coroner.

"I have seen the address of the brother of the gentleman, with whom she lived as a servant somewhere near Hyde Park," he replied, with what seems, at first, to be a strange non sequitur.

"That was not what I asked you," the coroner responded; "do you think she went away with anyone else?" he clarified, referring to the period when Kidney was involved with Elisabeth, not to an episode in the past, before Kidney knew her.[5]

Why she retained the details, not of the employer for whom she worked more than twenty years earlier, but of his brother, raises many questions. However, it is extremely revealing that Kidney volunteered the information in the context of being probed on the subject of men with whom his partner may have had a relationship. In what form this address appeared is also mysterious. As Elisabeth could not write, the details would have been inscribed by another hand and given to her. Perhaps it was a letter, written by the man himself, carefully preserved over the decades. Elizabeth had also obviously spoken of him and their history to Michael Kidney. Twenty years is a remarkably long time to recall someone who had simply been the brother of her employer.

It may have been on account of this illicit attachment that Elisabeth eventually left the Hyde Park residence. Whatever the state of affairs, her employer (or perhaps his brother) provided her with a good enough reference to enable her to acquire work elsewhere.

By the winter of 1869, if not earlier, Elisabeth had found employ-ment working for a widow by the name of Elizabeth Bond. Mrs. Bond, as she was known to her two servants, ran a genteel lodging house, which rented furnished rooms to a respectable clientele at 67 Gower Street, around the corner from the furniture warehouses and shops of Tottenham Court Road. A Swedish maid, well-trained in a gentleman's household in Hyde Park, would lend a certain air of sophistication to Mrs. Bond's establishment, though Elisabeth's chores consisted of the usual drudgery. While Mrs. Bond and her widowed daughter, Em-ily Williams, managed the business, Elisabeth and her fellow servant passed their days and nights trudging up and down the three flights of stairs with their scuttles of coal and buckets of water and trays laden with supper and tea. Those whose grates she scrubbed and beds she made were firmly of the middle class. Mrs. Bond's lodgers at var-ious times included a lecturer and fellow of Corpus Christi College, Oxford; a Prussian merchant of "fancy goods"; a former brewer and his wife and daughter; a lawyer; and a widow "living on independent means." Among them, from 1868 through 1869, was also a German musician, Charles Louis Goffrie, and his daughter, who lived at and gave singing and piano lessons from Mrs. Bond's rooms.[6] Once more, Elisabeth found herself among musicians, her workdays lightened by melody and perhaps a remembrance of those who had once lifted her from adversity.

During one of those afternoons or mornings, when Elisabeth was sent out to fetch provisions or visit the post office, she may have stopped at a local coffeehouse for some brief refreshment when she was noticed by a forty-seven-year-old carpenter from Sheerness. It is impossible to say how their meeting occurred or how their relation-ship progressed, if John and Elizabeth's paths crossed on multiple oc-casions, on the street moving to or from work, or in the wooden stalls drinking a dark, sugared brew. Whatever the case, by the early months of 1869, they had become engaged.

Nothing is known about John Stride's appearance — if he was a man of commanding good looks, or just plain and respectably turned out. By his late forties, he was certain to have been turning gray. What then did a very pretty twenty-five-year-old housemaid, who may have recently been the mistress of her rich employer's brother, see in a modest maker of furniture nearly twice her age? In her midtwenties, Elisabeth knew that she would have to marry soon, and John, who had lived as a bachelor for many years, likely had put money aside. Perhaps too, after her tumultuous past, John's affections seemed refreshingly genuine. She had experienced the harm men could do, and John Stride must have seemed a safe choice.

Interestingly, they were married neither in a Methodist chapel nor a Lutheran church, but rather at the Anglican church in Elisabeth's parish — St. Giles-in-the-Fields, its lobster tail of a spire poking through the London soot. On that day, March 7, 1869, Elisabeth stood before the altar with no one from her life, neither family nor friend — to act as her witness. While Daniel Fryatt signed his name to the register alongside that of his constant customer and companion, the church sexton was made to perform this role for Elisabeth. There was nothing from her past that could intrude on her wedding day. She even chose to cite a false name for her father, "Augustus Gustafsson." Her experience was one typical of an immigrant, one who wished no shadows or remembrances to fall upon this new chapter. How much her husband understood of her tragic experience in Gothenburg and the disease, which she still carried, is unknown.

The Strides' marriage marked another fresh beginning in both of their lives. Their union was sealed by the birth of a business venture and a move to another part of town: Poplar, roughly six miles away, in the East End. This relocation would have been carefully considered. John Stride's intention was to open a coffeehouse, but the possibility of carpentry work at the docks also offered a failsafe in case the business venture failed. The area's thriving dockyards employed over two hundred full-time laborers and during the 1860s were undergoing an extension project that linked the North London Railway with the port. John's brother George, a dock clerk, had established himself and his family there, and the convenience of nearby family was likely an equal draw to a couple who expected to soon have children of their own. By 1871, the two Stride brothers were joined by a third, Charles, who settled in Limehouse.

Within months of their wedding, the Strides had opened their new establishment on Upper North Street, in the heart of what was called Poplar New Town. This grid of recently built nineteenth-century streets to the north of the waterside was a mixed area of modest villas, middle-class terraced housing, and lodgings for laboring families. According to the writer Jerome K. Jerome, who lived there as a child in the 1860s, it was a place of contrasts, where "town and country struggled for supremacy," where the surrounding marshes were still dotted with farms, and where herds of goats and cows might be driven through the streets. "Processions of the unemployed" moving between the docks and the workhouse were also a regular sight.[7]

In theory, the social composition of Upper North Street, with its grocers, apothecaries, dressmakers, and butchers, was no different from Munster Street, where John had studied Daniel Fryatt's efforts at keeping a coffeehouse. The teachers, masons, servants, shipwrights, and laborers who lived alongside the shopkeepers would have been the Strides' intended clientele, not the workers at the dockside. The coffeehouse's position across the road from Trinity Methodist Chapel was also strategic. The costs of the lease and the initial investment in the business were presumably covered by John's savings; Elisabeth too may have contributed. It is possible that John employed his skills as a carpenter to create or improve upon a traditional wood interior of plain booths, varnished partitions, and drop-leaf tables. With Elisabeth's experience as a servant, she and John would have run their family business together. Charles Dickens describes the ubiquitous sight in working men's coffeehouses of the "neat waitress" who was "economical of speech" but ever "ringing the changes between her two refrains of 'coffee and slice' and 'tea and a hegg.'"[8] A coffeehouse owner's hours were long ones, but the couple could keep their own clock, and, for the first time, Elisabeth's scrubbing, cooking, washing, and serving would have been performed not for an employer, but for the benefit of her husband and herself.

The difficulties the Strides were likely to have encountered came from competition with pubs. Despite the popularity of coffeehouses, not every working man was prepared to abandon alcohol and the jolly camaraderie of the local public house. While the coffeehouse may have had its dedicated adherents, a business could rise or fall based on its location: too many pubs and too few teetotalers nearby could close the shutters of even the most welcoming coffee room. By 1871, the Strides had learned this the hard way. They were forced to move their business to 178 Poplar High Street, where they hoped to attract a better trade. The failure of this first venture would have come at a cost. It appears that John returned, at least part time, to his former calling, to recover the loss. On that year's census, he reported his occupation not as a coffeehouse owner, but as a carpenter. Still, the Strides would not concede defeat and were just able to sustain their business.

In four years since they were married, no children had been born to the coffeehouse keepers. If Elisabeth had pregnancies, they were not brought to term, most likely on account of her condition. While her syphilis could not be communicated to John in its latent stage, there continued to exist a high risk of miscarriage and stillbirth. In an effort to bury her past, Elisabeth may have been too ashamed to confide her secret to John. Bringing syphilis into the marital home was considered a disgrace and a tragedy, but it was one for which errant husbands who visited prostitutes and who kept mistresses tended to be blamed. Medical texts generally addressed the problem from this perspective while partially exonerating the man for his conduct by claiming the root of the issue lay with the selfish immorality of those in the sex trade.[9] The possibility that a man might choose to marry a woman with a sexual past, who had been exposed to the disease, seemed unconscionable. Elisabeth's failure to become a mother in an era when a woman's identity and purpose was defined by this role would have been devastating to her, especially as society and the church would have ensured that she shouldered the blame for her own misfortune. Elisabeth's upbringing would have inculcated in her the belief that this was punishment for her sinful life. How John and his devout Methodist family viewed the situation is uncertain. While Stride maintained contact with his brother Charles, his wife, and his children during the early years of his marriage to Elisabeth, it seems that they began to drift apart after 1872. The Stride family appears to have been a divided one, and at no point were the fissures more evident than in the wake of the death of their revered patriarch.

In the early 1870s, William Stride was approaching his ninetieth birthday. Stubborn and determined until his last, he never once missed a meeting of the Sheerness Pier Commission. However, by the end of the summer of 1873, his health had begun to falter. On September 6 he died in the home he still shared with his son Daniel, and was attended by his daughter Sarah Ann. For one who had played such a prominent role in the development of Sheerness, the obituary in the local paper was rather sparing in words. It described him only as one "who was generally respected throughout the town."[10] No catalogue of his great deeds or selfless acts of charity appeared and, perhaps more revealingly, no mention was made of a devoted and grieving family.

With the exception of Daniel, no one among the Stride children had dedicated more of his or her adult life to their father than John. If anyone had a reason to expect something from William Stride's will, it was his second-eldest son, who had forgone marriage until his forties and remained in Sheerness at the expense of his income and future financial security in order to serve his family. However, when the will was read on the thirtieth of that month, it was found to contain a number of surprises.

Daniel was handsomely rewarded with property. His father left him five houses on Stride's Row and two houses on Victory Street, which included an additional "plot of ground, a stable, a coal shed, a workshop and a garden." William Stride's daughter Sarah Ann Snook, who had made her life only three doors down from her father, was also favored with two houses on Stride's Row. John's affluent brother Edward, who had remained in Sheerness, trained as a surgeon, and become the star of the family, was bequeathed a house on Stride's Row as well.[11] John received nothing, not even a mention or acknowledgment.

William Stride had played a vindictive game of favorites, sending a clear signal from beyond the grave as to who among his progeny had pleased or dishonored him. John's eldest brother, William James, who had been born deaf and struggled financially as a laborer in Sheerness all of his life, was similarly excluded, as were all the sons who had abandoned their father for London.

It cannot be a coincidence that John and Elisabeth were forced to sell the lease of their coffeehouse within months of William Stride's death. The collapse of their first endeavor on Upper North Street was likely to have left a debt, while attempting to buoy their fortunes with a second failing business would only have increased their arrears. In order to keep his concern afloat John may have had to borrow money, quite probably against the promise of inheriting property. When his father's will left him disappointed, there was nothing more to be done but to shut the door for good on his ambitions and to attempt, in whatever way he could, to keep a roof over the couple's heads.

LONG LIZ

IT WAS NEARLY 8 p.m. The sky had darkened, and the moon had risen over the flat, silvery Thames. On the evening of September 3, 1878, summer was in retreat, and more than eight hundred passengers on board the *Princess Alice,* a pleasure cruiser filled with day-trippers and those returning from their holidays in Sheerness, were headed back to London. On deck, the ship's band played a rousing polka, and couples gathered to dance and sing. Children chased one another across the slippery wooden decks, out of reach of their parents and nannies. Gentlemen read their newspapers and watched the passing shoreline — warehouses, docks, and factories disappearing into night's shadow. As they approached North Woolwich Pier, it never occurred to those lulled by the gentle evening and the music that they were moving directly into the course of the *Bywell Castle,* an 890-ton iron-clad coal freighter. By the time both ships realized that a collision was imminent, it was too late. The sharp point of the *Bywell Castle*'s bow plunged knifelike through the *Princess Alice,* tearing through the engine room and shearing the vessel in half. Within minutes, both parts of the ship were sucked into the depths of the sewage-filled Thames; panic-stricken passengers clung to its sides as it went under. The river was filled with bobbing heads, gasping for breath and crying out to loved ones across the black water. Parents held tight to their drowning children; women's heavy skirts and metal bustles made it almost impossible for them to fight the pull of the tide. The *Bywell Castle* threw down ropes and lowered the few lifeboats stowed on board, but its crew was otherwise impotent to save the lives of so many.

More than 650 died in the tragedy, the greatest loss of life sustained in any Thames shipping disaster. The number of survivors was never confirmed, though estimates placed it between 69 and 170. Those who lived faced the horrific task of helping to identify the dead, who were daily pulled from the clasp of the murderous river. Entire families perished on the night of September 3. Many children, whose parents had gone off for the day, were left orphans. Wives and husbands were widowed; some had watched helplessly as a loved one swallowed water and slipped beneath the waves.

The *Princess Alice* disaster traumatized London. The story spread furiously among the communities surrounding the East End docks. Many had witnessed the events firsthand — seen the bodies, the wreckage — or listened with horror as others described what they had observed. As the impact of the tragedy was felt equally among those from Sheerness, the news of it must have landed especially hard on the Stride brothers in Poplar and Limehouse, who would have anxiously scanned the growing lists of the dead, searching for the names of family or friends and neighbors. Elisabeth took in the magnitude of the calamity with keen interest as tale after tale circulated in the newspapers and among those she knew.

By the time of the *Princess Alice* disaster, Elisabeth's own life was in turmoil. Following the collapse of John's final attempt to maintain his coffeehouse, their marriage had turned sour. The ensuing financial hardship and possibly other factors, such as the couple's inability to produce children, may also have contributed to the friction growing between them. It is likely that drink had also begun to play a role.

In March 1877, eight years into their marriage, it appears that Elisabeth left John. Although this separation was to be temporary, she had nowhere to turn, and rather than opt for the workhouse casual ward, she chose to take her chances on the street. On March 24, she was picked up by the police under vagrancy laws, either for begging or sleeping rough, and forcibly taken to the workhouse. After this sequence of events, the Strides were reconciled, but their arguments and difficulties continued. Two years later, when John had fallen ill, Elisabeth appealed for aid from the Swedish Church, and in 1880, her name appears in workhouse records, once at Stepney Union in February, and a second time at Hackney Union in April, where the word "destitute" was written beside her entry.[1]

It was during this period, if not as early as September 1878, that Elisabeth alighted upon an ingenious method of supporting herself. If John could not provide for them, then she would have to use her wits to survive. A keen student of human nature, Elisabeth watched and listened and cogitated. As the autumn of 1878 wore on, she had heard a litany of horror stories about the victims of the *Princess Alice* disaster. Noticing how these sorrowful tales of loss had led to outpourings of pity and offers of material compensation, she invented a narrative of her own. At the time, the newspapers were filled with information about the generosity of Londoners, who had raised more than £38,246 as part of a relief fund.[2] Victims, survivors, and their families were urged to come forward with claims, and Elisabeth may have been inspired to do just this. In the weeks following the calamity, many were playing this game. On September 29, a twenty-one-year-old woman named Elizabeth Wood was sent to prison for a month after defrauding a Woolwich coffeehouse owner on the pretext that she had survived the disaster but lost her family.[3] Similarly, the Princess Alice Fund rejected fifty-five applications for assistance from "those with no good reason." Elisabeth Stride's name does not appear among the list of survivors and, unless she employed an alias, neither was she successful in acquiring charity from the relief fund. It's far more likely that her gains were made simply by peddling her story to concerned individuals.

Elisabeth's tale was an elaborate one, colored with detail and drama designed to beguile the listener. She claimed that she had been aboard the *Princess Alice* with John and two of their nine children. She appears to have told some people that John was employed on the ship, and she and her children were accompanying him that day. When the pleasure cruiser was struck, they were separated; John had attempted to save the children, but he and the two young ones were snatched away by the river and drowned. Elisabeth, who found herself within one of the ship's collapsing funnels, saw that a rope had been dropped by the *Bywell Castle,* and grabbed for it. In scaling her way to safety, she was kicked in the mouth by the man above her, which damaged her palate. Remarkably, she survived, or so she told those rapt by her story of courage. She went on to say that life as a widow was fraught with hardship. As she was unable to support her seven remaining children, she had placed them in the care of an orphanage in South London run by the Swedish Church. In the end, she had nowhere to turn but to a friend of her husband's, and there she still found herself in dire financial need.

It is likely that Elisabeth knitted this story together from others she had heard, or lifted it wholesale from a person she had known. John Stride's wife had never borne nine children, or if she had, the true tragedy may have lain in the fact that none survived birth. She may have instead endured nine failed pregnancies, or perhaps she had simply borrowed the number from John, who was one of nine siblings. Whatever the case, in the ensuing years Elisabeth would retell this tale enough times to convince everyone around her of its veracity. It would be the first step in rewriting her history and reframing what would become a malleable identity. She would also use it to distance herself from her husband; during periods when she was separated from him, she claimed he was dead.

In April 1881, the couple were again reconciled, though this time the reunion lasted only a handful of months. The census for that year found their circumstances considerably compromised. When once they occupied several rooms above their coffeehouse, their living space was now reduced to a single room in a house on Usher Road, in Bow. By December, John and Elisabeth had apparently agreed to part permanently. Like William Nichols and John Chapman, John Stride may have also consented to pay his wife a small maintenance as a formality of making their separation official. From this period, Elisabeth took up residence in Whitechapel, first on Brick Lane, and then, following a stay in the workhouse infirmary for bronchitis, at the lodging house to which she'd return repeatedly over the next six years: 32 Flower and Dean Street.

According to the writer Howard Goldsmid, "Flowrydean Street," as its habitués called it, was no "rose by any other name," but rather "one of the worst of the East-end slums." It smelled "unwholesome" and looked "uninviting."[4] The Associated Press journalist who visited in 1888 described it in slightly more flattering terms, claiming that "for the East End" it had "a fairly presentable appearance."

> One side of the street is mainly occupied by a huge pile of modern buildings, intended for occupation by the families of artisans, and rented almost exclusively by a colony of middle-class Jews. The other side presents a far more dingy appearance. The brickwork of the houses is blackened with age, and doors and windows alike present the only too familiar aspects betokening the abode of the extreme poor.[5]

According to the article, all of the buildings on the dilapidated side of the street were registered lodging houses, and number 32 had beds for a hundred "dossers." While Goldsmid described these dormitories as crawling with insects and rodents, "shamefully overcrowded, very-ill-ventilated, and . . . foul-smelling and unhealthy," the AP journalist believed number 32 "seemed to look uncommonly comfortable" inside. Certainly, Elisabeth preferred it to other lodging houses, and over the years, came to regard it as a sort of base.

While living at 32 Flower and Dean Street, Elisabeth supported herself through "charring." A charwoman, "the lowest trade of domestic — even lower than the maid of all work," was an occasional servant who came to a home for a few hours to perform tasks for families who couldn't afford live-in staff. The charwoman was generally older than the housemaid, "between 40 and 60," and usually, as evidenced by her "dirty mob-cap, battered bonnet . . . tucked-up gown and bare, red arms," impoverished.[6] In addition to the two shillings she would receive for a day's work, Elisabeth might also receive food: toast and tea, scraps of the family meal, or even a provision of sugar.

In the East End, the Jewish community, which comprised the majority of the population between Whitechapel High Street and Hanbury Street, relied on the services of gentile charwomen to assist them during the Saturday Sabbath. As religious custom forbade Jews from engaging in any form of work from sunset on Friday to sunset on Saturday, a charwoman was hired to light the fires, switch on the gas lighting, and cook and serve meals. As recent immigrants who had escaped persecution in Russia, Prussia, and the Ukraine, most families here did not speak English; Elisabeth learned to communicate with them in Yiddish. In fact, it is possible that she had acquired the rudiments of this language in Gothenburg. Haga, the working-class district where she had lived, was also the home of the city's Jewish community.[7] Working for Jewish families would also offer Elisabeth the security of knowing that fellow immigrants were not usually eager to discuss their pasts, and therefore were unlikely to make many inquiries into hers.

Living apart from John, in a different neighborhood, away from the West End and from Poplar, gave Elisabeth the opportunity to become whomever she wished. She had learned that shedding an identity was as simple as moving somewhere new. While she resided in Whitechapel, she was Elisabeth the widow and Elisabeth the disaster victim. She could be many things to many people; the farmer's daughter had become a servant, and the servant had become a man's mistress and a fallen woman. The fallen woman had become a prostitute, and then a rescued Magdalen. She had found herself an immigrant, a foreigner in a new land. She had likely been the paramour of a rich man and then the wife of a struggling carpenter. She had been a coffeehouse keeper and a workhouse inmate. She was Swedish, but she could speak English well enough to fool people into believing it was her first language. She may also at times have claimed to be Irish and used the name Annie Fitzgerald. When she chose to, Elisabeth could even transform herself into another woman's sister.

In 1883, fate threw Elisabeth into the path of a woman named Mary Malcolm, a tailoress. It seems that the years spent squinting over a needle had ruined what remained of Mrs. Malcolm's eyesight. Her attraction to the bottle probably did not help matters. One day, perhaps on the street or in a pub, she glimpsed Elisabeth Stride and was convinced it was her estranged sister, Elizabeth Watts. Mary had probably called out her sister's name, and Elisabeth Stride had conveniently answered to it. The mistaken identity stuck, in part because Elisabeth was all too pleased to use this new relationship to her advantage.

When the tailoress gave her account of events, it appears she conflated the two women's stories, weaving the details she understood of Elizabeth Watts's life with those Elisabeth Stride had told her of her recent past. She claimed in her inquest testimony that her sister was colloquially called "Long Liz" and that she had lived with a man who ran a coffeehouse in Poplar. She also stated that she knew Elisabeth's husband had died in a shipwreck, though recalling the precise circumstances proved problematic. As it happened, Elizabeth Watts's second husband had genuinely died as a result of a shipwreck on the Isle of St. Paul, but these facts became entangled with Elisabeth Stride's lies about the *Princess Alice* disaster. Knowing that her real sister had led a checkered life, which included at least two marriages and a period spent in an asylum, Mary Malcolm was inclined to believe that the bedraggled, impoverished woman she had met was this same person.*

From the time Mrs. Malcolm first encountered "her sister," she claimed that drink was Elisabeth Stride's primary failing. She was always in need of money, and Mary "had her doubts" about what she did for a living. However, as family, she felt compelled to assist her. For the next five years, the two women met at least once a week, and sometimes more frequently. Mrs. Malcolm handed over two shillings to Elisabeth every Saturday at four o'clock on the corner of Chancery Lane. Occasionally she gave Elisabeth clothing as well. Regardless of appearances, Mary did harbor some doubts about Elisabeth. In fact, during the five-year period she met with her, she insisted on keeping Elisabeth at an arm's length. Mrs. Malcolm had never invited "her sister" into her home, claiming, "I was always grateful to get rid of her." When asked if her husband or anyone else had known about her meetings with "her sister," she confessed, "No, I kept that from everyone. I was so ashamed."[8]

Mary Malcolm's shame in part may have stemmed from her persistence in maintaining the relationship with Elisabeth in spite of her

---

* Elizabeth Watts had been married to a wine merchant in Bath, but it appears his family disapproved of the union and set about trying to get rid of her. She was placed in an asylum, and her children were taken away from her. Her husband eventually moved to the United States, though she seemed to be under the impression that he had died.

concerns. So long as Mary did not scrutinize Elisabeth too closely, she could continue to fool herself, while Elisabeth successfully managed to hide from Mary the true circumstances of her life.

In October 1884, Elisabeth received word that John, whose health had been deteriorating for some time, had been admitted to the Stepney Sick Asylum. There, he died of heart disease at the age of sixty-three. He was buried on the thirtieth of the month, and within weeks, Elisabeth's life rapidly spiraled downward.

Certainly it is no coincidence that by November 13, Elisabeth was arrested on the Commercial Road for soliciting.[9] That she was also charged with drunk and disorderly behavior betrays her anguished state of mind. The desire to numb herself and her rage at the world were natural. Frederick Merrick, the chaplain of Millbank Prison, observed that most of his female inmates "loathed" selling sex on the streets and that "their repugnance to it could only be stifled when they were more or less under the influence of intoxicating drinks."[10] For her offenses, the judge gave Elisabeth a prison sentence of seven days' hard labor. Following this, there is no evidence that she was ever arrested again for soliciting.

It was after John's death that Elisabeth met and took up residence with another man, Michael Kidney. Kidney was a waterside laborer, a dockworker who loaded and unloaded vessels and earned some extra income as a volunteer in the army reserve. In his midthirties, he was several years younger than his new paramour but always assumed, based on her appearance, that they were roughly the same age. It is believed that the two met on the Commercial Road, though whether it was by accident or while Elisabeth was soliciting is uncertain. The relationship soon became a firm one, and the couple rented a series of dingy furnished rooms together, first on Devonshire Street and then on nearby Fashion Street. Like Elisabeth, Michael enjoyed drinking to excess, and he was no less angry or violent than she was when intoxicated. In January and June 1887, Elisabeth made complaints to police about Kidney's brutality, though, like many women with an abusive partner, she later dropped the charges.[11] However, Elisabeth was by no means a passive victim in her relationship. According to Michael, in the three years the two cohabited, Elisabeth left him twice and was gone, he estimated, "altogether about five months." "She always returned without my going after her," he boasted, because "she liked me better than anyone else."[12] On the occasions when she left him, Elisabeth regularly sought out a bed at the familiar surroundings of 32 Flower and Dean Street. The couple's relationship was a complicated one, which was likely to have come unraveled not only on account of Elisabeth's drinking and Kidney's violence, but also due to infidelity. By the end of their time together, Michael was suffering from syphilis, for which he received treatment at Whitechapel infirmary in 1889. He would not have contracted this from Elisabeth, who was no longer contagious by the time she was living with him.

Interestingly, over the course of her many visits with Elisabeth, Mrs. Malcolm didn't have an inkling of these tribulations. She claimed that she never knew Elisabeth to be involved with a man and that she had only a vague understanding that her "sister" was living in a lodging house, "somewhere in the neighbourhood of the tailors and Jews at the East End." However, she did know that Elisabeth was undone quite frequently by drink and that she had come before the magistrate and "been locked up" on account of it.[13]

From roughly 1886 until her death, there does appear to be a distinct change in Elisabeth's behavior. Her arrests for drunken disorderliness and obscene language increased markedly. By the end of summer of 1888, Elisabeth had been charged on no fewer than four occasions over three months. While this can undeniably be attributed in part to her dependency on alcohol, there may have been another contributing factor. It had been over twenty years since Elisabeth had contracted syphilis, and the disease would have potentially been entering its tertiary and final phase.

Neurosyphilis, or cerebral syphilis, as it was known in the late nineteenth century, presents in a variety of different ways when the disease begins to attack the brain and nervous system. The French physician Alfred Fournier, who conducted a study of the progress of the disease, identified "epileptic fits" as its first manifestation. Interestingly, as Mary Malcolm mentioned in her inquest testimony, Elisabeth had recently begun to suffer from such "fits." This confused Mary, as she had never known her sister to have epilepsy.[14] Apparently, Elisabeth's seizures were so bad that there were occasions when the police had let her off charges on account of her condition. Had Elisabeth actually suffered from severe epilepsy throughout her life, it is unlikely that she would have been able to maintain her positions in service, or that Michael Kidney and others who knew her would have failed to mention any such condition at the inquest. It is also unlikely that the seizures were a sham. The police and magistrates would have seen every trick in the book to avoid a prison sentence and were unlikely to fall for any act that Elisabeth might feign.

In addition to seizures, neurosyphilis can lead to paralysis in some victims and dementia-like symptoms in others. A victim's memory may falter, and the sufferer may become prone to hallucinations and delusions. Behavior becomes erratic, if not irrational, inappropriate, or violent. If Elisabeth was indeed suffering from the early stages of neurosyphilis, then her heavy drinking was likely to have disguised these symptoms, or at least offered an easy explanation for her increasing episodes of violence and obscene language. It is also possible that her symptoms themselves drove her to increase her alcohol intake in order to quell the pain or sense of disorientation.

Whether or not Elisabeth's disease was to blame, her behavior while she lived in Whitechapel was decidedly secretive and deceitful. The scam she perpetrated on Mary Malcolm, as well as her insistence that she was a survivor of the *Princess Alice* disaster, may have demonstrated to her the gullibility in human nature. In the manner of some of the most experienced con artists, she appears to have learned how to milk this weak spot for financial gain. In her testimony, Mrs. Malcolm mentioned that Elisabeth had told her she had "a hollowness in the right foot," caused by "an accident when she was run over by a machine" three years earlier. She had told Mary that she intended "to get some money" for it, but Mrs. Malcolm could not say "whether she ever got the money."[15] However, after viewing Elisabeth's body, she noticed that the "hollowness" had mysteriously disappeared, a development for which Mary could not account. Mary Malcolm also raised another peculiar incident. She claimed that Elisabeth had one day left a naked baby girl outside Mary's door. "I had to keep it until she fetched it away," Mary continued. She was under the impression the infant was

Elisabeth's child, which she had had with a policeman.[16] Michael Kidney, when questioned about this, was entirely baffled; "she never had a child by me and I never heard of her having a child by a policeman," he commented.[17] The child was unlikely to have been Elisabeth's, but rather one she had acquired temporarily from an acquaintance or a "baby-farmer" for the purposes of begging.* The addition of an infant, swaddled, crying, and hungry in its "mother's" arms, was a well-known ruse designed to tug on the heartstrings and purse strings of passersby. Elisabeth later returned for the baby. When Mary asked after it again, Elisabeth lied, saying that she had taken the girl to Bath, to live with the family of her first husband.†

Aside from Mary Malcolm, Catherine Lane, the wife of a laborer, was the only other person who claimed to know Elisabeth for a substantial period of time. Lane stated that they had met when Elisabeth first came to stay at 32 Flower and Dean Street, around 1881–82. She saw Elisabeth nearly every day during that time. As the lodging house was the nearest thing Elisabeth had to a permanent home, she made a habit of coming by to visit even while she was living with Michael Kidney. However, given the constancy of their association, it's also surprising how little either Catherine, or Elizabeth Tanner, the deputy lodging-house keeper at number 32, actually knew about Elisabeth's life. Neither knew her surname or her age. Whereas Michael Kidney believed her to be in her thirties, Elisabeth had chosen to tell Ann Mills, another resident at the lodging house, that she was "over fifty years of

---

* "Baby-farming," as it was called in the nineteenth century, was the practice of accepting the care of an infant or infants while the mother worked. Parents, who paid a small fee for the child to be looked after, often never returned to reclaim it, thereby making this a convenient way of disposing of an unwanted baby. As the care of the abandoned child eventually outstripped the fee originally paid, a caretaker might find that it was more expedient to let the infant die from neglect or sell the child on to someone else. The practice of baby-farming continued into the twentieth century.

† After Mary Malcolm gave her testimony, the real Elizabeth Watts, the sister from whom she'd been estranged, appeared. It turned out that she had been living with a new husband (her third), a Mr. Stokes who worked at a brickworks in Tottenham, in North London. She confirmed that she had not seen Mrs. Malcolm in years and that Elisabeth Stride must have been impersonating her. In the course of the inquest it also emerged that her first husband, whom she thought was dead, was actually alive and well in the United States and that Elizabeth Watts was now married bigamously.

age."[18] No one seemed to know where she had been born. In addition to peddling her stories about the *Princess Alice*, Elisabeth chose to tell her friends that she was from Stockholm. Only Sven Olsson, the clerk of the Swedish Church to whom she applied regularly for charitable handouts, had a grasp of her true history from the details recorded in the church's ledgers. Sadly, in all of the time she spent in Whitechapel, Elisabeth's friendships appear to have never taken on any more than an ephemeral shape, where even those who thought they knew her were kept at an arm's length.

In late September 1888, Elisabeth returned once more to 32 Flower and Dean Street after she and Michael Kidney had what Catherine Lane described as "words." By now, Elisabeth was accustomed to these cyclical separations. She gathered her possessions and spoke to a neighbor, a "Mrs. Smith," whom she asked to look after a Swedish hymnbook while she was away.[19] Possessions of value were never safe in a lodging house, and 32 Flower and Dean Street was no different. It was here, on the twenty-sixth, where the social reformer Thomas Barnardo claimed to have encountered her in the communal kitchen, along with several other women. As a campaigner for children's welfare, Barnardo had come to speak with the women about their experiences with children in lodging houses and how their lot might be improved. Instead, the female residents were more eager to discuss the Whitechapel murders, about which they "seemed thoroughly frightened." At one point, a "poor creature who had evidently been drinking exclaimed somewhat bitterly; we're all up to no good and no one cares what becomes of us. Perhaps some of us will be killed next! If anybody had helped the likes of us years ago we would have never come to this!"[20] With hindsight, Barnardo claimed that he believed the woman who spoke those words might very well have been Elisabeth Stride. In truth, they all might have been Elisabeth Stride, and certainly Elisabeth strove to be all of those women — everyone and no one. She was anonymous: a woman with a mutable story, a changeable history, someone who had recognized that the world didn't care about her, and chose to use that as a weapon in order to survive.

The day of September 29 was no different from any other for Elisabeth. The whitewashers had been in to smarten up the walls of 32

Flower and Dean Street. She and Ann Mills had cleaned the rooms after the men had finished. For completing this task, Elizabeth Tanner gave her six pence. Elisabeth then went to the Queen's Head Pub on Commercial Street for a drink, where the deputy keeper saw her again. At the inquest Tanner mentioned in passing that Elisabeth had gone out "without a bonnet or cloak," a point that would not have been lost on newspaper readers.[21] In the slums, women who wished to show that they were available sexually often appeared "in their figure," without items of clothing obscuring their appearance. However, it was equally well known for women selling sex to dress "gaudily" and for even the poorest to wear plumed and decorated hats. If Elisabeth had gone to the Queen's Head Pub in order to solicit, she did not meet with much luck, as she and Tanner walked back to the lodging house together around 6:30. Presumably it was at this time when she may have paid the deputy keeper for her bed. Just as the newspapers reporting on Polly Nichols's and Annie Chapman's last movements were riddled with contradictions and inconsistencies, the same can be said for Elisabeth Stride. While some publications, like the *Western Daily Press,* affirmed that she did pay Elizabeth Tanner in advance for her stay that night, others, like the *Daily Telegraph,* stated the opposite. If Stride had paid for her bed, then her intention when she left number 32 that evening was certainly to return. Knowing that she would be out for at least several hours, she asked Catherine Lane to mind a length of green velvet that she had acquired, perhaps with a view to pawning it. Finally, before she stepped out the door, she sought to smarten up her appearance and borrowed a brush to rid the muck from her only set of clothes.

Precisely where Elisabeth went and with whom is one of the more puzzling mysteries surrounding the deaths of the five canonical victims. As Elisabeth evidently avoided telling anyone details about her current or past life, it is impossible to conclude with much certainty what her designs were that evening. During the inquest, no one was able to say if she was involved with a man, or men, other than Michael Kidney. No one could comment on her typical habits — which places were her usual haunts and who might have been her regular companions, or if indeed she had any. Instead, her death merely left more questions about a woman whom no one could claim to have known at all. It is possible that Elisabeth may even have wanted it that way.

Only a handful of demonstrable facts are known about what she did that night. From the autopsy report, it seems that she had eaten some potato, bread, and cheese. It is almost certain that she would have had a few drinks as well. At some stage in the evening, she had acquired a corsage, or nosegay — a single red rose tied with some maidenhair fern, which she or someone else attached to her bodice. She also had been carrying some cachous, or hard sweets, for freshening the breath. Either these had been purchased for her, or she had enough spare change to buy them. She had presumably gone out to socialize or to meet someone — possibly this was a prearranged occasion, or possibly not. She may have gone out with the intention of soliciting, or in the hope of finding a longer-term partner — or both. At the time she was wearing what the *North London News* described as "a rusty black dress of a cheap kind of sateen with a velveteen bodice over which was a black diagonal worsted jacket with fur trimming," adding that her black crepe bonnet was too large for her; Elisabeth had stuffed the back of it with "a folded copy of a newspaper . . . with the object of making the article fit closer to the head." Interestingly, the reporter also remarked that Elisabeth's mode of dress was "entirely absent of the kind of ornaments commonly affected by women of her station."[22]

In the wake of her murder, a number of people came forward claiming to have sighted her that night, but due to poor lighting and the proven inaccuracy of witness perceptions, none of these claims are in any way verifiable.* Additionally, by the occasion of what came to be called "the double event" — the murders of both Elisabeth Stride and Catherine Eddowes on the same night — the residents of Whitechapel were desperate to offer what assistance they could to end the

---

* In 1896 the wrongful conviction of Alfred Beck by witnesses who all incorrectly identified him as the notorious fraudster called John Smith assisted in demonstrating the fallibility of the witness identification procedures used by the police during this period.

murderer's bloody rampage. With hindsight, the silhouette of any woman who had been seen in a doorway or on the street that evening with a man took on the form of Elisabeth Stride, an individual whose face these witnesses had never seen clearly and whom they didn't know. Of all of the purported sightings, only one is most likely to have been Elisabeth.

At around 12:45 a.m., a Hungarian man by the name of Israel Schwartz was walking along the Commercial Road and turned onto Berner Street. As he did so, he saw a man and woman having a disagreement. The woman stood facing the street, with her back toward the gate leading to an area called Dutfield's Yard. As Schwartz proceeded up the road, the dispute became increasingly more heated. The man grabbed the woman, turned her around, and threw her onto the footway. The woman screamed three times, though not especially loudly. At this point, Schwartz, who did not want to interfere in what he believed was a domestic dispute, crossed the road. Just then, a man who had been standing in the darkness beside a pub lit a pipe and moved in Schwartz's direction. Uncertain if the man was attempting to chase him off, Schwartz now began to panic and broke into a run. As he fled, he thought he heard the woman's attacker cry out the word "Lipski" — a reference to Moses Lipski, a notorious murderer and also a term of abuse often leveled at Jews.

Fifteen minutes later, Louis Diemschutz, a seller of costume jewelry, was on his way home when he discovered Elisabeth's body lying in Dutfield's Yard. When he found her, she lay on her side, facing a wall, in what looked like the fetal position. She held in her fingers a paper wrap of cachous. Diemschutz thought she appeared as if she had fallen asleep.

At the time of the coroner's inquest, both the police and the press believed the woman Schwartz had seen was likely to have been Elisabeth, due to the narrow window of time in which the sequence of events occurred. However, whether the assailant that Schwartz saw was the same man who would eventually murder her with a single cut across her throat can never be confirmed. Indeed, the question as to whether Elisabeth Stride was truly a victim of the malefactor known as Jack the Ripper, or the subject of another man's violence, is as likely to remain as much of an enigma as will she.*

Over the course of her life, Elisabeth had been a variety of things to many people; she had been both dark and light, a menace and a comfort. She had been a daughter, a wife, a sister, a mistress, a fraudster, a cleaner, a coffeehouse owner, a servant, a foreigner, and a woman who had at various times sold sex. However, the police and newspapers saw only another victim: an "unfortunate" who resided in a Whitechapel lodging house, a drunk, degenerate, broken-down woman far beyond the blush of youth. They depicted her passing as sad and unnecessary, but no great loss. These impressions, when set in typeface, would become fixed and for the most part unchallenged. There were no dissenting voices to object to this portrait and no attempt was made to paint a fuller one. No one cared to find her Swedish family and tell their story. No journalist sought out her in-laws, or possessed any true curiosity about her past, about the gentleman in Hyde Park, Mrs. Bond on Gower Street, or the customers in Poplar who had sat on the benches of her coffeehouse. Eventually, the opportunity to truly know Elisabeth Stride would slip away with her killer into the shadows.

<hr />

Sven Olsson would have read about the murder of two women in the early hours of September 30 long before he suspected that he knew one of them. As the clerk at the Swedish Church and the keeper of the reading room, he had seen Elisabeth Stride pass through the doors on a number of occasions. She was like many of their other impoverished parishioners: far from home, isolated, and in distress. Johannes Palmér, the church's priest, found his posting to this degraded part of London dispiriting and, at times, infuriating. He had grown weary of thieves invading his church and contending with what he called the "parasitic" beggars, among whom Elisabeth Stride would have numbered.

---

*The question as to whether Elisabeth Stride was murdered by the Ripper or by someone else has long been a subject of debate among experts.

Olsson did not find the poor as tiresome as did his priest, and so when the police approached him to identify someone who they believed was part of the Swedish community in the East End, he did not hesitate to lend his assistance.

A hymnbook that he had given to Elisabeth Stride had been found among her possessions. After the trials she had endured, Elisabeth was unlikely to have felt the stirrings of devotion that the book was intended to arouse. Nevertheless, she kept it. She did not pawn it, as she had everything else. It held something of significance to her, perhaps some shadowy remembrance of a farmhouse in Torslanda.

Sven Olsson must have understood that Elisabeth had no blood relations in England. There was no mother or brother to claim her, to mourn for her, to speak for her at the inquest, or even to provide her true name: Elisabeth Gustafsdotter. It fell to him, a stranger, to be all of this for her.

After he said his piece at the inquest, after all his accented words were scrutinized by the coroner and the jury, Olsson felt he owed Elisabeth Stride one final duty.

There was no one to pay for a hearse and ponies to parade her casket around the East End. The newspaper described her funeral as "sparse." She was lowered, without any fanfare, into a pauper's grave on October 6, at the East London Cemetery in Plaistow. Sven Olsson stood by to bid her farewell and utter a prayer for her in Swedish.

PART IV

KATE

April 14, 1842

September 30, 1888

SEVEN SISTERS

O N A M I L D morning in June 1843, George and Catherine Eddowes, burdened with baskets and bundles and whimpering children, boarded a canal boat in Wolverhampton. A journey by train to London would have been far quicker, but such a convenience was considerably beyond the means of the family of eight. Walking the distance, which would mean tramping along the country lanes from dawn until dusk for the better part of a week, was an unrealistic option for six children under the age of ten. Traveling by barge, alongside what few possessions the Eddowes may have owned, was the only sensible choice.

The family spent roughly two days crowded onto the broad, flat vessel, which they shared with fellow passengers as well as the bargeman and a heap of bulky cargo: boxes, trunks, pieces of furniture, and barrels. If it rained, a small enclosed cabin, partially occupied by a coal stove, offered the only shelter. However, the sights along the Grand Union Canal would have kept the children occupied as the barge wound through Birmingham and the industrial landscape of the West Midlands. Leaving behind the familiar slag heaps and furnaces, the Eddoweses traveled through the unfamiliar scenery of southern England toward the capital, bisecting villages, weaving between farms, passing through green and yellow fields bright with wildflowers, spying ancient churches and country estates as they progressed. The intricate system of locks, which caused the boat to rise and fall with the water levels, as well as the sturdy workhorse that pulled them along, would have fascinated the nine-year-old Alfred and his sisters: eight-year-old Harriet, seven-year-old Emma, six-year-old Eliza, and four-year-old Elizabeth. The youngest sibling, Catherine (Kate), born the year before, on April 14, was not old enough to later recall any part of the journey, or even the circumstances that forced her family to leave Wolverhampton in the first place.

Kate, or "Chick," as her family called her, was scarcely nine months old when the shape of her father's life began to change. For two generations, the Eddowes family had given their sons to the tinworking trade, one of Wolverhampton's principal industries. As described in *The Book of Trades* of 1820, a tinplate man was expected to not only forge "kettles, saucepans, canisters of all sorts and sizes, milk pails, lanterns, etc." from sheets of tin but also to be proficient in coating ironware with a protective rust-resistant layer of the molten material. As a skilled profession, tinplate men would have been expected to enter their line of work at the age of fourteen through a seven-year apprenticeship, though by the early nineteenth century with the introduction of machinery, such traditional practices were on the wane. George Eddowes, who would have been among some of the last young men to have received the benefit of this form of intensive training, began his in 1822, at the Old Hall Works. Here, George and his younger brothers, William and John, toiled beneath the same roof as their father, Thomas, who in later years would be celebrated as the factory's most senior worker. Under the sharp eye of his apprentice master, George would have learned how to wield "a large pair of shears to cut the tin into a proper shape and size" and "how to apply heat so as to solder the joints of his work." For six days a week, from six o'clock in the morning until six at night in the summer, and from eight until eight in the winter months, he labored with his fellow apprentices at their workbench, learning the difference between the hammers for planishing, hollowing, and creasing, and when to use "the large or small anvils, the beak irons, chisels, gouges, knippers, plyers, squares and rules." Only at the end of this rigorous period of instruction, which concluded when the apprentice presented a piece of tinware of his own creation to his examiners, was he granted the right to officially practice the trade. By the end of that seven-year period, the tinplate man had acquired not only an essential set of skills, but also a keen sense of identity as part of a community of fellow craftsmen.

Since 1767, the Old Hall Works, a decaying Elizabethan manor house encircled by fields on the outskirts of Wolverhampton, had sat at the heart of tinworking life. The streets that radiated from it — Dudley Street, Bilston Street, and farther west, into the more rural surrounds off Merridale Road — became the traditional quarter of the tinplate man and the "japanner": those who decorated and shellacked the tinware with elaborate painted designs. Men who had trained together as apprentices and then worked together in the factories also lived side by side in the weathered cottages and "back-to-back" houses that lined the streets. Families mingled and intermarried. Gossip spread quickly, especially in the local tinworkers' public houses, the Merridale Tavern, the Swan, and the Red Cow.

It was at the Red Cow that the Friendly Society of the United Operative Tin Plate Workers of Wolverhampton, or the "Tin Man's Society," had been meeting regularly since 1834. Concerns over the introduction of machinery had led to labor unrest in the 1820s; sensing that future conflict with the factory owners was inevitable, the organization began to draw up a strategy to protect the workers' interests. All members were expected to contribute no less than five pence and no more than six shillings per week for a strike fund. Additionally, they compiled a "book of rates," standardizing pay for their work, and by 1842 requested that all six of Wolverhampton's tin factories sign up to it. Most employers followed suit, including William Ryton, the owner of the Old Hall Works, who was often celebrated among his peers as "a well-known friend to the working classes."[1] Unfortunately, not all of the town's tin factory owners bore a similar reputation or regarded standardized pay to be in their interests; especially not Edward Perry, the man who had only recently employed George Eddowes and his brother, William. The response of the Tin Man's Society was to call a strike, and by January 1843, Perry had "no less than thirty-five men . . . out of his employment."[2]

Edward Perry was no friend of the working man, and he would not abide labor action under any circumstances. Over the course of his career as a factory owner, he would use foreign workers, death threats, spies, and imprisonment to break strikes. Perry prided himself on possessing "a good knowledge of the rights of . . . labour, and especially of the laws relating to conspiracy." Most important, "he felt sure the ignorance and the enthusiasm of . . . working men would give him an advantage."[3] On this occasion, he was determined to pursue, personally and with force, each employee who was in breach of contract. When Perry learned that his men were being enticed away to London under the protection of the union, he set out after them. With the assistance of informants and detectives, he tracked his errant employees to the metalworkers' pubs of Clerkenwell and hauled them back under warrant. Once they were arrested for contravening the terms of their employment, he had them tried and sentenced to two months of hard labor at Stafford Prison.

Much as he had hoped, Perry's decision to make no concessions began to divide the community of tinplate workers and japanners. Angry, hissing crowds of tin men began gathering outside the court building whenever Perry took the stand to prosecute his employees, and it was not long before the dispute degenerated into violence.

As dedicated members of the Tin Man's Society, the Eddowes brothers were among the thirty-five men who unlawfully walked out of Edward Perry's factory. It was the brothers, along with a handful of other Society members, who sought to pressure their colleagues into joining the protest, promising that the organization would pay them "15 shillings a week as long as the calamity [the strike] lasted." On January 9, Richard Fenton, "one of Perry's men" who had refused to strike, was enjoying his ale at the Merridale Tavern when allegedly William Eddowes and two other tinworkers pushed through the door and began accosting him.

Later, witnesses at the trial believed that he "and his party had come in for a row."

"You have a brother out on strike, you shabby devil!" Eddowes was reported to have shouted. He then "up with his fist and struck Fenton, and kicked him." Within moments, a group of at least nine tinworkers, including William Eddowes's wife, Elizabeth, set upon Fenton, kicking and beating him and crying, "We'll murder him, murder the bastard!" as Fenton attempted to flee upstairs.[4]

According to the magistrate who presided at the trial, Fenton had been fortunate to escape with his life. William, perhaps shaken by the severity of his own actions and the prospect of imprisonment, went into hiding, leaving his wife, Elizabeth, to appear at the trial.

Unfortunately, this incident was but the first of the Eddowes family's misfortunes. On February 15, Edward Perry ordered a notice to be printed in the *Wolverhampton Chronicle*. Perry stated that he and two other factory owners were aware that "daily secret meetings" were being held for the purpose of "inducing our men to leave our employment," and he offered thirty pounds "to any person who shall give such information as may enable us successfully to prosecute any parties conspiring, by payments of money or otherwise, to prevent us carrying on our respective trades, to withdrawing our men or to compel us to alter our methods of carrying on our businesses, or to submit to their terms." By March 24, the newspaper ad had come up trumps. Whoever the informant was, he had pointed his finger at George Eddowes.

At the trial that followed, Perry took the stand and directed his fire at his former employee. "The defendant," he said, "had been a ringleader" and "was a complete firebrand." Perry wanted Eddowes gone and went on to claim that "he had coerced the others and had it not been for him, no strike would have taken place."[5] The judge had sympathy for the beleaguered factory owner and immediately sentenced George to two months' hard labor. According to the *Wolverhampton Chronicle*, Eddowes demonstrated no remorse for his purported crimes, nor indeed any concern that he was leaving behind his wife and six young children. Instead, "he retired . . . with something like an air of bravado and a readiness to undergo . . . punishment."[6]

While Kate Eddowes's father may have hid his anxiety at the prospect of spending the next two months plodding the prison treadmills, he would not display it openly. As a committed union man, George Eddowes would have known the risks he faced when he became an agitator and would have expected the union to reward him and his family for their sacrifice. Equally, he would have recognized that his days of working alongside his friends and family in Wolverhampton were now at an end.

⸺◦◦◦⸺

The Eddowes family made their entrance into London along the gray, effluent-tainted waters of the Thames, passing through an archway of dangling cranes that framed the docks of Bermondsey. The small house in which they settled, at 4 Baden Place, was set a safe distance from the polluted waterfront. George Eddowes would have paid extra to situate his family nearer to the open green spaces and market gardens that flourished between the factories and warehouses. Although the area's housing was not of the highest caliber — it was plagued by poor drainage and ventilation and a lack of running water — the family was not subjected at close range to the eye-watering fumes of chemicals spewn from the local tanneries, dyers, and breweries. A lungful of relatively fresh air was one of the few privileges the expanding family could enjoy.

Had George been a single man or even one with a modest collection of children, his move from Wolverhampton might have been the making of the family. The union was likely to have been responsible for getting him his new job at Perkins and Sharpus, a large tin- and copperware manufacturer on the northern side of London Bridge. As a "skilled mechanic," George was entitled to a better rate of pay than was a general laborer — one of the many porters, carmen (deliverymen), or dockworkers who populated the neighborhoods of Bermondsey. According to *The English Book of Trades,* in the 1820s, a tin-plate man, "if sober and industrious," could "with ease earn from 35 shillings to 2 guineas in a week." However, it is likely that by midcentury, George would have expected to receive a weekly wage of approximately three pounds and nine pence from his new employer.* Such an income would offer a family with two or three children a degree of certainty that the rent would be paid, the hearth fires would be lit, and that a choicer cut of meat might appear on the table. As the writer

---

* This is roughly one pound, seven shillings, and five pence to two pounds, two shillings in about 1820. The sum above accords with the full-time wages Edward Perry was paying in 1842.

C. S. Peel describes, in London, a man could "rent a neat little house of six rooms," one of which he would probably let out to a lodger, who would pay twenty pounds per year. The children would "probably go to an Endowed school or a British Day [school]. There will be occasional jaunts to [the seaside at] Gravesend or Margate: sound boots, Sunday best." With a reliable workingman's income to support them, George's two or three children could rise in society. If they had a good education, his boys might become clerks or shopkeepers, his daughters, schoolmistresses or the wives of clerks and shopkeepers. However, a burden of six children blocked that route to improvement. Indeed, it is unlikely that such a hopeful scenario so much as crossed the minds of George and Catherine Eddowes, who were both born into large families whose needs far exceeded the stretch of their fathers' wages.*

According to the social reformer Seebohm Rowntree, phases of "want and plenty" marked the life cycle of the working classes. Household income ebbed and flowed according to the number of mature earners residing under a single roof. While a young man lived with his parents and had employment, he might enjoy "comparative prosperity," a situation that would "continue after marriage until he has two or three children, when poverty will again overtake him." Most workingmen then entered "a period of poverty that will last perhaps for ten years, ie; until the first child is fourteen and can earn wages." But Rowntree also noted that "if there are more than three children, it may last longer." For a working-class woman, this pattern was the same, though she typically contributed less before her earning potential was further crippled by the onset of childbearing and domestic obligation.

The experience of Kate Eddowes's mother, Catherine Evans, mirrored this pattern. As the second of seven children born to an impoverished Wolverhampton latch-maker, little care was taken over her schooling before she was sent to work. By the time she entered her teens, she had acquired experience as a kitchen maid and eventually worked her way up to become a cook at the Peacock Inn, one of the premier hostelries in Wolverhampton. However, in 1832, at roughly

---

* George Eddowes was the third of twelve children.

age eighteen, her short career there was curtailed. Matrimony in the nineteenth century spelled the beginning of a woman's true calling: motherhood, and in this regard Catherine proved exceptionally dutiful. In the first five years of her marriage, she produced four children; the eldest, Alfred, was mentally disabled and suffered from epileptic seizures. While many women of the laboring class continued to work after becoming mothers, whether by taking in washing or mending or by going out to factories or laundries, it is possible that Alfred's condition and the rapid succession of births that followed his arrival prevented Catherine from contributing to the family's income. Whatever the case, if either she or George had possessed access to reliable information about contraception, their lives, and those of their children, might have been entirely different.

It is often erroneously thought that the Victorians, those who are charged with inventing the covered table leg, were too strait-laced to contemplate, let alone write about, the reproductive lives of married couples. Nothing could be further from the truth. In the first part of the century, Francis Place, Robert Dale Owen, and George Drysdale each published works on methods by which men and women could "restrict family size." Suggestions varied from coitus interruptus to (reusable) "French letters" constructed from sheep's gut, to spermicidal douches and "contraceptive wads" placed inside the vagina. However, while this information was discreetly communicated to the literate middle classes, who could afford books, it was not successfully circulated among the working classes. Neither George nor Catherine Eddowes could read, nor is it likely they even knew that such books existed, or where to get them. The acquisition of "French letters" would have proven equally baffling, if not totally beyond the means of a family scarcely able to make ends meet. At any rate, conception and its prevention were widely believed to be a woman's responsibility. Like her mother and grandmother and most of the women in her community, Catherine would have been conditioned to accept perpetual childbearing as the lot of a wife. Contraception, when it was used, all too frequently came in the form of her husband's exhaustion or illness. In times of desperation, herbal tisanes and douches with spermicidal or abortifacient properties could be concocted, if a woman possessed the time, the money, or the moral courage to acquire the ingredients. In many cases, she had none of these resources.

All these factors — poverty, lack of information, and a sense of obligation to perform the role of a dutiful wife — resulted in what the nineteenth-century maternal rights campaigner Margaret Llewelyn Davies called "a life of excessive childbearing." Its toll on the physical, emotional, and material well-being of women like Catherine was enormous. In large families, like the Eddoweses, where the addition of another mouth to feed became almost an annual occurrence, resources grew increasingly stretched. In real terms this meant less food on the table; a thinner soup, a forkful of offal, a slice of bread in watered-down milk. In such circumstances, it was the mother who was expected to go without. Regardless of whether she was pregnant or breastfeeding, "at a time when she ought to be well-fed . . . ," she would "stint herself, in order to save; for in a working-class home, if there is saving to be done, it is not the husband and children, but the mother who makes her meal off the scraps which remain over, or plays with the meat-less bones."[7] Contemporary experts frequently remarked on how malnourished mothers were and the high incidence of miscarriage, stillbirth, and births of enfeebled infants who failed to thrive in the first year of life.

Nevertheless, women like Catherine, forced to contend with the demands of an infant and young children while simultaneously maintaining the home for her husband on ever-diminishing pay, could not permit themselves the luxury of reducing their duties during pregnancy, or delivery. Even with occasional help from female relations and neighbors, a woman was expected to be on her feet, engaged in "the incessant drudgery of domestic labour," right up to the moment of birth. If she couldn't pay for assistance during her period of recovery, she had no choice but to be "back at the stove, at scrubbing and cleaning, at the washtub, in lifting and carrying heavy weights" within days of giving birth. Such strain could have serious repercussions, including hemorrhages, severe varicose veins, and crippling back problems.

None of these factors impeded the expansion of the Eddowes family, which continued at a steady pace in the wake of their move to London. The following year saw the birth of a seventh child, Thomas, who was soon joined by George in 1846 and John in 1849. Two further girls, Sarah Ann and Mary, were born in 1850 and 1852. By the arrival of William in 1854, Catherine had given birth twelve times, though only ten of her children survived beyond their teenage years.* It must have seemed that whenever an older child flew the nest to earn a wage, a new, crying, demanding tiny sibling replaced her. In order to accommodate this growth in number and the accompanying adjustments to the household budget, the Eddoweses relocated at least four times between 1843 and 1857; for the most part they moved no more than a street or two away from their original address, on Baden Place.† This in itself is an indicator of the family's standing in the community. It seems that despite their often difficult financial circumstances, the Eddoweses made good on their rent and paid down whatever debts they owed to the local shopkeepers. Unlike less fortunate families, such as those of unskilled laborers with irregular work, George, Catherine, and their children never had to "do a flit" in the night, disappearing to some other neighborhood, leaving their unpaid bills behind them. This would have been a matter of great pride to the family, a mark of respectability. Catherine, like other wives of her status, would have attempted when possible to put aside money for lace curtains, a sideboard for crockery, or a carpet to lay down on Sundays. Ideally, all of the children of a hardworking skilled laborer would own a pair of shoes, and it is unlikely that the "seven sisters" of the Eddowes clan (as they came to be known) were permitted to mix with those boys and girls who ran barefoot through the streets.

As much as it was possible given the practical hardships of manag-

---

* Both John and William died within a few months of birth. On nineteenth-century birth certificates, the cause of an infant's demise is often described as "convulsions," a term that seems to report what a parent observed in the last moments of a child's life. A different cause appears on John's documentation: "cyanosis," a condition caused by abnormalities of the heart, the lungs, or the blood. In the case of a young child, the cyanosis would have been congenital or brought on by external conditions. The sulfur-laden coal smoke of urban industrial districts and the damp, close living quarters sucked the vitality from many adults and children, leaving their weakened lungs vulnerable to respiratory disease.

† Birth records, the 1851 census, and later, workhouse examinations have the family living at 35 West Street from 1849 until at least 1851, 7 Winter's Square in July 1854, and 22 King's Place from roughly April through December 2, 1857.

ing an army of children, it seemed that at least George, if not Catherine, wished their offspring to benefit by some sort of education. Although they were under no legal obligation to send their children to school, Elizabeth, age twelve, Kate, age ten, Thomas, age eight, and George, age six, are cited on the 1851 census as scholars.* Yet this does not guarantee that they actually attended school. Working-class parents would sometimes claim that their progeny were receiving an education in order to keep up appearances. How much instruction Kate's four elder sisters received is questionable since none but Emma could write, let alone read, as evidenced by the cross they marked in place of a signature on their marriage certificates.

Illiteracy and a poor level of education were hardly unusual among the daughters of the working class at this time when 48.9 percent of English women could not even sign their name.[8] Regular school attendance was not deemed essential when a girl was of more use assisting her mother at home or earning a wage. As the educational reformer James Bryce commented in the 1860s, "They can help in the house-work and mind the baby . . . Hence it often happens that girls are not sent to school till long after the age when systematic instruction ought to have begun, and . . . they are frequently kept away upon slight grounds." Those "slight grounds" might be the birth of a sibling, the illness of a family member, or a wide range of other circumstances. Such an event might remove a girl from school for several months at a time, if not permanently. In larger families, in which the eldest children were expected to assist in the rearing of their younger brothers and sisters, birth order often determined how much schooling a girl often received. While Catherine's attention was likely occupied by her infants, it would have been Harriet, Emma, and Eliza who took turns minding Alfred, as well as the smaller children; the older girls would also help with cooking meals, shopping, and doing the laundry and the cleaning. These obligations would shift each time a daughter entered employment; then, the next eldest would be called upon to lend as-

---

* According to the census-taking practice in that year, children were designated as "scholars" if they were "above five years of age and daily attending school, or receiving regular tuition under a master or governess at home."

sistance at home. While the constant juggling of wage earners with mother's helpers would have placed many obstacles in the four elder sisters' paths to an education, it had the effect of leaving Kate's open.

It is unknown who alerted George Eddowes to the availability of places at the Bridge, Candlewick and Dowgate School, little more than a few minutes' walk from the gates of Perkins and Sharpus. This charity, established to provide education for the poor children in the area, had recently extended its admissions policy to accept the sons and daughters of those who worked nearby. Upon learning this, George sought to enroll Kate at the Dowgate School.

In the 1840s, the Dowgate School accommodated "not less than 70 boys and 50 girls"; at times, a waiting list existed. Although the education offered there adhered to the religious-based National System, the teaching was much more focused and rigorous. Boys and girls were taught separately, though both were instructed in reading, writing, and arithmetic, as well as the Bible and music. Girls were given additional lessons in needlework. To be granted a place at this school would be an honor for any child of a working-class family. Although Dowgate was not a boarding school, its pupils undertook a full day of structured learning, seven days a week, from 8 a.m. to 12 p.m. and 2 p.m. to 4 p.m. in the spring and summer months, and from 9 a.m. during the autumn and winter months. On Sundays they were required to attend no fewer than two church services, usually at St. Paul's Cathedral, in whose shadow the school stood. Cleanliness and respectability were enforced absolutely. Each child was to wear a uniform, laundered and provided by the school and made by the female pupils. Both boys and girls were responsible for mending their clothing, and no child could enter the schoolroom in the morning without a clean face and hands. A special sink was installed to ensure that this standard was upheld, and a sum was budgeted each year for the purchase of soap. Teachers were also expected "to attend and see the children's hair is cut every six weeks."[9]

The intention of the Dowgate School, and others like it, was to create a better sort of working-class person — one who valued themselves and the principles of Christianity and who would go forth into the labor force dignified, clean, thoughtful, and obedient. When students reached the age of fourteen and completed their schooling, Dowgate strove to place them in a respectable industry. Boys were offered positions with architects and engineers, or given work as clerks in banks or businesses, while girls were prepared for roles in domestic service. Successful pupils who persevered at their new trade and were commended by their masters or mistresses became eligible to receive prizes from the school, amounting to as much as five pounds, and Dowgate's minute books are filled with such stories.

Ultimately, one of Dowgate's objectives seems to have been to separate the child as much as possible from the demeaning circumstances of his or her daily life, where they were viewed as another pair of hands, rather than a scholar. The demanding schedule, seven days a week, kept children away from their families but for dinner and bed; it also limited a child's exposure to any vices that the home might harbor. A parent who put a child forward for such an opportunity knew that the Dowgate School offered a stepladder out of the cycle of poverty.

It is unknown why George and Catherine determined to send Kate, in particular, to the Dowgate School. Birth order certainly played a role, but it is likely that Kate also demonstrated an aptitude for learning, a spark that set her apart from her brothers and sisters. In later years, Emma recalled her sister's youthful personality as being "... lively ... , warm hearted and entertaining,"[10] while other acquaintances remarked that Kate "possessed an unusual degree of intelligence."[11] Because the school admitted children as young as six, it is probable that she began her education there in 1848, possibly alongside Emma. Every morning and every evening after 4 p.m., Kate would have crossed back and forth along London Bridge, just like her father. Dressed in the blue-and-white uniform she had stitched herself, she would weave her way between the leather market and Guy's Hospital, between factories and tanneries, squinting against the sun in summer and swathed in a wool cape in winter.

It is difficult to know what exactly were Kate's experiences at the Dowgate School; her name does not appear in any of the minutes that record exceptional or poorly behaved pupils. It might be assumed that she was an average and obedient student. As a charity, Dowgate attracted the interest of a number of benefactors who wished to see the children excel, but who also believed that education should be imparted with kindness. The trustees instructed the master and mistress to "abstain as much as it is possible from inflicting severe chastisement." Instead, during the period that Kate would have attended the school, prizes were made available by wealthy subscribers to encourage good behavior: "A book was to be awarded to the boy who had best conducted himself and a work box to the girl in a like manner." The master and mistress decided to "leave the award of the prizes to the children themselves . . . so that they had selected the boy and girl who were really the most worthy."[12]

The school's eminent donors were also eager to offer the children special opportunities. On June 26, 1851, Edmund Calvert, the owner of the nearby Calvert and Co. Brewery, hosted a day's outing for the 124 pupils at the Bridge, Candlewick and Dowgate School to the recently opened Crystal Palace, in Hyde Park. The spectacle of the Great Exhibition, one of the first world fairs, housed within a magnificent glassplate structure, was unlike anything seen before in Britain. Resembling an enormous greenhouse, with an interior of 990,000 square feet, the structure towered to a height of 128 feet and housed more than 15,000 exhibitions from around the world. The array of objects on display was staggering. Masterpieces of technological advancement — printing presses, steam hammers, and locomotive engines — shared the space with vast porcelain vases from China, furs from Canada, a fifty-kilogram lump of gold from Chile, and the Koh-i-Noor diamond, which was kept in a cagelike safe, illuminated by gas jets. International exhibitors paraded in their native dress; men in turbans, embroidered robes, and gold-threaded textiles chaperoned their country's treasures. "Whatever human industry has created you find there," wrote the author Charlotte Brontë, of her visit. There were

great compartments filled with railway engines and boilers, with mill machinery in full work, with splendid carriages of all kinds, with harness of every description, to the glass-covered and velvet-spread stands loaded with the most gorgeous work of the goldsmith and silversmith, and the carefully guarded caskets full of real diamonds and pearls worth hundreds of thousands of pounds. It may be called a bazaar or a fair, but it is such a bazaar or fair as Eastern genii might have created. It seems as if only magic could have gathered this mass of wealth from all the ends of the earth — as if none but supernatural hands could have arranged it thus, with such a blaze and contrast of colours and marvellous power of effect.[13]

The Crystal Palace would have dazzled ten-year-old Kate Eddowes. That morning, she and her classmates, accompanied by the schoolmaster and schoolmistress, were conveyed by horse-drawn vans, specially provided by the brewery, "to the great centre of attraction." One hundred twenty-four little cap-covered heads were counted in and out, and guided in orderly lines through what must have seemed a fairyland. Children who had seen little beyond the basic interiors of their home and schoolroom would have been mesmerized by the circus-like swirl of the exotic. Then, after "having enjoyed themselves for some hours in the many attractions of the place, they were conveyed back at about six o'clock in the evening to the brewery." Here, "an excellent dinner was prepared for them," and they dined in the company of the heads of Calvert and Co. After toasts were made, the children rose to their feet and sang the national anthem "in a highly effective manner."[14] This would have been an exceptional occasion for the children of Dowgate School, and Kate would be unlikely to forget it or the splendors she had briefly glimpsed.

Childhood, for the sons and daughters of the Victorian laboring classes, was a short and fleeting phase of life, which was often curtailed abruptly by family circumstances. In Kate Eddowes's case, what schoolroom pleasures she may have enjoyed were to come to a conclusion by 1856. Kate's fourteenth birthday in April of that year, which would have ordinarily marked the end of her education, also coincided with the dissolution of Perkins and Sharpus, her father's employer. Whether George was easily able to find further work is unknown, but certainly there would have been an added urgency in seeing his daughter placed swiftly into employment. However, it is possible that the upheaval visited upon the Eddowes family in 1855 brought her days as a schoolgirl to a close earlier than this.

For the better part of 1855, Kate's mother, Catherine, was suffering from a terrible cough and fever. Her family would have watched her grow weak and thin. It is likely they knew the cause of her torment even before she received the diagnosis of consumption. One of the elder daughters would have nursed her, and George, with little choice in a house of three or so rooms now occupied by eight family members, continued to sleep beside his ailing wife as she perspired and sputtered up blood. By November, as the chill and damp set in, she had worsened. Kate was only thirteen when she lost her mother on the seventeenth of that month. Catherine, whose body had been ravaged by childbearing, physical labor, and poor nutrition, had, at forty-two, lived the average number of years for a woman of her class at that time.

A reorganization of household responsibilities followed in the wake of Catherine Eddowes's illness and death. In an account written in 1888, Emma claimed that as the second eldest, it was left to her to manage the home and look after Alfred and the four youngest siblings, all still under the age of twelve. However, these arrangements were only to prove temporary. In 1857, less than two years after tuberculosis claimed his wife, George too began to sicken.[15] The family expected the inevitable, and by September, the elder Eddowes daughters had begun to consider their futures. On the twenty-seventh, Elizabeth, at the age of nineteen, agreed to marry her beau, Thomas Fisher, a neighbor, then only eighteen years old and described as a laborer. Under other circumstances, George may have hoped for a husband with better prospects, but at least one of his girls would have been legally married and settled in a home of her own when he departed this life. While deathly ill, George, with the assistance of his daughters, attended the wedding, at St. Paul's, Bermondsey, on Kipling Street, a short but difficult walk from their home on King's Place. Here, he gave away Elizabeth and came forward as a witness, to put his cross upon the register beside his name. The occasion, during that gloomy autumn, would have been a bittersweet one, and would have marked out the final weeks in which the Eddoweses would ever live together as a family.

As the leaves reddened and dropped and October became November, the question of what would be done with Alfred and the younger children following their father's death loomed large for the two elder sisters. Emma's account, which appeared in the *Manchester Weekly*

Times, suggested that Harriet was already settled with (though not married to) Robert Carter Garrett, a "carman," or deliveryman.[16] Eliza had acquired a place in service, and the newly wedded Mrs. Fisher and her husband were running a bird shop in Locks Fields.[17] Emma recognized that she needed to support herself in full-time employment, so when an opportunity arose in a good household on Lower Craven Place in Kentish Town, north of the river, she left the care of the children and the nursing of her father to Harriet.

It may have initially been their plan, between them, to assume responsibility for their siblings, but as the family was so large, this would be no simple undertaking. The question of who would look after Alfred became "a constant source of trouble" for the elder sisters, but for some unspecified reason, Emma claimed they were most concerned about Kate. "We wished especially to get her away," she recalled. At fifteen, it is likely that Kate was profoundly affected by the loss of her mother, and the impending death of her father would surely have only worsened her grief. It is possible that Emma and Harriet believed their sister required more guidance and stability than they could provide, or perhaps they felt that Kate, bright and educated, was capable of further improvement under the watchful eye of the family. Whatever the case, Harriet had a letter sent to her uncle and aunt, William and Elizabeth Eddowes, in Wolverhampton, "to see if she could get Kate a situation away from London." Her relations agreed to this but were unable to provide the train fare. With time running short, Emma, who never failed to paint herself as the most resourceful among the sisters, took matters into her own hands and approached her employer. "My mistress," she recalled thirty-one years later, "upon learning our unfortunate position, paid Kate's fare to Wolverhampton." And that was that. Whether Kate had any say in the matter that would ultimately come to determine the course of her life is doubtful.

Given the family's limited resources, the fate of the other Eddowes children was a foregone conclusion. Neither Elizabeth and Thomas Fisher nor Harriet and Robert Garrett had the means to support thirteen-year-old Thomas, twelve-year-old George, seven-year-old Sarah Ann, five-year-old Mary, or twenty-five-year-old Alfred. On December 9, a week after the death of their father, perhaps even on the day of his funeral, Alfred and the three youngest were sent to Bermondsey Union Workhouse as orphans. Thomas joined them there the following day. It cannot be imagined that George went to his grave easily in the knowledge that the seams that held his family together would be torn apart upon his death.

As for Kate, alone on a Wolverhampton-bound train, December 1857 marked the end of her childhood. She would leave behind all she had ever known for a place she did not remember, to live among strangers with whom she shared nothing but a surname.

THE BALLAD OF KATE AND TOM

A STRANGER TO WOLVERHAMPTON would never have guessed that the romantic sixteenth-century moated manor house, surrounded by the fields off Bilston Street, housed one of the city's hives of industry. Like virtually everything in this town, the once proud home of a family of wealthy wool merchants had given itself to the advances of commerce and progress. Notwithstanding the carefully laid out flower beds and ornamental goldfish ponds, the Old Hall Works was no different inside than any of the other factories that lined the streets and filled the courtyards of the soot-choked town. Its former kitchens were "utilised for tinning . . . goods"; its large open fireplace contained "vans of molten metal and grease," while "the kitchen floor was strewn with pans and dish covers in the process of tinning." The grand oak staircase, which sat at the center of the house, "instead of leading to the state ballroom, now led to warehouses where women and girls were employed in wrapping up goods."

Onto the south part of the mansion, a functional modern brick extension had been built, which was filled with the constant thump and hiss of steam presses in the stamping room. In the polishing shop adjacent to it, women stood for as many as twelve hours a day, repeatedly rubbing shellacked japanware to a brilliant finish. Nearby in what were called "the lions' cages," the red-hot japanning stoves were stoked, while two powerful engines rattled and chugged beside a boiler and a burnishing mill.

Amid these furnaces and machinery was a room filled with vats of acid over which a collection of women, known as "scourers," wielded what were called "pickling forks." With their hair tightly bound inside their caps, and their clothing protected by heavy aprons, they used their long-handled tongs to dip a piece of recently forged tinware into an oxide bath in order to prepare it for the japanning process. Once the debris had been stripped off, the piece would be dried in sawdust. This entire process would then be repeated, again and again, from 7 a.m. to 7 p.m. in the summer and 8 a.m. to 8 p.m. in the winter, six days a week. Burning eyes, raw throats, and the occasional industrial accident were all to be expected.

Work as a scourer was a good position, William and Elizabeth Eddowes would have lectured their niece Kate, and they had done her proud by securing it for her. Three generations of Eddoweses had toiled at the fires and workbenches of the Old Hall Works, including her father, and after the industrial disputes of the 1840s, the factory owner, Benjamin Walton, welcomed the family back into his workforce and offered them a fair wage. However, a factory job as a scourer was not likely the "situation" that Kate's sisters, Emma and Harriet, or even the Dowgate School had envisioned for a pupil who had been educated for a life in domestic service.*

A new chapter of Kate's life had begun as her train from London had passed through the deadened, scorched landscape of the West Midlands, a region that had recently come to be called "the Black Country." An industry of chain-making, brick-baking, and steel-forging had arisen from the land, fed by a thirty-foot-deep vein of coal that ran through the countryside. Those who did not graft in factories or before furnaces, hammered at the seam itself, drawing forth the lifeblood

* George J. Barnsby, *Social Conditions in the Black Country* (Cheshire, UK, 1980), pp. 14–15. Curiously, nearly three-fourths of women under the age of twenty in the industrial regions of the Midlands were employed as servants rather than in factory work, so Kate herself may have been surprised to discover where circumstance had landed her.

that sustained the engines. By day the chimneys rained soot; by night the forges glowed demonically through the darkness. Even for those accustomed to horrific scenes of misery, the spectacle presented by a journey through the Black Country could come as a shock. Dickens described the hellish spectacle: "On every side, and far as the eye could see into the heavy distance, tall chimneys, crowding on each other, and presenting that endless repetition of the same dull, ugly form, which is the horror of oppressive dreams, poured out their plague of smoke, obscured the light, and made foul the melancholy air." The approach to Wolverhampton was crowded with "mounds of ashes," beside "strange engines that spun and writhed like tortured creatures clanking their iron chains, shrieking in their rapid whirl from time to time as though in torment unendurable, and making the ground tremble with their agonies."[1] Although Kate had grown up in the shadow of London's tanneries and factories, this new environment shaped by heavy industry would have seemed as foreign and strange to her as did her family in Wolverhampton.

It is likely that the first time Kate had ever met her father's brother, William, and his wife, Elizabeth, was when she, with her small collection of childhood possessions, came to live at their house at 50 Bilston Street. Her cousins — William, age thirteen; George, age seven; and five-year-old Lizzie — would have stared at her with hesitant and curious eyes. Sarah, the eldest, at fourteen, would have made a perfect companion, someone with whom Kate would have shared a bed and her thoughts. Kate would also have been introduced to her grandparents, Thomas and Mary, who lived around the corner, and her uncle John and his four young children. How willing the Eddowes clan had been to embrace their London relation is unknown. Another mouth to feed was never an entirely welcome prospect, though at fifteen, Kate was certain to earn her own keep and contribute to the household income. The sad loss of both parents was commonplace enough, and no excuse for not pulling one's weight; Kate would have been put out to work without delay.

By the time Kate entered her late teens, her cousin Sarah had left the family home to become a servant, but her position within the family was soon filled by the birth of Aunt Elizabeth's final child, Harriet.

After working long hours, Kate would have been called upon to assist with domestic duties as well; cooking, cleaning, and looking after her cousin Lizzie as well as bringing in the extra shillings. It was probably at about this period in her life that Kate began to acquire what her uncle described as "a jolly disposition": a fondness for drinking and keeping what he called "late hours."[2] The tinworkers' public house, the Red Cow, stood only a few doors down the road from her home, a convenient escape from the close quarters and family pressures beneath her uncle's roof.

As an outsider, the extent to which Kate ever felt a true sense of belonging among the Wolverhampton Eddoweses is questionable, and by the summer of 1861 she had grown both restless and reckless. According to members of her family, the turning point came when Kate was caught stealing from the Old Hall Works.

While passing through the drying rooms or packaging areas, it would not have proven too difficult to slip a tin card case, a small box, or a pen tray into a pocket or within her garments. Not every pawnshop was scrupulous about determining the origin of the objects it accepted in exchange for money. Someone weary of laboring over an acid bath day upon day might have felt that such a risk was worth taking. Unfortunately, the Old Hall Works was full of eyes, and at least one pair fell upon Kate.

Kate was scolded and dismissed, but she was not brought before the magistrate. This was probably because of the Eddoweses' longstanding relationship with the factory owners. The mortification she had caused her family was extreme and the shock of her actions reverberated from Wolverhampton to London as Emma and Harriet, the architects of her new life, received word of her disgrace. Back at 50 Bilston Street, the recriminations would have been thunderous. In later years, Sarah Eddowes, who became Mrs. Jesse Croote, the wife of a Wolverhampton saddler and horse dealer, recounted the family drama to a newspaper reporter.[3] According to Sarah, this incident would come to define Kate's future life, and the Wolverhampton Eddoweses would neither forget it nor forgive her for it. At nineteen, Kate once again packed her belongings to make a new start. On this occasion, she herself determined her destination and set out for Birmingham, a fourteen-mile walk to the south. There she hoped to find refuge with a more sympathetic member of the family.

For many years, Wolverhampton's renowned Peacock Inn, where Kate's mother had once stirred sauces and baked pies, was also a venue for bare-knuckle boxing matches. Throughout the 1850s, the inn yard was regularly cleared, sod laid, and a ring pitched for prize fights. Among those to appear was the English heavyweight champion and local hero William Perry, also known as the "Tipton Slasher," as well as Joe Goss, who went on to make his pugilistic fortune in the United States. It is likely that here too Tom Eddowes, also known as "The Snob," fought his way into his niece's heart.

Bare-knuckle boxing had been big business in England since the eighteenth century. Jack Broughton had attempted to formalize the sport and lend it a sense of gentlemanly and patriotic merit. With the patronage of the Prince of Wales, boxing schools intended to "impart the art of pugilism" appeared in London. A burgeoning sports press helped to create a buzz around prize matches by publishing pre-fight taunts between participants. British men of all classes were hooked, and matches governed by Broughton's rules became popular nationwide. Contestants stripped to the waist, wrapped wadding around their fists, and slugged it out for cash.

Fighters generally came from working-class backgrounds, and the Midlands contributed a number to their ranks. A few pugilists carved out full-time careers in the sport, but many more were amateurs, who occasionally put aside their leather aprons and laid down their tools to step into the ring. Tom Eddowes was one of these. A shoemaker, or "snob," by trade, Eddowes supplemented his income through the exercise of brute strength.

Born in 1810, Uncle Tom had already seen his best fighting years by the time Kate watched him raise his fists. But because prize money of up to twenty-five pounds a side was at stake, Thomas Eddowes did not go eagerly into retirement. As late as 1866, the country's foremost sports newspaper, *Bell's Life in London*, was advertising a match between "Ned Wilson and Tom Eddows (alias The Snob)," two "old Birmingham men" who had spent years cultivating their boxing talent.[4]

Just as it is today, the early-nineteenth-century boxing match was as much theatrical entertainment as it was a sports competition. Before the introduction of the Marquess of Queensbury's rules in 1868, boxers were permitted to wrestle as well as throw punches.[5] Posed at the center of the ring, in a bare-chested display of physical prowess, competitors would have appeared as heroic actors on a stage, while the prospect of a large prize fight, announced in bills plastered about town, would have seemed as thrilling as the arrival of the circus.

The designated day followed an established order of events. A crowd of men in top hats and flat caps would gather, eagerly checking the time, fiddling with their watch chains, tucking their hands into their waistcoat pockets. Eventually, the combatants would appear, one after the other, each accompanied by a second and a bottle-holder responsible for refreshing and sponging down the fighter between rounds. The pugilists would shake hands, and a coin toss would decide who could choose his corner. Once these formalities were concluded, the men would strip down and "have their drawers examined" to ensure that there had been no "insertion of improper substances." Only then could the fight officially commence.

While it would not have been expected for "respectable" ladies to be present at such matches, the attendance of working-class women would have been neither encouraged nor entirely frowned upon. It is likely that Kate watched her uncle from amid the crowds, slightly starstruck; not only by his strength and talent as a fighter, but by his ability to command the attention of a rapt audience. Whatever relationship they formed, whether it was one based on a niece's admiration of an older family member, or common interests, Kate came to believe that her Uncle Tom would offer her the sort of home and sympathy she did not find in Wolverhampton.

In 1861, Tom Eddowes and his wife, Rosannah, were living at the heart of Birmingham's industrial center. Across the way, Eldridge & Merrett's pin works, an imposing brick mill with thrusting smokestacks, pounded out tiny steel pins and needles. At Brooks & Street, a few doors down, brass wire was woven into sieves and spark guards, while at Thomas Felton's manufactory, carriage lamps and chandeliers were smelted into shape. The smaller workshops along Bagot Street were occupied mostly by toy makers and gun makers, the trade that lent its name to the area: the Gun Quarter. Birmingham differed little in appearance from Wolverhampton. Brick had been built upon brick, and all of it was smudged with thick black coal dust.

The Eddoweses' residence, in a courtyard off Moland Street, was situated amid the incessant thud and chug of heavy machinery. There would scarcely have been a quiet hour in the day when an engine did not crank loudly or a cloud of smoke did not hang over them. Mercury and other metals discharged from manufacturing plants made the neighborhood's water unfit to drink; residents relied on deliveries from a cart. Their courtyard house, constructed of late-eighteenth-century brick, would have seen its share of wear after nearly a hundred years. With a room on both the first and second floors, as well as a ground-floor kitchen and a cellar, the house would have provided sufficient enough space for the couple and their two youngest children: sixteen-year-old John, who made brass tubing at a local factory, and twelve-year-old Mary, who remained at home to assist her mother. When Uncle Tom was not throwing punches in the ring, he was driving nails into shoes, either in a room partially converted for that purpose or in a nearby workshop.

In nineteenth-century working-class families, distant relations would receive a welcome proportionate to their ability to contribute practical or financial support to a household. Whatever plan Kate had made for living in Birmingham, work was an inescapable part of it. But if she had hoped to avoid returning to factory drudgery, she was to be sorely disappointed. Kate knew tinwork, and Birmingham had plenty of it. It wasn't long before Uncle Tom had found her a position much like the one she had left behind in Wolverhampton. No longer a scourer, Kate now sat at a long table with polishing cloths, rubbing newly shellacked japanware trays and working their surfaces to a high sheen, so that somewhere, in a house with a parlor, a serving maid could deliver tea to her mistress on an object pretty enough to make the visitors envious. Kate's hours would have been the same: rising at dawn or in early darkness, home for supper, and then to sleep, in a bed shared with her cousin Mary, in a room divided by a curtain from the snores of John, or Kate's uncle and aunt. It did not matter where she fled — to Wolverhampton or Birmingham, to the household of a pugilist or a tinplate worker. She could expect that this routine would command her life until she married. Then it would be her own mother's life; the pain of childbearing, the weariness of child rearing, worry, hunger and exhaustion, and eventually, sickness and death.

⊗

The wet Indian heat smothered the listless soldiers of the 18th Royal Irish Regiment. As they rested in the shade of Asirgarh Fort's ruined mosque, they played cards, polished their boots, and listened to stories. There were always stories to be told: stories from back home in Ireland, stories from the jungles, battle stories, stories of willing women with wanton smiles and dark skin or twinkling eyes and fair faces.

The man his commanding officers called Thomas Quinn would listen to such tales with a keen interest. Quinn, or Thomas Conway, the name he received at birth on November 21, 1836, in County Mayo,[6] was a collector of and later a peddler of stories, though he never recounted the tale explaining the reason for his change of name. Men who wished to escape their past, whether a broken marriage or a situation far worse, frequently assumed a new identity when they "took the Queen's shilling" and enlisted. In October 1857, Thomas Conway had done just that.

When he marked a cross by his name on the enlistment roll, Conway likely knew he was destined for India. Word had reached Britain in September of the rebellion of British East India troops near Delhi, which had grown and threatened to spread through the north of the country. The Sepoy Mutiny supplanted the Crimean War in newspaper headlines as British troops, scarcely recovered from the sieges of the Black Sea, left for the dust of the subcontinent. The call for reinforcements became urgent, and Thomas had received barely a month of training before he, along with the rest of the second brigade of the 18th Royal Irish Regiment, boarded the steamship *Princess Charlotte,* bound for Bombay. For a young man on the eve of his twenty-first birthday, who had seen little beyond rural life and sod houses, this would prove to be the greatest adventure of his life. India would offer him a rich harvest of stories.

The journey by sea took three months, but not one of the sights he glimpsed along the way — not the flying fish or the sharks or the swells of the Cape of Good Hope — was nearly as alien and exotic as India. When the men landed at Bombay, many Irish and English recruits found themselves completely bewildered by the hectic, colorful scenes. They gawped at women wrapped in bright silk saris, wearing nose rings, and jingling with bangles. They were bewildered by the bold scent of ginger and garlic and by the dozy buffaloes shuffling through the marketplace. At times the extreme differences in culture and climate proved too difficult to adjust to, and many found themselves succumbing not only to "the rigours of the weather" but to "the melancholy of homesickness."

It was the former rather than the latter that felled Thomas Conway during his Indian adventure. The humidity entered his chest. He coughed and wheezed so much during marches that he was eventually sent to the army hospital in Madras, where the cool breezes were expected to revive him. Unfortunately, the mutiny was put down before he managed to recover. Upon his return to Dublin in 1861, the army's senior medical officer examined him and soon determined that he would never recover. Conway's "Physical disability and continual infirmity" was diagnosed as "the result of former illness, principally rheumatism and chronic bronchitis." To make matters worse, the doctor also detected that Conway, age twenty-four, suffered "from a disease of the heart." As a consequence, it was recommended that he be discharged; his papers noted, rather favorably, that the soldier's disorder was "partially, if not entirely attributable to military service and climate and not intemperance or other vice."[7]

With a bad heart and a weak chest, Thomas could neither soldier nor return to casual labor, the occupation which had sustained him prior to joining the army.* While this news would have been disquieting for a young man without formal training in a trade, his consolation would come in the form of a pension, to be paid twice yearly. Generally,

---

* It is possible that Conway had asthma, a medical condition not properly recognized until the 1960s. It is also likely, as the medical officer's notes seem to imply, that while in India he had contracted rheumatic fever, which weakened his heart.

privates' pensions, especially for those like Thomas Conway, who had served only four years and six days, were menial sums, enough to supplement a worker's income, but not to replace it. According to his records, he was eligible to receive six pence per day, an amount that over the years was reassessed and adjusted upward or downward by one penny, based on any improvement in his medical condition.[8] Thomas would be forced to find some way of subsisting that did not involve swinging a hammer, mowing hay, or lifting burdensome loads.

As a child in rural Ireland, Conway would have come to know the chapmen, or chapbook men, peddlers who plodded the roads through County Mayo, visiting farms, taverns, and turf-roofed houses. Chased by dogs and followed by curious children along his route, the chapman carried a linen pack filled with an assortment of useful goods and materials for those without access to a nearby shop. Part vagabond, part town crier, part wily salesman, the chapman was viewed with a mixture of suspicion and welcome. He moved from village to settlement to town, collecting and sharing information, news, and gossip wherever he landed, which was for some villagers his most essential role. However, a good hawker knew his business and understood how to make the most out of every stop. Farmers' wives and daughters were enticed by scissors, combs, thimbles, knives, ribbon, thread, buttons, and even brooches and small toys, which he spread over the kitchen table. He also carried an array of printed material, in particular, chapbooks — short pamphlets decorated with woodcut engravings, which recounted everything from fairy tales to biographies, poems, and short stories. At the taverns and pubs, the chapman might pull out his collection of broadside ballads — songs printed on a single large sheet, which told of the loss of love or detailed the story of a bloody crime. These lyrics were usually set to a well-known tune, so a purchaser could throw down a penny, grab the broadside, and launch into a new song over a pint of ale.

The chapbook seller's life was entirely peripatetic. Each day began with an empty stomach and no promise of a bed. *The History of John Cheap the Chapman,* a chapbook usually found in the pack of most chapbook peddlers during the first half of the nineteenth century, offers some insight into the daily life of those who took to the road with their wares. The narrator of the tale makes it clear that the hazards and discomforts frequently more than outweighed the adventures. Falling into a ditch or a sewer, escaping the wrath of a farmer's dog or the horns of a bull, were among the ever-present dangers. He grumbles over the inconvenience of sleeping on wheat sacks, in a field of kale, or beside a cow on a cold winter's night. He barters with farmers' wives for a bowl of soup or cabbage and often complains of "travelling all day and getting neither meat nor bread nor ale, going from house to house." Nonetheless, peddling offered a degree of freedom rare in other walks of life. There was something romantic in slipping the ties of a typical nineteenth-century existence. Wandering, living by his wits, encountering different sorts of characters, and visiting new places, a chapman was beholden to no one, not family, community, church, or employer. For some, that liberation was thrilling.

Not surprisingly, life as a chapman appealed to single men without families, though, much like modern traveling salesmen, marriage was certainly seen as no impediment to pursuing this profession. Those thought most suited to it were former soldiers, who, it was believed, were already accustomed to long marches and hardship.

Becoming a chapman must have seemed a logical choice for Thomas Conway, who since his teens had been no stranger to a nomadic existence. The Great Famine, which devastated the Irish countryside in 1845–52, fell hardest upon County Mayo. By 1851, nearly 30 percent of the population of the region had died or immigrated. Thomas was no exception. At the time he enlisted in 1857, it appears he had already moved across the Irish Sea to Yorkshire, where he had been working as a casual laborer near Beverley. Upon his discharge from the army, on October 14, 1861, he claimed his pension, paid a visit to relations in Kilkerry, and returned to England, this time to Newcastle, where he stood a better chance of making a living. With the money he'd been paid, the young Irishman purchased goods to fill his pack and set out on the peddler's path, which took him south to Coventry and then to London, before he arrived in Birmingham by the summer of 1862.[9]

The stories differ as to how Kate Eddowes and Thomas Conway met. According to one account, at twenty years of age, she was "a nice looking girl with a very warm heart." He was a gray-eyed Irishman with light brown hair and a talent for telling tales. Both Sarah Croot and Emma Eddowes claimed that Kate met him in Birmingham, but Uncle Tom Eddowes insisted, with a certain displeasure, that this was not the case. It was not under his watch that "she formed the acquaintance of this man Conway." Whatever the truth was, nine months into her life in Birmingham, at about the time she would have met Thomas Conway, Kate declared a sudden desire to return to Wolverhampton, the direction in which Conway was headed.

Thomas Conway certainly cut a romantic figure, with his tales of tigers and fragrant jungles, with his songs and his sack of stories. His engaging patter would have enchanted strangers in every pub and marketplace. He was footloose and went where the wind blew him. It was understandable that Kate, jolly, outgoing, and open, would find him attractive and his lifestyle a possible alternative to the drudgery of her situation.

The Eddoweses were not pleased by this turn of events, and Kate discovered as much when she appeared back at Bilston Street. Thomas Conway was never well liked by Kate's family — not by William and Elizabeth, her cousin Sarah, her Uncle Tom, or even her sisters in London. It is no mystery why. Judged medically unfit by the army and with no real occupation, as well as no home, no family, and no reliable income beyond a paltry pension of six or seven pence per day, this Irish drifter was like a figure in a Victorian cautionary tale about whom young women were warned. Any liaison with his kind was seen as a ticket to poverty, starvation, and the workhouse. Worse still, if Conway had offered to marry Kate, he demonstrated no real hurry to exchange vows.

Still, this did not discourage Kate's attachment: she was, according to an account of events in the *Black Country Bugle,* completely "infatuated with the handsome, poetical Irishman." Aunt Elizabeth eventually gave her an ultimatum: end the affair with the penny-ballad salesman, or leave the house.* Kate chose the latter and moved into

---

* It is also believed that when Kate returned to Wolverhampton, Elizabeth and William banned her from the house and sent her to live for a short while with her recently widowed grandfather, around the corner.

a lodging house with Thomas. The timing of this rupture was important; by July of that year, 1862, she was pregnant.

While the Eddowoses would have been ashamed and embarrassed by their niece's predicament, pregnancy out of wedlock was not unusual. Among the more privileged classes, chastity was considered a measure of a young woman's character and her worth on the marriage market, but virginity did not hold the same significance for the working classes. Their lives were governed by practical concerns. The innocent femininity cultivated in middle- and upper-class girls was not expected of their working-class sisters. Commentators of the period expressed concern that sexualization of the laboring classes occurred at a very young age on account of cramped domestic arrangements. With living space in short supply, and family members, other relatives, and even visitors sharing bedrooms and beds, bodily privacy and modesty were luxuries they simply could not afford. The sights and sounds of sexual activity were part of everyday life; temptation and experimentation were a consequence of exposure. In addition, lack of room at home pushed young teenagers outside, beyond the watchful gaze of parents. As a young woman told the pornographic writer "Walter," "There are lots of girls about . . . their mothers don't care what they do . . . when they's about thirteen or fourteen years old they won't be kept in, they is about the dark streets at night . . ." She went on to explain that "the girls went with the coster boys who are their sweethearts" and that "a virginity was a rarity at fourteen years old." Henry Mayhew made similar discoveries when interviewing teenage girls employed in "slopwork," or the manufacture of cheap clothing. One confessed to him, "I am satisfied that there is not one young girl that works at slop work that is virtuous, and there are some thousands in the trade."

At a time when sexual relationships tended to result in pregnancy, many couples waited until conception or even birth to marry. However, others among the laboring class might reject marriage altogether and instead choose to cohabit. Those in certain professions, such as ballad sellers and costermongers (sellers of fruit and vegetables), whose work required mobility, were more inclined to the latter arrangement. In theory, a certain fluidity in relationships could suit both the man as well as the woman. The need for a man to follow work, sometimes quite far afield, left the woman he was partnered with free to form another relationship closer to hand. Because of these dynamics, many couples did not feel the need to legitimize their union in a church, although a significant number regarded their bond as permanent and remained together for life, or at least for extended periods. As nineteenth-century journalists and social reformers discovered, working-class communities tended to refrain from probing the circumstances of their friends' and neighbors' relationships and lived by a simple rule: if a couple said they were married and behaved accordingly, then they were. "Ask if the men and women living together ... are married, and your simplicity will cause a smile," wrote the social crusader Andrew Mearns. "Nobody knows. Nobody cares."[10] However, this is also not to suggest that attitudes toward cohabiting couples were not full of contradiction and nuance. Landlords and employers, who in many cases belonged to the same social class, could be quick to evict or dismiss those discovered not to be legally wed, and women naturally bore the brunt of any social persecution, especially if illegitimate children were involved. Whereas a man might walk away from cohabitation and suffer no ill consequences, a dependent woman, with reduced earning potential and mouths to feed, might find herself instantly plunged into penury.

When Kate threw in her lot with Thomas Conway, she would have been fully aware of the risk involved. Yet life with him seemed preferable to her present circumstances. Sarah Croot intimated that the couple did not remain long in Wolverhampton, and soon after set out together toward Birmingham.

Joining forces with Kate would have had advantages for Thomas. In addition to having a woman at his side to cook and do his laundry, Kate might prove to be a useful business partner. In rural areas, a man could easily work on his own selling chapbooks and assorted small items door to door, but in larger villages, market towns, and cities, he needed a different approach. Public visibility was important to making sales.

Conway and Kate belonged to a class of peddlers whom Henry Mayhew described as "flying stationers" or "general paper sellers." There were different types. The "running patterer" walked through the streets and squares, shouting out titles and summaries of broadsides and chapbooks. The "standing patterer" sought out a patch on the corner of a street or outside a pub and with a silver tongue seduced buyers from across the road with tales of accidents, scandal, battles, horrors, and executions. Both the standing patterer and the running patterer were often accompanied by a female "chaunter," who would assist by singing or reciting passages of a ballad as her male companion flogged the broadside to passersby. Together the couple might also perform duets or engage in theatrical repartee. As an extrovert who had been taught music at school and loved singing, street performance would have suited Kate's inclinations far better than factory work.*

When Thomas Conway set out to make his living as a chapbook seller, he may have aspired to write his own material but had no means of achieving this aim. As the cross he marked on his army discharge papers demonstrated, Thomas was illiterate. Kate was not. Whatever inspiration he had gathered from his adventures in India (and such stories made for highly popular ballads in the 1850s and '60s) would had to have been dictated and transcribed before he had met Kate. Allowing her to take on this role made the entire endeavor more economical. One can imagine the couple hunched over a pub table; Kate with inky fingers acting the scribe to Conway's poet, furiously scratching out words, arguing, recomposing, and singing the verses to themselves. Under such circumstances, it would be difficult to conceive that Kate did not have a hand in the composition of these works.[11]

Although Kate had escaped a conventional life, her chosen path was not necessarily as happy or carefree as she might have hoped. Pattering in towns and selling chapbooks door to door in rural areas did not pay especially well. Mayhew wrote that the average earnings taken in by such a vendor were roughly ten to twelve shillings a week. In order to earn twelve shillings, one had to be willing to write and sell anything: ballads, chapbooks, poems, and pamphlets. Illness, drunkenness, or any other unforeseen situation would have made this impossible. Itinerant life had its miseries: sodden, frozen, filthy cloth-

* According to the *Times*, 5 October 1888, Kate was noted for singing. Singing and music were also taught to all pupils at the Dowgate School.

ing, a rumbling belly, and often a lack of shelter. For Kate, occasions for enjoying a bath or wearing freshly laundered clothes would be limited. In rural areas, the couple might successfully beg for a bed, but in cities they had to depend on crowded, unpleasant lodging houses and the workhouse casual wards, if they didn't sleep rough. What little Kate and Thomas possessed they carried with them, which made them prey to robbers and tricksters. To brave the hazards of a gypsy existence while pregnant would be even more wretched. It is hardly a wonder then, that in April 1863, in her ninth month of pregnancy, Kate found herself knocking on the workhouse infirmary doors at Great Yarmouth, in Norfolk.

For a woman who had no guarantee of a bed, a workhouse infirmary where she might go to bear a child would have seemed a welcome respite. By the 1860s, all workhouses accommodated destitute expectant mothers, though the guardians in many cases sought to distinguish between "deserving married women" and "the fallen," who arrived to bear children out of wedlock. When Kate appeared at the gates, she gave her name as Catherine Conway and claimed she was married to "a labourer." Thomas may have accompanied her there, or more likely placed her in the care of the workhouse while he set out in search of work.

Although Conway could rest assured that his "wife" had a roof over her head, the workhouse infirmary was by no means a safe haven for childbirth. Dedicated maternity wards were an exception; most women in the throes of labor were placed in the general ward, alongside patients with a variety of ailments and contagious diseases, from tuberculosis to smallpox and syphilis. Sanitation was universally appalling. The Poor Law reformer Louisa Twinning reported that during her visit to a women's ward, she discovered that a broken lavatory had been left to degenerate into an open sewer, cleaning was performed without disinfectant, and infants were delivered without the use of soap and water. At the infirmary at Yarmouth Workhouse, where Kate gave birth to her daughter, Catherine "Annie" Conway, on April 18, 1863, the gas jets were regularly left on to keep rats away. However unpleasant the setting, Kate likely found it far preferable to delivering her first child in the mud by the side of a road. The presence of tiny

Annie Conway would slow the couple's progress through town and country only slightly. In fact, an infant strapped to Kate's back or nestled against her breast might move people to offer the family an extra loaf of bread or a comfortable place to rest. In the years that followed Annie's birth, the couple continued to roam, traveling as far north as Newcastle, then down to Hull before returning to Coventry. Briefly, in June 1864, they stopped in London, perhaps Kate's first visit back since her departure from the city. Over the course of the family's wanderings, Kate would become accustomed to laying Annie down to sleep in stable stalls and churchyards, against walls, or under trees as the rain thrashed, drenching her clothes as she attempted to shelter her infant. This mode of life could never have felt entirely satisfying, though she must have found something that sustained her; the joy of performance, the singing and the storytelling, and the composing of tales. And drink would have helped too, when money allowed for it.

If it was at Conway's insistence that they tramp the country from end to end in search of success, then ironically enough, he was to find it back in Staffordshire, directly under the nose of the Eddowes family.

In the dawn-touched hours of January 9, 1866, spectators bundled in scarves and shawls began to gather in the yard at Stafford Gaol. There had not been a hanging for a "crimson crime" for some time, so people had risen especially early and come from the surrounding towns and villages to watch a murderer, Charles Christopher Robinson, twitch and wiggle like a fish on a line. The vendors of tea and coffee and hot milk had set up their stalls. The crowd filled their stomachs with currant buns, boiled eggs, sheep's trotters, and cakes. Although the popular enthusiasm for public executions had begun to wane by the 1860s, a hanging could still rouse as much excitement as a fair or a market day. Workers from factories and mills would have stopped by on their way to work; neighbors met and chatted, and hawkers came to sell their wares. Among those elbowing and jostling for a good view of the drop, Kate and Thomas Conway had set out their pitch.

Hanging days were big business for ballad and chapbook sellers, who belted out the murderer's supposed lamentations in rhyme and song. Nothing sold better than criminal tales, and as soon as an execution was announced, every penny bard and printer in the county scrambled to get a version of the story in ink. Often, these "true" last confessions, some purportedly spoken on the gallows, were being sold in the prison yard before they were even uttered. Executions would have been Kate and Thomas's bread and butter. Much of the travers-ing that they did would have been in order to reach the county towns in which these events were scheduled to take place. However, this hanging would have been of particular importance to the couple, as Charles Christopher Robinson was Kate's distant cousin.

Like Kate, Charles had been left an orphan and was raised in the home of Josiah Fisher, a relation who worked as a house agent in Wolverhampton. As a man of some standing and wealth, Fisher acted as the guardian to another family member in distress, Harriet Seager, the sister of his son's wife. As Seager was close in age to Charles Rob-inson, a romantic attachment developed, and eventually the couple became engaged, though Harriet remained wary of her fiancé's quick temper and tendency to be jealous. On August 26, 1865, Robinson was spotted wandering about the garden in a fury, unwashed, unshaven, and wearing no more than his shirt. After he found his sweetheart, an argument ensued; Robinson attempted to grab and kiss Harriet. She ducked his advances, and he slapped her. The couple parted angrily — Robinson was not prepared to forgive Harriet for quarreling with him. A short time after, a servant spotted him striding downstairs to the scullery with his razor. Frantic noises and a gunshot alerted the house-hold that something was wrong. They discovered Robinson, howl-ing and screaming; he had unsuccessfully attempted to shoot himself and was about to draw a razor across his neck. At his feet, in a pool of blood, lay Harriet Seager, "with a gash in the throat that had laid the spine bare."[12]

How well Kate knew her cousin is unknown, but she and Conway would have been determined to make something of this connection. Wolverhampton Archives possesses a copy of one of the only publica-tions believed to be linked to the pens of Thomas Conway and Kate Eddowes: *A Copy of Verses on the Awful Execution of Charles Christopher Robinson for the Murder of his Sweetheart, Harriet Segar of Ablow Street, Wolverhampton, August 26,* written to be sold at the hanging in 1866.[13] The ballad takes an interesting perspective. Whereas many authors would have written a dramatic account of the killing or shaped the events into a tale of murderous love, the lyrics instead paint Robinson as a remorseful figure, worthy of pity.

> Come all you feeling Christians,
> Give ear unto my tale,
> It's for a cruel murder
> I was hung at Stafford Gaol.
> The horrid crime that I have done
> Is shocking for to hear,
> I murdered one I once did love,
> Harriet Segar dear.
>
> Charles Robinson is my name,
> With sorrow was oppressed,
> The very thought of what I've done
> Deprived me of my rest:
> Within the walls of Stafford Gaol,
> In bitter grief did cry,
> And every moment seemed to say
> "Poor soul prepare to die!"
>
> I well deserved my wretched fate,
> No one can pity me,
> To think that I in my cold blood,
> Could take her life away,
> She no harm to me had done,
> How could I serve her so?
> No one my feelings now can tell,
> My heart was so full of woe.
>
> O while within my dungeon dark,
> Sad thoughts came on apace,
> The cruel deed that I had done
> Appeared before my face,
> While lying in my prison cell

Those horrid visions rise,
The gentle form of her I killed
Appeared before my eyes.

O Satan, Thou Demon strong,
Why didst thou on me bind?
O why did I allow thy chains
To enwrap my feeble mind?
Before my eyes she did appear
All others to excel
And it was through jealousy,
I poor Harriet Segar killed.

May my end a warning be
Unto all mankind,
Think on my unhappy fate
And bear me in your mind.
Whether you be rich or poor
Your friends and sweethearts love,
And God will crown your fleeting days,
With blessings from above.

While Kate would have watched nooses tighten around the necks of many villains, to have witnessed the execution of a blood relation would surely have proven a different experience. Whether or not Kate was affected by the sight of her kinfolk, clad in mourning, their veils drawn about their faces, will never be known. Neither will it be known if they recognized her, the impertinent chanteuse bellowing her verses into the chilly air, declaiming the injustice of murder.

If the *Black Country Bugle* can be believed, Kate and Tom's ballad turned an exceptional profit that day. The couple fared so well that they were able to "return from Stafford in style, booking inside seats on Ward's coach with the proceeds." The takings allowed Conway to invest in a donkey and cart and order another four hundred copies from his printer in Bilston, which the couple then sold "at their regular pitch on the following Monday." It is said that Thomas rewarded

Kate "with the price of a flowered-hat." "Such was their lifestyle," continued the piece, "that they lived for a spell in lodgings at Moxley," a village outside Wednesbury. This was the stroke of good fortune that Conway had been hunting for. Rather than rest on his laurels, it is suggested that he set his sights on a permanent move to London, "where his rhyming talents . . .would be even more fully appreciated."[14]

The veracity of the *Black Country Bugle*'s account of the couple's lives has always been thought questionable, but Thomas Conway's pension records confirm that the pair began to spend more time in London from this period. Their decision to settle in the capital may have been driven in part by Conway's ambitions, but also by other factors. If Kate had learned anything since the death of her parents, surely it was that her true family were not those who lived in Wolverhampton. London was the home of her youth and the home of her sisters, and after years of roaming, it was now time for the prodigal daughter to make her return.

HER SISTER'S KEEPER

E MMA HAD ALWAYS attempted to do what was correct. As the second-eldest girl of a large brood, she had been handed bawling infant after bawling infant. She had been taught to stir the soup, change
the baby's filthy diapers, and keep the toddlers from the hot coals and
the carriage wheels. She had kept an eye on her brother Alfred, helping him when he had seizures, offering protection to an older sibling
who could not return the favor. It was Emma who nursed her dying
mother, Emma who sought to comfort her sick father. It was Emma
who learned to read and write, and then went out to service in order
to support her brothers and sisters. It was Emma who agonized over
how these orphaned children were to live when they no longer had a
home. Emma sent Kate to Wolverhampton, hoping for the best, while
she continued in her post, dutifully scrubbing, washing, and serving a
middle-class family and quietly saving what she earned. Around 1860,
at the age of twenty-five, she met James Jones, a neighbor of her sister
Harriet, who lived in Clerkenwell. James and his family were tallow
chandlers, or those who made and sold candles, once an esteemed profession with its own guild in the time before gas lamps and domestic
gas jets began to extinguish the trade. Emma did what was expected
of a woman of her era: on November 11, she married the man who had

courted her. Only after that did the children begin to arrive: six in total.

In Kate's absence, her four elder sisters' lives continued to grow and twist closer together like the roots of trees. Throughout the 1860s, the women who had guided and mothered her had all managed to relocate from Bermondsey, south of the river, to Clerkenwell, a working-class district set around the meat market at Smithfields. They each married in the same church, St. Barnabas, and three of them lived no more than a few streets apart. Eliza had wed a local butcher, James Gold, in 1859, and Harriet and Robert Garrett at last had solemnized their union in 1867, after a period of cohabitation that produced no children. Only Elizabeth lived on the opposite side of the Thames, in Greenwich, where she had settled with her husband, Thomas Fisher. In spite of the cares that accompanied a constantly growing family and the responsibilities of housekeeping, the sisters remained in regular contact, sharing gossip and news. One day, the news was that Kate had returned to London.

The fifteen-year-old motherless girl whom Emma had dispatched like a package to unknown recipients had come back a full-fledged woman, with a child of her own and a man she called her husband. Kate was, however, careful about revealing to her sisters many details about her life. Initially, she told Emma that she and Thomas Conway had been settled in Birmingham, choosing to omit the stories of her vagrant's existence. Her marital status and the lack of a wedding ring were likely to have raised questions as well, as would have the tattoo of Thomas Conway's initials, which was inked crudely onto her forearm.

Although they would become fashionable briefly in the late nineteenth century, in the middle of the Victorian era, few symbols were more associated with society's lowest element than the tattoo. Traditionally, body art had been the preserve of sailors who had traveled to parts of Asia and Oceania where it was common to decorate the body with ink. The practice of tattooing followed the seafarers back to Britain, as did their reputation for poverty, vice, and criminality. Soldiers too were known to have initials, regimental insignias, and other designs permanently drawn on the limbs and torso. Thomas Conway would have been no stranger to the sight of inky snakes, hearts, crosses, and sweethearts' names etched on the biceps of his army companions. However, while men might be forgiven for defacing their bodies as a mark of their manliness and spirit of adventure, tattooing among women was not regarded with such lenience: a tattoo on a woman's body not only flouted conventions of feminine purity and beauty, but also rendered her masculine. Getting a tattoo was dirty and painful; in the nineteenth century it involved a needle, a pot of ink, and a sustained succession of pricks. Any woman who would have sought out such an experience was seeking to challenge her "natural delicacy" and to permanently alter her God-given appearance. Much like many of Kate's decisions — to cohabit with a man, to bear a child out of wedlock, and to lead a nomadic life — acquiring a tattoo was deeply subversive. It is likely that the suggestion had come from Thomas Conway, who may have had her initials marked on his arm too. Perhaps by these means the couple solemnized their commitment to one another on their own terms, without wedding bands and a church service.

Whatever Harriet, Emma, Eliza, and Elizabeth whispered among themselves about their sister, Kate's appearance in London seemed to signify a desire to make alterations to her life. By 1868 she and Thomas were settled in what was described as a "clean and comfortable" small house at 13 Cottage Place, in an area off Bell Street in Westminster. This house was a significant distance from Clerkenwell, a choice that may reflect Kate's complex relationship with her family, which regularly swung between intimacy and antagonism. Whether her siblings were present that same year to assist her with the birth of her second child, Thomas Lawrence Conway, is unknown, but by March 1869, Kate was content to name a newborn daughter after her eldest sister, Harriet.

If Conway had brought his wife and child to London in order to further his ambitions, within three years, his hopes had stalled. Though the capital offered a wide market for the sale of ballads and chapbooks, Thomas never seemed to establish himself securely there. By the late nineteenth century, London was home to hundreds, if not thousands of individuals singing and selling their songs on the street. Worse still, Westminster, where they lived, was cited as one of the primary haunts

of such peddlers, who had earned a reputation for doing as much begging as they did singing.[1] In the past, such a setback would not have
hindered Conway and Kate; they would simply have cut their moorings and drifted north or south, in the direction of prospective work.
Now, however, young children anchored them in a single place. In
spite of his heart condition, Thomas returned to physical labor in order to make ends meet. For a time, he worked as an assistant to a brick-
layer; this succeeded in making the rent and paying for meager meals.
But these comforts were short-lived. The job and money did not last,
and neither did food. Soon the infant, Harriet Conway, suckling at her
mother's empty breast, began to wither. Within three weeks, Kate reported the infant's death from malnutrition; she felt the child's final
convulsions as she held her in her arms.

It may have been this incident that, by the end of the year, prompted
Thomas to leave London in search of work. That winter he headed
north, toward Yorkshire, to look for employment. In his absence,
Kate took seven-year-old Annie and two-year-old Thomas to Abbey
Wood, near Greenwich, possibly to live with her sister Elizabeth and
her family. As the Fishers were eight in number by 1870, this arrangement could only have been temporary, and inevitably, by January 20,
Kate, Annie, and little Thomas found themselves standing before the
gates of Greenwich Union Workhouse.

What initially began as an expedient method of contending with
a problem rapidly evolved into a way of life for Kate. Over the next
ten years, whenever faced with misfortune, Kate placed herself in the
care of a board of guardians. On August 15, 1873, she gave birth to another son, George Alfred Conway, in the maternity ward of Southwark
Workhouse. Records suggest that the length of her sojourns varied, in
some instances lasting for weeks and others for several months. On
each occasion, Kate was accompanied by one or more of her children.

For a destitute woman, entering the workhouse with her children
presented a number of complications. According to the Poor Law,
single mothers with illegitimate children were not entitled to receive
"outdoor relief," or parish handouts designed to assist poor families
who lived in their own lodgings. Authorities feared that providing financial support to immoral women in their own homes was tanta-

mount to a state subsidy of prostitution. Although they were aware that many poorer women like Kate cohabited with monogamous common-law partners, no real distinction was made between this type of "fallen woman" and acknowledged prostitutes. As far as "respectable society" was concerned, a mother had borne her child through either a legal union or a sinful coupling. Once the woman and her children were inside the workhouse, the board of guardians was at liberty to discriminate between the decent and the damned, to separate the so-called fallen women from impressionable young girls or to feed mothers who had borne an illegitimate child on a punishment diet of watered skilly.

After they had passed through what was known as "the archway of tears," the admission routine for families would have been the same for all, regardless of the mother's marital status. Everyone was separated by gender and age, stripped of clothes and possessions, ordered into the bath, and handed a workhouse uniform. According to the stipulations of the Poor Law, children under the age of seven were allowed to remain with their mother, sleeping in her filthy, hard bed and playing beside her on the bench as she picked oakum. Children between seven and fourteen years of age were removed from their parents, or the one parent who had brought them to the workhouse, to live in separate school facilities. Though families were strictly segregated, parental "interviews" were permitted with children in the dining hall once a week, so long as the sons and daughters remained on site. In November 1876, when Kate arrived at Greenwich Union Workhouse in anticipation of the birth of her fourth child, Frederick, two-year-old George Alfred was allowed to remain at her side, but Annie, who was then thirteen, and Thomas, age eight, were dispatched to the Industrial School in Sutton.*

In spite of its terrifying reputation, the workhouse was often able

---

* Frederick William Eddowes was born at Greenwich Union Workhouse infirmary on February 3, 1877. Kate, who had been claiming she did not have a husband or male partner to support her from the time she first started accepting relief from Greenwich Union, had to continue with this charade by not disclosing the identity of Frederick's father. If she had given the name of the child's father, the parish would have pursued Thomas Conway for support (which he was unable to provide) and inevitably discovered Kate's ongoing deception.

to effect some good, especially for destitute children. The Poor Law Union insisted that workhouses provide girls and boys with lessons in reading and arithmetic for a minimum of three hours daily, helping many children to acquire at least a semblance of education. Authorities hoped to give children born into poverty an opportunity to step out of the trap that had caught their parents and grandparents. To further this aim, the government made provisions in 1857 for the expansion of what were called Industrial Schools. Removing young paupers from both the corrupting influence of the workhouse and the unwholesome environment of urban centers, these establishments were intended to offer a practical education to poor children. Boys were taught trades such as shoemaking, tailoring, carpentry, and music; girls were educated in the domestic arts, such as needlework and knitting, to prepare for life in service.

The school that Annie and her brother Thomas attended at Sutton absorbed most of the workhouse children from the southeastern London parishes and boasted a capacity of up to a thousand pauper scholars. In the 1870s, its facilities, considered state-of-the-art, included expansive kitchens, a laundry, washrooms, a boiler room, and a steam engine to pump fresh water into the school's tanks. In addition to open, spacious stairwells, dormitories, and classrooms, there were workshops for learning trades as well as a farm where students were educated in agriculture. Compared to Dowgate, the small charity school that Kate had attended, the facilities offered far greater scope for a child to improve his or her prospects. According to the memoirs of the otherwise anonymous "W.H.R.," a former pupil at Sutton, the compassionate encouragement offered by some teachers was matched by the brutal violence of others. However, as a whole, Sutton offered cleaner beds, more plentiful food, and a cheerier environment than Greenwich Union Workhouse. There were also opportunities for song and musical performances on the harmonium. The regimen had an overwhelmingly positive impact on W.H.R. "At Sutton," he concluded, "I was thoroughly de-pauperised, for come what would in a fair way, I was determined never again to enter the workhouse as a pauper."[2]

The success of the Industrial School at Sutton can also be measured in terms of its impact on Kate's younger brothers and sister — Thomas, George, and Mary — who were sent there from Bermondsey Workhouse after the death of their father. Within several years, George Eddowes had been trained as a shoemaker, while Thomas Eddowes had been taught music and was sent to join the band of the 45th Nottinghamshire Regiment of Infantry in Preston. Mary too succeeded well enough in her "domestic studies" to warrant placement as a servant.* Had Kate been a year or so younger in 1857, she too may have benefited from a Sutton education and the course of her life may have taken a very different turn.

By the late 1870s, Kate's problems appear to have become twofold. Like many working-class women, she was caught in a vicious circle: Conway had to leave London to find work, but in doing so, he left his common-law partner and their children without support. No amount of women's labor in a factory, a sweatshop, or a laundry, selling items on the street or doing piecework from home, would ever bring in an amount adequate to cover a family's needs and keep it from the workhouse. Worse still, when Thomas Conway did return, he was violent.

Conway's absences and the extreme hardship the family faced in attempting to feed themselves and maintain a home had begun to lead to physical altercations when the couple was together. Kate's sisters and her daughter noticed a dark pattern emerging. Although Emma claimed that "on a whole, they lived happily together," the "quarrels between them" became difficult to ignore. According to both Annie and Emma, the pair's disagreements were exacerbated by Kate's "habit of excessive drinking," while Thomas was committed to abstinence. It appears that the couple "could never agree" on this point, and both Annie and her aunts eventually came to believe that where her drinking and her relationship with Conway were concerned, Kate was the author of her own misfortunes.

This attitude was not out of step with Victorian working-class sentiments about domestic violence; frequently the woman was blamed

---

* Sarah Ann was not so fortunate. She appears to have developed a mental disorder and was removed to an asylum.

for the beatings she received. A certain degree of violence within the home was thought to serve a disciplinary function. Husbands felt no remorse for administering a chastising slap, while wives were often made to feel that they had "asked for it."[3] The catalogue of offenses that might cause a husband to raise his hand against his wife was extensive: the use of foul language, the rejection of his sexual advances, disobedience, impertinence, or simply challenging his superior role within the family. However, nothing figured more prominently in cases of domestic violence than alcohol. A drunken man was just as likely to beat his wife as was a sober husband who disapproved of his wife's intoxication. A wife's perpetual drunkenness was often used successfully by a spouse as a defense in trials against a claim of assault.[4] In 1877, the very year that Kate and Thomas Conway's union began to fracture under similar circumstances, a legal textbook, *Principles of Punishment,* described wife beating as a crime that "varies infinitely in degree of criminality." Whereas some serious cases might warrant imprisonment, most incidents of physical abuse were, according to the author, so "trifling as almost to permit of justification."

There were, however, limits to this attitude, and not everyone in a community or a family was prepared to turn a blind eye. While neighbors and friends might tactfully avoid direct physical intervention during a domestic dispute, communities closely monitored warring couples by checking up on the woman or by reminding the man that they could hear what he was doing. Most action was taken indirectly, usually by offering the woman shelter when she needed to avoid her husband's wrath. The Eddowes sisters chose to deal with Kate's deteriorating domestic situation in this manner.

In the year between November 1876 and December 1877, Kate was in and out of workhouses and casual wards on at least seven separate occasions. On August 6, she was arrested for drunk and disorderly behavior and sent to Wandsworth Prison for fourteen days.* In every

---

* Wandsworth Prison, Surrey: Register of Prisoners, Series PCOM2 Piece number 284; Wandsworth Prison, Surrey: Register of Prisoners, Series PCOM2 Piece number 288. Kate also appears in the prison records for August 1878 on the same charge, drunk and disorderly behavior.

instance, including her incarceration, she brought some or all of her children with her. As Kate's life fell to pieces, Emma was there to help gather them. According to an interview in the *London Daily News,* in the worst of times, Kate had fallen into the habit of appearing at her sister's door and begging her for help. Emma recalled that her sibling's face appeared "frightfully disfigured" from Conway's beatings. Kate, with her emotions loosed by drink, often gave way to sobs. "I wish I was like you," she would cry.[5] Although Emma's life, contained in a few shabby rooms in Bridgewater Gardens, might not have appeared worthy of envy, to her younger sister it would have represented everything Kate had failed to become.

The situation only worsened. In December 1877, she was arguing furiously with Conway again. Shortly before Christmas, she left him and took ten-month old Frederick with her to the casual ward for the night.* Some form of temporary reconciliation had been reached by Christmas Day, which Kate and her family spent with her sisters and their families. Unfortunately, the festive celebration did not go well. The Eddowes women were shocked by Kate's battered appearance. Emma recalled that "Both her eyes had been blackened" and that she bore "a dreadful face." She was equally horrified by Thomas's attitude. "The man, Conway," as she referred to him disdainfully, "appeared to be attached to her," though Emma found it difficult to fathom how any affection could exist between the two, especially when Kate so obviously "suffered from his brutality." Much to Emma's disgust, Thomas exhibited no shame for his actions and remarked openly and with a sigh of exasperation, "Kate, I shall be hung for you one of these days."[6] Whatever occurred during that gathering — Kate's excessive drinking, or something else — the sisters came to the conclusion that Kate was no better than Thomas Conway. Shortly thereafter, a rift developed, and Emma and Harriet broke off relations with their sibling altogether.

In 1877 she took Frederick, her infant, with her. I am indebted to Debra Arif for this information.

* Workhouse admission records also indicate that Kate was pregnant during the summer and autumn of 1877 for the sixth time. There is no indication that the pregnancy was brought to term or resulted in a live birth.

Like many women caught in the cycle of domestic violence, Kate always returned to Conway. The couple experienced periods of peace and discord, chaos and harmony, and their children suffered the consequences. Their perpetual financial distress made it necessary for the family to move frequently, from Westminster to Southwark and Deptford, occupying single rooms and lodging houses as necessity demanded. Annie had, however, grown old enough to look after her younger siblings and mind the home, so Kate was able to work. Sometimes this included laboring at a laundry or a bit of charring for her better-off neighbors, but toward the end of the 1870s, it appears that she and Thomas returned to hawking ballads together.

In 1879, their regular patch was Mill Lane, a small commercial street near the army barracks at Woolwich, frequented by an assortment of vendors and peddlers catering to residents and soldiers. On October 4, eleven-year-old Thomas and his six-year-old brother, George, accompanied their parents as they pattered and sang out their wares. Eventually, both parents wandered off and instructed the boys to wait where they had been left, outside 8 Mill Lane. When it began to grow dark and no one returned for the children, questions were asked and the boys were escorted to Greenwich Union Workhouse, a place they had come to know well over the years. Nearly a week would pass before Kate could be located and made to reclaim her progeny.* This incident was followed by a similar one, on November 11. This time, the boys were escorted to the workhouse by police officer 251, who had found them "deserted by their mother" on the street.[7] On this occasion, Kate could not be found. Nearly a month later, the boys' sixteen-year-old sister was called upon to collect them.

---

* It's worth noting that there were in fact two Mill Lanes relatively near to each other: Mill Lane in Woolwich, which ran alongside the army barracks, and Old Mill Lane in Deptford, known as one of the area's worst slums. On October 17, 1877, Kate was brought into the local workhouse and an unusual note was written next to her entry on the admissions ledger: "pesters Mill Lane." This likely refers to Mill Lane near the barracks, where a military maternity hospital was located. Kate had recently given birth to Frederick, and it is recorded that he was with her when she was admitted on the seventeenth. In addition to hawking and begging along that road, it is possible that Kate made a nuisance of herself outside the maternity hospital, in hope of receiving charity.

Where Kate had disappeared to during that time is anyone's guess. Certainly, her behavior begs many questions about her state of mind and her use of alcohol. Earlier that year, Kate had suffered the loss of her infant, Frederick, a circumstance that may have only exacerbated her existing problems.

Kate and Thomas Conway's destructive and abusive relationship limped on into 1881. Although they are recorded on the census that year as living together with their two sons in Chelsea, in a room at 71 Lower George Street, by autumn, the couple had split up. When journalists later interviewed Conway and his daughter, neither could recall the precise date when this event occurred; however, Thomas was quick to paint himself as the victim. According to his version, he had found it necessary to leave Kate on account of her drinking, and he made certain to take his children with him when he went. The Eddowes sisters disputed this narrative. Elizabeth claimed that her sister had left Thomas "because he treated her badly," though Annie added that "Before they actually left each other she [Kate] was never with him for twelve months at a time."[8] The separation had been a long time in the making; when it came it offered respite to both parties.

For a time following the breakdown of her relationship with Thomas Conway, Kate appears to have turned to her sister Elizabeth for assistance, though this arrangement did not last for long. Much like Emma and Harriet before her, Elizabeth soon found her sister's behavior insupportable. In September 1881, Kate was once again charged with drunken disorderliness and dragged off the streets as she spewed obscenities at passersby. On this occasion, the magistrate spared her a prison sentence. However, where the law was forgiving, her family was not, and by the end of that year, Elizabeth too had broken off relations with her younger sister.

Now without Elizabeth, without Thomas Conway or her sons, without Emma or Harriet, Kate sought out the only remaining sister with whom she still maintained a bond: Eliza.

At some time prior to 1881, Eliza Gold had become a widow. Although she had been the wife of a butcher, a practitioner of a respected skilled trade, the family had struggled financially. Apparently no provisions were made in the event of Eliza's widowhood, and consequently, as was the case for so many women of her station in life, Eliza's circumstances were significantly compromised by bereavement. With no savings or pension and a son not yet old enough to earn a proper wage, Eliza had to attach herself to the affections of another partner as quickly as possible.* Little is known about Charles Frost, the man she came to call her second husband. Both had been widowed, and in the tradition of many working-class men and women who formed relationships following bereavement, they chose not to officially solemnize their vows. In an interview, Eliza claimed that her "husband" "worked at the waterside unloading cargoes of fruit" and occasionally sold penny-farthing books at Liverpool Street station.[9]

Until the death of James Gold, Eliza had always lived near her sisters, either in Clerkenwell or Hoxton, but widowhood and Charles Frost brought her to Whitechapel. At least since 1881, the Frosts inhabited a garret room at 6 Thrawl Street, with Eliza's son and a daughter from Frost's previous relationship. Eliza's new address was far from desirable. Whereas both the poor and the more comfortably off lived in Hoxton, Thrawl Street was one of the most notorious sinks of poverty in Spitalfields.[10] It was here that Kate came to visit her sister, almost certainly to beg a coin or two off her, if not a meal or a narrow space in one of their beds. For a time, Eliza must have given Kate some much-needed solace.

That year, whenever she had the four pence to do so, Kate rented a bed at 55 Flower and Dean Street, a lodging house around the corner from her sister. "Cooney's," as it later came to be called, was also the doss house of choice for John Kelly, the man who would come to fill Thomas Conway's empty boots. In John's words, which bear all the hallmarks of journalistic embellishment, he "first laid eyes" on Kate while she was staying there. After "being throwed together a good bit," the two took a liking to each other "and decided to make it a regular bargain."†

---

* Eliza bore three children, two of whom died before maturity.

† *Worcestershire Chronicle*, 6 October 1888. It's also possible that Kelly and Kate met through

If the Eddowes women had taken a disliking to Thomas Conway, their disdain for John Kelly seems to have been even greater. As far as Emma was concerned, Kate's life "went from bad to worse" when she left Thomas Conway; at least when she lived with her abuser "her home was clean and comfortable."[11] After taking up with John, she had no home, only a vile temporary bed at a doss house. Although Kelly was described as "quiet and inoffensive," which was more than could be said for Thomas Conway, in the eyes of Kate's family, he possessed one major failing that Thomas did not: he drank, heavily. Annie, who blamed her mother for tearing apart the family, was unequivocal about her feelings for John Kelly: "I've never spoken to him and I don't like him."[12]

Despite her family's sentiments, once free of her abuser, Kate settled into a happier, though no less erratic life. She and John shared a love of the bottle, and their conviviality made them popular with fellow lodgers at Cooney's.* According to newspaper interviews with those at 55 Flower and Dean Street, Kate was always ready with a song and didn't hesitate to spare her last four pence for someone who hadn't made their doss money. For a time, both she and John worked; Kate, like Elisabeth Stride, took on charring for Jewish families in the area, while John labored at the market — though this income was disappointing and rarely reliable.

Although the couple came to regard 55 Flower and Dean Street as their home, they, like most who inhabited Whitechapel's lodging houses, could not afford to spend every night there. Their income ebbed and flowed; sometimes there was money to pay for a bed, and sometimes there was not. At the inquest John made it clear that he and Kate might pass the night at Cooney's, at number 52 Flower and Dean Street, in the casual wards, or on the streets. Kate, who had spent much of her life slumbering with the night sky as her blanket,

---

Charles Frost. Both men claimed to work transporting and selling fruit in some capacity.
* Although John Kelly claims he was not a heavy drinker, a statement echoed by Frederick Wilkinson, the deputy lodging-house keeper, Kelly's answers at Kate's inquest indicate that when he had money, he drank to excess.

was well known among the rough sleepers in Spitalfields. In the wake of her murder, a handful of homeless women were among the first to come forward to identify her. She was cited as one of "10 to 20 houseless creatures who are without the means of paying for their beds" who regularly curled up in a shed off Dorset Street.*

Kate and John Kelly's hand-to-mouth existence did not permit them to linger for too long in any one place. Casual ward records indicate that, from 1883, the couple made regular excursions to Kent in order to find work, roaming between London, Dartford, Seven Oaks, and Chatham. Kate never abandoned hawking, which had become to her as much of a way of life as it was a means of earning an income. After twenty or more years of wandering, of sleeping in fields or passageways, she may have found this free existence more familiar and comfortable than a settled life could ever be. As she learned from Thomas Conway, a peddler was beholden to no one: not employers or landlords or even family.

After Kate took up with John Kelly, even her sister Eliza and Kate's own daughter, Annie, attempted to distance themselves from her. Annie had left home in her teens, choosing to cohabit with and later marry a lampblack packer called Louis Philips. According to Annie's statements at her mother's inquest, Kate hounded the couple, frequently appearing at their door, intoxicated and begging for handouts. The situation became intolerable, and the Philipses were forced to move in order to avoid her. Annie complained that so long as her mother drank, it was impossible to maintain a normal relationship with her. In August 1886, the situation came to a head. Annie, preparing to give birth to her third child, appealed to her mother for assistance. Kate agreed to be present with her daughter in her "period of confinement" but insisted on receiving pay for it. Annie grudgingly obliged, only to discover that her mother had taken the money and gone out "to get too much to drink." "The result," Annie commented, "caused unpleas-

---

* *Lloyd's Weekly Newspaper,* 7 October 1888. Although these women were able to identify Kate, they were not asked to testify at the inquest, nor did the police, who were searching for a murderer of prostitutes, seem to consider their statements to be important.

antness . . . we did not part on very good terms."[13] Little more than a week after giving birth, Annie had thrown Kate out and decided she would have no more to do with her. The Philipses moved from their home on 22 King Street in Bermondsey and did not leave a forwarding address.

Perhaps what Kate liked best about John Kelly was that, unlike members of her family, he demanded little of her. Although everyone who knew them, from Kate's sisters to the couple's friends at Cooney's lodging house, attested that the pair "had a sincere attachment for each other" and that Kate "never went with any other man," their connection appears to have been one based more on practicality than emotional intimacy.[14] John called Kate his wife, but she preferred to bear the surname Conway, belonging to the man to whom she insisted she was legally married. Although the couple behaved as spouses, Kate used John's name only when it proved convenient. John never seemed to ask too many questions of Kate. He kept his distance from her family, never inquiring about her relationship with Annie, never speaking to her about Thomas Conway, and apparently never venturing to intrude on Kate's inner thoughts. Despite living as her partner for seven years, he knew surprisingly little about her — not even that she had been born in Wolverhampton. As he and others confirmed at the inquest, they rarely argued; Kelly recalled only one occasion when "they had words" before Kate returned to him a few hours later.[15]

First and foremost, Kate and John Kelly were companions committed to each other's daily survival. By the time that Kate had found John, she had known the violence of Thomas Conway's fists, the scorn of her children and sisters, the deaths of at least two infants, and the trauma of her own parents' demise. She had experienced the degradation of the workhouse, the general disgust of society, and had grown acquainted with starvation and illness.* Under such circumstances, what

---

* The autopsy performed on Kate revealed that she was suffering from Bright's disease. Today this is referred to as acute nephritis and subdivided into three distinct forms, all of which result in significant damage to the kidneys. The disease's causes are not entirely known; it may be hereditary or brought on by other diseases such as lupus, strep, or other bacterial infections. Symptoms may include exhaustion, blood or protein in the urine, and water retention. In the nineteenth century, the disease was erroneously linked to alcoholism.

mattered most was the here and now: getting the drink that dulled the pain and the food that stopped the hunger. John Kelly's company, his protection on the street, and his occasional income made life easier. For a woman who had so little, this in itself would have proven comfort enough.

"NOTHING"

FOR THOSE LIVING in the poorer parts of London, the end of the summer meant one thing: the opportunity to earn some money and enjoy themselves in the Kentish countryside, bringing in the hop harvest. For many, hop picking was as close as they would ever come to having an actual vacation. It offered a chance to enjoy the fresh air, the campfire camaraderie, and the free barrels of beer and cider laid on by the farmers. Each September, thousands of city dwellers poured into the area; the marginally better off arrived by train, while many more walked the roads from London. In a good year, such as 1890, an estimated fifty to sixty thousand men, women, and children arrived for the hop harvest, where they were paid two pence a bushel for their labor and were housed in huts, sheds, or barns near the hop gardens.

With free accommodation and drink on offer, Kate and John Kelly were not about to miss this opportunity to fill their pockets and their bellies. They had been regulars among the hop pickers in the past years, and in the summer of 1888, joined the procession of Londoners heading south to Kent. Unfortunately, they and the others discovered an especially poor harvest that season. The *Echo* remarked that workers found "the hops were not considered worth picking" in many parts of the county. "After trying many quarters for work," laborers were forced "to walk back to London, having earned nothing."[1]

Kate and John had set out toward the end of August, to work in the orchards and berry fields where hands were needed to bring in the fruit harvest. This was part of their usual circuit through Kent, and the two would have been hawking as well as picking up odd jobs until the hops were ready for picking. Gradually, the couple worked their way to Maidstone, where they would have heard that the hop crop was slightly better. As a county town, Maidstone also offered Kate and Kelly an opportunity to acquire some necessities for the work ahead; John needed a new pair of boots, along with a jacket, which he purchased from a pawnshop. The two then headed to Hunton, a village about five miles away, where, like other prospective pickers, they soon discovered that the crop was so sparse that "outsiders could get nothing to do."[2] Disappointed, they decided to "hoof it back" to London.[3]

The pair arrived in town on the evening of Thursday, September 27. Having eaten and drunk their way through the money they had earned in the countryside, they were forced to seek lodgings that night at the casual ward at Thavies Inn, on Shoe Lane. After years on the tramp, Kate and John had become experts at selecting the best spike in which to lay their heads, and Thavies Inn was a favorite. In spite of the rules set forth in the 1882 Casual Poor Act, which required all inmates to be detained for a minimum of two nights, to complete a full day's labor picking oakum and breaking stones prior to release, Shoe Lane was more liberal in its approach, and was cited as a place to which "paupers flocked" because "detention and work are not enforced."[4] This concurred with John Kelly's account of events; he and Kate were released early on Friday morning, which then allowed him to find some work at Spitalfields Market. By that afternoon, he had earned sixpence, which would cover the expense of a night's lodgings for one of them, but not both. Later, John, not wishing to look like a negligent husband in the wake of his partner's murder, claimed in his official statement that he offered to tramp to Mile End casual ward while Kate took four pence for a bed at Cooney's. "No, you go and have a bed and I will go to the casual ward," Kate protested, according to John. However, what was actually agreed upon and what came to transpire is a bit more "muddled," as John himself admitted to the coroner.

Much of what is known about Kate and Kelly's movements in September comes from his confused account; several versions of which appeared in the newspapers.* Initially, he stated that Kate went off to Mile End at around 3 or 4 p.m. on Friday afternoon, to line up for a bed, but under questioning, he revealed that this was not in fact a truthful record of events. The coroner produced a pawn ticket for a pair of boots that John said he had put in hock, dated Friday the twenty-eighth. John was taken aback by this; originally he had claimed that he pawned the boots the next day, on Saturday morning, and bought food and drink with the two shillings and six pence it provided. "It was either Friday night or Saturday morning. I am all muddled up," he stated, as the lie began to unravel. He further revealed that it was in fact Kate who had pawned the boots that Friday night, while John stood in the doorway in his bare feet.† "Had you been drinking when the pawning took place?" the coroner asked him. "Yes," Kelly admitted sheepishly. His confession made it plain to the jury why his memory of the events was poor.[5]

In fact, neither Kate nor John would have eaten since leaving Thavies Inn that morning, and filling their rumbling stomachs with food and drink would have been foremost on their minds. The six pence that John had earned had evidently been spent buying alcohol, which accounted for the state he was in while he and Kate pawned his boots. According to John's testimony, "the greater part" of the two shillings and six pence they received was then used in purchasing provisions, which were to last them through the next morning.[6] The couple bought tea and sugar, which Kate loaded into her skirt pockets, and probably a few more drinks. By the end of the evening it would be apparent that they had run through most of the pawn money, and so they decided that John should have the four pence for a single lodging-

---

* Unlike the inquests for Polly Nichols, Annie Chapman, and Elisabeth Stride, some of the official reports from the coroner's inquest into Catherine Eddowes's death have survived.
† In the course of their wanderings in Kent, Kate had met with a woman calling herself Emily Burrell, who had given her a pawn ticket for a man's flannel shirt. Both the tickets for the boots and the shirt were kept at Joseph Jones's shop at 31 Church Street.

house bed. That night John Kelly stayed not at number 55 Flower and Dean Street, but at number 52, while Kate was most likely not among the casuals at Mile End. Not only is there no record of her admission, but Mile End did not share Thavies Inn's lax enforcement of regulations. Had Kate taken a bed there, she would have been detained for two nights in order to pick oakum. Instead she appeared to meet John the following morning at the unfeasibly early hour of 8 a.m. John apparently had been loath to mention that Kate almost certainly slept rough that night, perhaps even in the shed off Dorset Street.* However, in light of the recent murders in Whitechapel, he knew that an admission of this would not have reflected well on him.

The coroner and the jury were naturally skeptical of John Kelly's narrative, but not simply because many of his statements did not add up, but because they, like the police and the press, were convinced that the killer was targeting prostitutes. The testimony of those who knew Kate well did not, however, support the notion that she was in the sex trade. John Kelly, Kate's sister Eliza Gold, Kate's daughter, and even Frederick William Wilkinson, the deputy lodging-house keeper at Cooney's, provided no such evidence. Wilkinson, who claimed a seven-year acquaintance with the couple, stated with certainty that he "never knew or heard of [Kate] being intimate with anyone but Kelly."[7] The coroner also pressed John on this point. He claimed that throughout the time he had been with her, he never knew of her "going out for immoral purposes at night"; neither had she ever "brought [him] money in the morning after being out." He stated categorically that he would never have suffered such a situation.[8]

Unfortunately, while defending Kate's honor, John used a turn of phrase with a double meaning. When he stated his concern over their lack of doss money, he claimed that he didn't want to "have to see her

---

* John's response to the question about the anomaly of Kate's early release from Mile End was reported variously in a number of newspapers. In the account in the *Times* of October 5, it was said that he didn't know what the rules were at Mile End and if she could have discharged herself when she liked. It was also suggested that her early discharge was due to "there being some bother at the casual ward." In truth, John Kelly, as a habitué of London casual wards, would have known very well what was the routine for discharge at Mile End. It is almost certain that he was covering for his own negligence in allowing her to sleep on the streets.

walk about the streets at night." The coroner picked up on this immediately.

"What do you mean by 'walking the streets'?" he asked.

John clarified: "Well Sir, many a time we have not had the money
to pay for our shelter, and have had to tramp about."* "Walking the
streets," as explained by William Booth in his book *Darkest England,*
referred to the rough sleepers' never-ending nocturnal quest for somewhere quiet to rest before a patrolling constable moved them along.
According to Howard Goldsmid, rough sleeping and walking the
streets were a common way of life for those who frequented the lodging
houses on Thrawl Street, Dorset Street, and Flower and Dean Street.
When not lying "on the kerbstone, in the gutters, on heaps of rubbish, anywhere," they could be seen walking "up and down with their
hands in their pockets, and their dull sleepy eyes almost closed."[9] Regrettably, at the inquest, John's answer to the coroner's question about
"walking the streets" did little to dissuade many journalists from per-
sistently identifying Kate as a prostitute. According to the *Telegraph*,
which was echoing the prejudices of its era while also attempting to
tell a more salacious story, homeless women and women who sold sex
were one and the same. The newspaper reported that Kate regularly
bedded down on the street, or in a shed, alongside other "houseless
waifs, penniless prostitutes, like herself..."[10]

Wherever Kate had spent Friday night, she and John Kelly were
back at Cooney's on Saturday morning, making themselves comfortable in the communal kitchen and turning their minds once again to
finding their doss money. Eventually, this question compelled them
out the door and onto the streets. They walked south, in the direction
of Bishopsgate, probably with no particular destination in mind.

By early afternoon they were in the vicinity of Houndsditch, a
street at the center of the Jewish rag-selling trade, whose shop fronts
were usually draped with stained calico petticoats and frayed woolen

---

* *Morning Post*, 5 October 1888; also, the *Times*, 5 October 1888. Like so many statements made
in the course of the inquests, this one too had been transcribed in a variety of ways. John's
statement has also been written as "I mean that if we had no money to pay for our lodgings we
would have to walk about all night."

trousers. As John had pawned his boots the night before, it is possible that Kate had contemplated selling one of the many layers she wore beneath her chintz skirt and black cloth jacket. However, as it was Saturday, the Jewish Sabbath, the couple would have only met with closed shutters.

According to John, Kate then suggested that she would go to Bermondsey and attempt to get money from her daughter. This could not have been a serious proposal. It had been over two years since Kate had last spoken with Annie. She didn't even know her address. Like so much of John's story, the details of what happened here are "muddled" as well.

It's unclear where the couple had spent the afternoon until this point. Houndsditch was only a short walk from Flower and Dean Street, and many drinking establishments stood along the route. As residents of Whitechapel for seven years, Kate and Kelly would have had no shortage of acquaintances and convivial companions, many of whom would have been ready to "stand them a drink," or several, returning similar favors from Kate and John. After a round or so, Kate may have thought that attempting to find Annie somewhere among the streets of South London no longer seemed impossible.

When John and Kate parted, she assured him she would return by four o'clock. According to John, they hadn't a penny between them as he watched her bob down Houndsditch toward Aldgate.

Kate didn't get very far. In fact, she did little more than turn the corner, once or even twice, onto Aldgate High Street, before she encountered someone who undoubtedly owed her a drink or two. Kate was not the sort to refuse, and her resolve, as it often did, disappeared with the contents of her first glass.

∞∞∞

At 8:30 that night, a woman sat in a heap against a wall at 29 Aldgate High Street, paralytic from drink. She babbled and sang and cursed, drawing the inevitable gawkers, some staring with amusement, others with genuine concern. This was hardly an unusual sight in Whitechapel. A passing police constable, Louis Frederick Robinson, seeing the crowd, decided to investigate. He found, at the center of it, a pitiful figure, with a bonnet of black velvet and straw tied to her drooping head. She reeked of alcohol. Robinson asked if any of the spectators knew the woman or where she lived. No one answered, although some present knew precisely who she was and even ran off to tell John Kelly that his "wife" had been collared for drunkenness.

Robinson tried to lift Kate off the street, but her feet, laced up in men's boots, were as shambling as those of a marionette, and she soon slipped sideways out of his hold. Only with the assistance of a colleague, Police Constable George Simmons, was Robinson able to lead the inebriated woman to Bishopsgate Police Station. Following protocol, they needed to record her name in the ledger before putting her in a cell.

"What's your name?" Robinson demanded.

"Nothing," Kate slurred.

They placed "Nothing" in a cell, hoping she would soon sober up. Instead, she slid into a drunken slumber.

At around 9:55 p.m. and then several times after, George Henry Hutt, the jailer at Bishopsgate station, looked in on her. At about a quarter past twelve, Kate woke up and began to sing to herself. This continued for about fifteen minutes, until Hutt came to see her in the cell.

"When are you going to let me out?" she asked him, in a tired, raspy voice.

"When you are capable of taking care of yourself."

"I'm capable of taking care of myself now."

This certainly was not the case. If Kate was entirely incapacitated at 8:30, it was improbable that she was fit and sober by 1 a.m., when Hutt decided to release her. She may have seemed steadier on her feet when she was led from the cell to the station office, but their prisoner was still intoxicated.

"What time is it?" Kate asked the jailer drowsily.

"Too late for you to get any more drink," answered Hutt.

"Well, what time is it?"

"Just on one."

"I shall get a damned fine hiding when I get home," she muttered, knowing this was all for show. [11] When she lived with Thomas Conway, that would have been the truth.

"And serve you right, you have no right to get drunk," taunted Hutt, who, like Kate's sisters and her daughter, would have agreed with the era's thoughts on such a matter: that an errant wife deserved a beating.

Before discharging her, James Byfield, who was manning the desk, once more quizzed her about her name and address. Kate, who had spent the better part of her life attempting to decoy casual ward and workhouse staff by inventing and swapping around names and addresses, knew exactly how to play this game. By this stage in her life, her contempt for authority was second nature.

"Mary Ann Kelly," she lied. She gave her address as "6 Fashion Street" and claimed she had just returned from hop picking, more exaggeration than fib, perhaps. [12]

The police officers then handed her back the contents of her pockets, an assortment of necessities that Kate would have always kept on her person: six pieces of soap and a swatch of flannel, a small comb, a table knife with a white handle, and a metal teaspoon, her tin boxes of tea and sugar, an empty tin matchbox, a piece of red flannel that she used for keeping her pins and needles, a thimble, and a collection of menstrual rags. She refilled her skirts with her other possessions suitable for hawking: an empty red-leather cigarette case, two short black clay pipes, and a ball of hemp.

Once she had assembled herself, Hutt showed her out.

"This way, Missus," he said, pushing open the swing door. Kate followed the passageway to the exit door. Hutt then politely reminded her to "pull the door to" when she left.

"All right," Kate replied. "Good night, Old Cock."

To Hutt's irritation, she pulled the door only partially shut. He watched as she turned left out of the station, toward Houndsditch. [13]

At 1 a.m., Kate's first thought would be to determine the whereabouts of John. As he had been penniless when they parted, she had no reason to believe he would have been able to pay for a bed at Cooney's. At any rate, by that hour the deputy keeper would be ejecting anyone who failed to produce their doss money. She had last seen John around

Houndsditch, and her hazy-headed instinct would have been to return there, to ask those still in the drinking dens if they knew of his whereabouts.*

The streets, with their handful of hissing gaslights, would have been as black as pitch in the earliest hours of September 30. Kate was accustomed to navigating the dark, and she knew the byways and passages of Whitechapel as well as she knew the bottom of a bottle. She had stumbled through them drunk on many a night. Here and there, lights were still burning, guiding her as she circled Houndsditch and wended her way along Duke Street, searching for a familiar face. Although it was late, Whitechapel's streets were never entirely empty. There would always be people about — those like her — the drunk, the dispossessed, and the homeless — as well as the criminal. Some were in search of dark corners; others wandered toward their bed. After about twenty minutes, Kate must have concluded that her search was not likely to yield the answers she was seeking. She was tired and would have reconciled herself to spending another night sleeping rough. By now, for this forty-six-year-old woman, the routine was a familiar one. Kate knew how to sleep beneath the stars, how to find a less-painful way of laying her head against a hard wall, how to ignore the muck that gathered in her skirts or the trickle of wastewater that rolled over her feet.

She found a spot in the far corner of Mitre Square, away from the lamps dropping pools of light. Here, she lowered herself down, her back against the wall, as if it were a chair supporting her. As she did so, the assorted objects in her peddler's pockets must have moved against one another. Among them were several small tin boxes filled with sugar and tea and pawn tickets. For one who carried no mementos of her family, who seemed determined to outrun a painful past and sever all ties, did these little items taunt her? Would the unexpected scent of tin remind her of Wolverhampton or the Old Hall Works or even

---

* In fact, John Kelly was at Cooney's. He had managed to procure four pence for his bed since parting with Kate; when someone told him that Kate had been arrested, he asked Wilkinson for a single bed.

her father? For all of her good humor, her singing and jolliness, Kate's heart must have been sodden with injury.

Kate closed her eyes against the night and reached for whatever respite she could find. Like all those without moorings, who drifted or "walked the streets," she understood that it was only a matter of time before someone came along and moved her on.

On the morning of September 30, a little girl came racing up the stairs to the top floor of 7 Thrawl Street. She banged on the door and called out to her neighbor, "Mrs. Frost," that there was a gentleman to see her on the street and a police inspector with him. Mrs. Frost, who was also known as the widow Eliza Gold and, prior to that, Eliza Eddowes, moaned from her bed. She was very ill and could not get up. She promptly sent the child away.

The girl returned to the men below and reported the message. The police inspector sent her back up the stairs again to implore Mrs. Frost to come down immediately, because the business was urgent. This time, he gave the little girl a message to report: "you must tell her that her sister is dead and she is required to identify the body."

Shaken to the core, Eliza came down to the street. Weak and sick but fully dressed, she was supported by a neighbor and her own son George. Together with the police inspector and John Kelly, they proceeded to the mortuary on Golden Lane.

When the coffin lid was drawn back, Eliza let forth a stream of anguished wails. The intensity of her distress was such that it was necessary to lead her from the room.

It was some time before she could compose herself enough to speak. Eliza claimed that though Kate's face had been disfigured, she recognized her sister's features perfectly well. The killer had not stripped her of that which distinguished her as an Eddowes. She burst into violent sobs once more as she related this to a journalist at the mortuary. "Oh my poor sister," she cried, "that she should come to such an end as this!"

In spite of their financial circumstances, the Eddowes family did not allow Kate to be dropped into a pauper's grave; neither would the

residents of Whitechapel permit her to be laid to rest without a re-
sounding sendoff. Hundreds filled the streets for the funeral procession on September 8. In some places the crowds were so thick that
they slowed the progress of the glass hearse and the mourning carriage
that followed behind it. At Ilford Cemetery, where Kate was interred,
nearly five hundred people gathered to pay their respects. Among
them were members of the Eddowes clan who had not seen one another in years. In removing a family member, sisters, daughters, cousins, and aunts were pulled more tightly together; an act of reunion,
which closed the now empty space at their center.

PART V

MARY JANE

c. 1863

November 9, 1888

MARIE JEANETTE

IN THE EARLY 1880s a gentleman in search of the carnal pleasures on offer in London's West End might find them rather more difficult to come by than in previous years. The Haymarket, once London's whirling circus of vice, had been silenced in the previous decade. The doors to the decadent gilt-and-crimson Argyll Rooms, where wealthy "swells" swallowed champagne and danced until midnight with silk-swathed prostitutes, had been shut. The lights had been extinguished in Piccadilly's "night houses," the after-hours venues where the "fast set" and their "frail companions" repaired for cigars, food, and drink. Gone were the accommodation houses, where they might seek a convenient room afterward. Even the brothels, decorated with mirrors and damask, were shuttered. As a result, vice was forced to become fashionably discreet.

Wealthy gentlemen, especially those favored by the well-dressed prostitutes living in St. John's Wood, Brompton, or Pimlico, might be fortunate enough to receive an invitation to a private ball. A set of function rooms would be hired at a venue somewhere between Oxford Street and Marylebone for a group of about eighty guests: forty men and forty women. Each male guest would pay for a woman's admission, which then covered the cost of the venue, the band, and the supper. To the casual observer, this gathering of gentlemen in top hats and evening dress, and beautiful young women in ball gowns and jewels, hinted at nothing untoward. As the sexual adventurer known only as "Walter" recorded in his memoirs, there was little that could be described as "immodest" or irregular about the occasion, with the exception that "no introductions were needed, and men asked any woman to dance . . . and women did not hesitate to ask men to dance . . ." However, following supper, the tone changed: "the dancing became romping, and concupiscence asserted itself . . . Suggestive talk was now the order of the night, bawdy words escaped, the men kissed the women's shoulders as they waltzed, one or two couples danced polkas with their bellies jogging against each other, suggestive of fucking."[1] Eventually the evening came to an end; couples peeled off and departed in their carriages, to continue their revels in private, at the women's lodgings in the leafy suburbs.

It was into scenes like this that a woman calling herself Mary Jane Kelly arrived at some point in 1883 or 1884. The stories she told about herself likely contained some truth and some fiction, but no one has ever been able to ascertain which parts were which. She may have borrowed aspects of her identity from someone she knew, or reinvented herself altogether, a phenomenon that was fairly common for women of her profession.

According to one version of her tale, Mary Jane was born in Limerick around 1863. Her father, a man thought to have been called John Kelly, took the family across the Irish Sea to Wales when she was very young and settled for a time either in Caernarvonshire or Carmarthen, where he was employed as the foreman of an ironworks. She claimed to have been one of nine children: six brothers who appear to have been younger and still living at home in 1888, and one named Henry, who, strangely, was called John or "Johnto" and served in the 2nd Battalion of the Scots Guard. Mary Jane also had a sister, who she said was "very fond of her" and led a respectable life traveling "from marketplace to marketplace" with her aunt. Mary Jane claimed that at the age of sixteen, she had married a coal miner (or collier) named Davis or Davies who died in an explosion a year or two later. Following his death, she went to Cardiff, where she had family. While there, she spent "eight or nine months in the infirmary" and then fell in with a cousin "who followed a bad life." Without admitting to it directly, she implied that this relative drew her into a life of prostitution. At some time around 1884, if not slightly earlier, she came to London "and lived in a gay house in the West End of the town."[2]

Mary Jane's story, as she presented it to her erstwhile lover, Joseph Barnett, amounts to nothing more than a collection of disconnected snapshots. To others who knew her, Mary Jane offered slightly different versions of this tale. To one, she claimed that "she was Welsh, and that her parents, who had discarded her, still resided at Cardiff." She stated that it was from there that she had come directly to London. "There is every reason to believe that she is Welsh, and that her parents or relatives reside in Cardiff," reported another. Intriguingly, this source went on to say that Mary Jane arrived in London as early as 1882 or 1883 and came from a "well-to-do" set in Cardiff. She was described as "an excellent scholar and an artist of no mean degree."[3] Two other individuals, her landlord and a city missionary, claimed that Mary Jane had told them she was Irish and that she received letters from her mother, who still resided in Ireland.[4] To confuse matters further, a neighbor stated that Mary Jane frequently spoke to her about her family and friends and that "she had a female relation in London who was on the stage." Mary Jane told other people that she had a two-year-old child, who would have been born around 1883.[5]

Not a single statement made by Mary Jane about her life prior to her arrival in London has ever been verified. In 1888, inquiries were made both in Limerick and in Wales, to no avail. The search for a brother in the Scots Guard also yielded nothing. As news of her murder spread across the UK and around the globe, not one friend or relation from the past appeared to recognize Mary Jane Kelly's name or any part of her history enough to have come forward. In subsequent decades, attempts to research her history have proven equally fruitless; no Kellys or Davieses or Mary Janes match up in censuses or parish records in Wales or in Ireland. The only likely conclusion is that the tale of Mary Jane Kelly's life, including her name, was entirely fabricated.

In the nineteenth century creating a new identity for oneself was relatively straightforward. A move to another town or even to another district and a change of moniker was easy enough. Inventing a new persona based on a manufactured history, an alteration in dress and manners, allowed many to pass successfully through different social strata, either above or below them. However, a higher quality of education and the indelible mark that it left on a person was far more difficult to either falsify or hide. An individual's schooling came across not only in their ability to read or write, but in their speech, their bearing, their interests, and often in their artistic or musical accomplishments. While the poor had access only to the most basic instruction, the rising middle classes sought to distinguish themselves socially by investing in the education of their children so that their progeny might bear the stamp of respectability.

According to those who knew her, this distinction seems to have made itself apparent in Mary Jane, who it was said came "from a well-to-do family." One of her landladies remarked on her high level of "scholarship" while also commenting that she was a capable artist. This statement was made at a time when training in drawing was given to girls at fashionable young ladies' schools, and did not feature in the average school curriculum.* A girl from a large, impoverished rural family would have had no access to instruction in such skills, or the money to purchase the materials, nor would she have been likely to receive the encouragement necessary for becoming an artist. More interesting still, no one who knew Mary Jane noted any regional accent, and those who inquired about her origins had to be told she was Welsh or Irish. If Wales or Ireland had once flavored her speech, its traces were not readily discernible, possibly owing to elocution lessons. "You would not have supposed if you had met her on the street that she belonged to the miserable class as she did," remarked a missionary who knew her in Whitechapel; "she was always neatly and decently dressed, and looked quite nice and respectable."[6] Mary Jane may have been telling the truth when she claimed to Joe Barnett that her father was a "gaf-

---

* In contrast to these comments, some have questioned whether Mary Jane was even literate. Numerous newspapers paraphrased and misquoted Joseph Barnett's inquest statement about "reading newspapers to her." The definitive version of his statement, as it appears in the official Coroner's Inquest document, reads, "she had on several occasions asked me to read about the murders."

fer," one in a position of authority at the ironworks. It is possible that Barnett mistook her meaning and that Mary Jane's father was in fact the owner of the business or played some role in its management. This certainly would have placed her in an altogether different social class.

Although Mary Jane insisted that she had been legally married at sixteen to a miner named Davies or Davis, no record has ever been found to confirm this. If she had indeed become romantically entangled with a man, it was more likely as his mistress or common-law wife. This too may accord with the suggestion that Mary Jane bore a child around 1883, roughly at about the time it is said that she spent eight to nine months "in an infirmary" in Cardiff. Like everything in Mary Jane's narrative, this too is questionable. No trace has been found of the birth of a child, nor is there any indication as to its fate. Such an extended stay at a publicly funded general hospital in the 1880s was highly unusual; it is more probable that Mary Jane stayed at a private institution, perhaps a reformatory for "fallen women" or an asylum. A middle-class family might consider either option appropriate for a daughter who had transgressed social norms by engaging in sex outside marriage.

At the time, Cardiff had at least two refuges for fallen women: the Protestant House of Mercy and the Catholic Convent of the Good Shepherd. Both took in young women in their teens and twenties from the lower classes. On occasion, middle-class girls participated in their rehabilitation programs, which mainly consisted of religious instruction and training in domestic skills and needlework. However, some middle-class families regarded sexual behavior outside marriage as evidence of a mental disorder, to be dealt with by trained doctors. At this period Cardiff did not have its own mental hospital but instead sent its patients to the United Counties Lunatic Asylum in Carmarthen, a town where Mary Jane also claims to have spent part of her life.

Although the precise chronology of this period is cloudy, Mary Jane appears to have told Joseph Barnett that it was following her stay in the "infirmary" that she fell in with her badly behaved cousin. Both asylums and refuges for fallen women often failed to rehabilitate their inmates, making Mary Jane's claim sound feasible. Unfortunately, Joe Barnett never elaborated upon what Mary Jane meant by her cousin's "bad life." Was she part of a sporty "fast set"? Was she a prostitute or a man's mistress? Was she a madam? And was she the connection that facilitated Mary Jane's move to London?

Of all of the holes in Mary Jane's account, none is so gaping as that which explains how or why she left Cardiff for a "gay house" in the West End of London. Travel or a change of residence to another city or town was not something a single woman embarked upon haphazardly in the nineteenth century. London, though linked by rail to Cardiff, was still a considerable distance from Wales, both physically and culturally. Generally, an unmarried young woman came alone to London for only two possible reasons: a job had been arranged for her or someone connected to her through social or family ties lived in the city. Either or both of these possibilities must have guided Mary Jane to the capital; otherwise, as a newcomer, it would have been difficult to negotiate immediate entry into the middle to upper ranks of the sex trade. Personal contacts in a new and confusing city would have been just as essential to women in the higher end of the sex trade as they would be to anyone in "respectable" society wishing to be introduced to the right circle. An acquaintance may have given Mary Jane the name of a "landlady" who offered women introductions to gentlemen. Alternatively, she may have arrived with a lover from Cardiff or with the intention of joining one in London.

By the last quarter of the nineteenth century, it was no longer common for prostitutes to live where they practiced their trade. Those who walked the pavements of Piccadilly, the Haymarket, and Regent Street tended to make their homes in the outlying parts of the capital. For poorer women this was frequently the East End, while those who catered to the middle classes and above often opted for locations such as Chelsea, Pimlico, St. John's Wood, and certain streets in Knightsbridge and Brompton, where Mary Jane Kelly took lodgings.

Since the middle of the century, the little streets extending from Knightsbridge Barracks to Brompton Road, as far west as Brompton Square, had acquired a reputation as a haven for army officers' mistresses, actresses, and the artistic set — those who indulged in sin discreetly behind shutters and dark velvet drapery. In 1881, the oblong Brompton Square, with its green center, appears to have been the favored address of a number of female heads of household describing themselves as "lodging house keepers."* Number 15, inhabited by two "actresses," was a house owned by Mary Jefferies, one of the most formidable madams of the Victorian age; she catered to aristocrats, politicians, wealthy capitalists, and at least one member of the royal family. This was only one of the procuress's many properties in Brompton and Chelsea; her network of residences and women extended across west and north London. Jefferies operated her business from a safe distance, like a puppet mistress, arranging for her "girls" to meet clients by appointment at various locations, thereby keeping her own hands clean. Although the "French woman" with whom Mary Jane came to reside was unlikely to have possessed such an empire, she probably ran her concern in a similar manner: her "boarders" were offered opportunities to make the acquaintance of gentlemen.

Procuresses who ran middling to upmarket businesses facilitated introductions to men, but by the latter part of the century, clients did not necessarily come to their premises in search of women. In some cases assignations were arranged through an exchange of letters or a conversation, while others occurred by chance meeting. On one occasion "Walter" gained an introduction to a discreet Marylebone brothel disguised as a shop by exchanging glances with its madam while on a train. After he struck up a conversation, she informed him that she was a dressmaker and employed only the prettiest girls at her place of business. Before disembarking she handed him a card and invited him "to call and try on her gloves." Walter was certain that she drummed up a good amount of trade by approaching men in railway carriages and other forms of public transportation.[7] One of Mrs. Jefferies's methods of exciting interest in her latest recruits was to drive to the Guards Club in her landau and distribute personal invitations to meet her young la-

* http://Booth.lse.ac.uk Booth/B/362, Arthur L. Baxter's notebook: Police District 27, Brompton. In mapping areas of wealth, deprivation, and crime in the 1890s, Arthur Baxter, one of Charles Booth's inspectors, mentioned that Beauchamp Place, located across the Brompton Road from the square, was noted for its "respectable knocking shops." Many of the buildings were inhabited by prostitutes who worked in Piccadilly and brought their clients home. Nearby Pelham Place was also noted for its "colony of foreign prostitutes." Baxter commented that on the whole, the prostitutes in this area were of a higher caliber and mostly solicited in the West End.

dies. Officers in the most elite regiments, from wealthy and titled families who had money to spend and time to kill while in barracks, were notably good customers. When considering Mary Jane's proximity to the Knightsbridge barracks and the area's association with regimental mistresses, a number of such men may have been among her clientele, perhaps including the Henry or "Johnto" she mentioned, who was in the 2nd Battalion of the Scots Guard. "Johnto" may not have been her brother at all, but rather an officer and a former lover with whom she maintained a correspondence when his postings took him abroad.*

The men who sought the company of women like Mary Jane through a procuress would expect to commit to an evening of entertainment in addition to receiving sex. Walter's dressmaker-madam introduced him to a young woman working in her shop called Sophy, whom he met formally in an adjoining house. The madam informed him that he would not be having sex with her on the premises; rather, he was to pay the madam five pounds up front and then take Sophy to dinner the following night. Five or six years earlier, men like Walter might have met someone like Sophy or Mary Jane at the Argyll Rooms before taking them to an accommodation house, but now, evenings often began at venues like St. James's Restaurant, known as "Jimmy's," at 69 Regent Street or at the Café de l'Europe on the Haymarket. Here, women and their male companions sat down to dine in smoke-filled, mirrored, and palm-fronded rooms and were tended by French and Italian waiters known for their discretion. After gorging on oysters, deviled kidneys, and roast beef and washing it all down with bottomless glasses of champagne, Moselle, and hock, the couple would travel

---

* Despite extensive research into the names of those serving in the Scots Guards, no one has turned up a Henry or John or Johnto Kelly among the enlisted privates. In spite of inquiries, no one from the Scots Guard came forward in response to the description of Mary Jane Kelly in 1888 either. If Mary Jane's story as told to Joseph Barnett is to be believed, the likelihood of a poor, working-class boy based in rural Wales joining a London-based Scottish regiment is remote. The 2nd Scots Guard was based at Westminster barracks during the second half of the 1880s, with periods spent abroad in Egypt, the Sudan, and Dublin. It is more likely that Mary Jane met an officer from the regiment through her professional connections, and this man may have acquired a fondness for her. Referring to former lovers with whom one still maintained contact as "brothers" or "cousins," in order to disguise an intimate history from a new lover, was a ruse commonly employed by women in the sex trade.

by hackney cab or in the gentleman's carriage to an equally discreet hotel, or back to the woman's lodgings. Such assignations might not end the next morning, nor did they have to begin at a restaurant. A trip to the theater, the music hall, the races, or any number of other destinations might be involved, until the gentleman exhausted himself sexually, grew tired of the woman's company, or found that duty called him elsewhere. In exchange for the pleasure of her company, he expected to be billed accordingly. The "price" for her company generally included the purchase of "trinkets" as well as cash. In addition to the "five pounds up front" demanded by Walter's dressmaker-madam, Sophy also managed to negotiate "three sovereigns and a new dress" as compensation for the night's activities.

Arranged meetings were only one method by which those in the sex trade did business. Women of all ranks made themselves accessible to potential clients through public display. This included appearing in the promenades and galleries of certain music halls and theaters, as well as streetwalking. In the years that followed the closure of the Argyll Rooms, the West End's smartly dressed prostitutes and their louche companions decamped to the Alhambra Theatre in Leicester Square. One social explorer, Daniel Joseph Kirwan, described the scene on a night in 1878, as he moved beyond a group of "young ladies smoking cigarettes" and entered the promenade. This he found "choked with men and women, walking past each other, looking at the stage, drinking at the bars, chafing each other in a rough way, and laughing loudly."[8] He was surprised to discover that the men seemed "of a good class," while the women were "cheerful, pleasant-looking girls, of quite fair breeding, and of a far better taste in their dress than the honest wives and sweethearts of the mechanics and shopkeepers, who sit in the place of virtue, within the painted railing."[9] However, the Alhambra catered to all ranks of prostitute, and on that night, a police sergeant estimated there to be "at least 1,200 women of the town" present. Upon ascending into the gallery, Kirwan noticed that the mood changed, that "the clamour and the smoke made the place unbearable," and that there was "not the slightest disguise in the conduct of the females." Worse still was the gallery above that one, where "the riffraff collected"; encountering this sight prompted him to remark that "when a woman goes to the sixpenny gallery in the Alhambra she is indeed lost beyond all hope of rescue."[10]

When not passing an evening in the Alhambra or venues like it, West End prostitutes of the middle ranks also sought custom through street solicitation. The Haymarket, Regent Street, Piccadilly, and the smaller streets that flowed from them into Leicester Square and Soho formed the parade ground along which women devised their individual circuits. A slow, meandering progress might begin at Piccadilly Circus and proceed up Regent Street, where a woman would take her time gazing at the shop windows, seeming to admire the hats, china, or toys on display while cautiously glancing to either side, to note whether the male passerby who slowed his gait and joined her was a genuine shopper, a potential john, or a police constable. If she had no luck, she might cross the road and proceed southward, perhaps stopping at the Café de l'Europe, where she might meet the eye of a gentleman and his friends. Failing this, her course would perhaps take her eastward down Coventry Street to Leicester Square, to stop in at the Alhambra. Somewhere along this route, at least once that night, a man would step close to her and tip his hat. He may have noticed that she raised the hem of her skirt an inch or so too high as she crossed the road and stepped onto the curb; however, as the busy West End was also filled with respectable shop girls leaving their places of employment for home and maids out on errands for their mistresses, he had to be careful. Even the seasoned philanderer "Walter" commented that he often found it difficult to differentiate between a prostitute and "a virtuous girl." One he followed all the way from Bond Street to Piccadilly, uncertain of whether to approach her, because "she was so neatly dressed like a superior servant, that I couldn't conclude if she were gay or not . . . she seemed to look at no one when stopping and looking at shops. When she did, I also stopped and looked, standing by the side of her."

In this quarter of London, it was obligatory for a potential client to make the first approach and for the woman to respond, either with flirtatious feigned horror or acceptance. Eventually, Walter leaned in toward the young woman and spoke to her.

May I go home with you?
    She looked at me as if half astonished, then after hesitation, *Yes,
but I live three miles off —*
    Let us get into a cab —
    Oh no, I can't take you home.

The situation was remedied when Walter hailed a cab and then found them "a snug accommodation house" ten minutes away.[11]

While the area around Piccadilly and Leicester Square formed the semi-respectable, high-class heart of the city's sex trade, prostitution was present in most parts of the metropolis, and in other corners of the West End. In the early 1880s, the area between the Strand and Charing Cross station was still a haunt for streetwalkers, as it had been for well over a century; other West End streets, such as Brewer Street and Lisle Street, just to the north of Leicester Square, became noted for older and cheaper women.[12] Prostitution had also begun to move nearer to train stations, into areas with transient populations, hotels, and lodging houses, such as Euston and Victoria. However, Mary Jane, a young woman in her early twenties and at the height of her career, would have found no obstacle to making a good living in the center of town, at the top end of the sex trade. With a fashionably stout, five-feet-seven-inch figure, blue eyes, and long luxuriant hair, she possessed physical attractions that allowed her "to drive about in a carriage" and "lead the life of a lady." She referred to herself as Marie Jeanette and accumulated "numerous dresses of a costly description." Those who gathered at the Alhambra, at the Café de l'Europe, and at Jimmy's would have undoubtedly known her well.

Mary Jane would be accustomed to well-dressed gentlemen making her offers and promises — to entertain her at the races, to buy her gloves and jewelry, to spoil her with fine food and drink. The savviest women in the sex trade understood that their youthful allure was fleeting and that in order to capitalize on their worth it was essential to seize every opportunity put before them. So when "a gentleman" offered to take Mary Jane to Paris, she agreed.

Like everything that Mary Jane Kelly recounted to Joseph Barnett about her past, the circumstances surrounding this particular proposal, the name of the gentleman involved, or any other detail concerning the trip was not revealed. How she came to know this man and whether he was a client or a serious romantic prospect or an acquaintance or someone who came to her with a business offer are unknown. However, what is certain is that the visit to Paris was not what it appeared to be on the surface. Mary Jane's French landlady-procuress may have played a role in what transpired. At this time, international travelers sent their luggage separately to their intended destination, so Mary Jane packed most of her expensive wardrobe in a trunk; evidently she expected her madam to forward it to her address in Paris. The trunk was never sent, and perhaps its absence was the first thing that alerted Mary Jane to the possibility that she had been deceived.

By the last quarter of the nineteenth century, the trafficking of women between Britain and continental Europe had become a lucrative enterprise. The expansion of rail networks and shipping made it cheaper and easier for people to travel and goods to be shipped. It also allowed those "goods" to reach a wider range of markets and cater to particular tastes. Just as London became a receiving hub for young women from France, Belgium, and Germany, English girls were procured and shipped out to brothels in these and other countries. A former trafficker, in an interview with the newspaper editor W. T. Stead, estimated at least 250 British women were sent to Belgium and northern France in 1884 alone. Of those, two-thirds were abducted after accepting a position in service abroad or a sham proposal of marriage.[13] Often, they were plied with drink or doped, given false travel documents, and bundled onto a train.

In 1879, Adelene Tanner, a recently unemployed domestic, was horrified to find herself in this position. It had all begun innocently enough when John Sallecartes, a "respectably dressed man" with a foreign accent, struck up a conversation with her in a railway waiting room.[14] By chance, Adelene encountered "Sullie" again and on this occasion agreed to join him for a drink at a hotel in Soho. A more experienced young woman, someone like Mary Jane, who knew the sex trade, would have immediately sensed what was happening, but nineteen-year-old Adelene was a virgin, and a sheltered one. Sullie saw to it that the girl's glass of wine was regularly refilled and soon "she could scarcely remember what [she] said." He also took the opportunity to introduce her to his business partner, a handsome Belgian called Frederick Schultz, who, like Sallecartes, was a *placeur,* or recruiter for continental brothels. With the room spinning, Adelene was then presented to the man who would be her pimp. This was Édouard Roger, a Frenchman, who after a short conversation told her that he had "taken a great fancy to [her]; that he would like to take her to Paris, and if after seeing his grand house, carriages &c. [she] would like to be his wife, he would marry [her]."[15] The intoxicated, bedazzled servant enthusiastically agreed. Of course, Adelene, along with two other young women tricked by Sullie and Schultz, was not destined for Paris, but for Brussels and the locked rooms of a *maison close,* a state-sanctioned brothel. Before departing England, all three were issued false identities. Upon arrival in Belgium, they were warned that they had just participated in an illegal activity, and if they ever attempted to flee Roger's house, they would be arrested immediately.

It has been suggested that out of all of those duped into foreign prostitution, at least one in three women who agreed to go abroad was already working in the sex trade and "anxious for a change." W. T. Stead, in an 1885 series of articles, "The Maiden Tribute of Modern Babylon," explored the murky world of the trade in women and underage girls. He recounted the story of "Amelia Powell," who found herself transported from London to a brothel in Bordeaux. While never openly admitting to it, Amelia insinuated that she had worked as a prostitute after leaving her husband placed her "on the verge of destitution." She claimed that "a friend in an honest position" was eager to introduce her "to a certain Greek" who ran a cigar shop on Regent Street. This man promised that he could get Amelia and three other women "excellent situations" in Bordeaux. It did not take much persuading to get her to go. Amelia explained why: "I grasped the suggestion . . . as affording the means of escaping from the associations and sufferings with which I was so painfully familiar in London."[16] However, they were not long in Bordeaux before the reality of their "excellent situations" was made clear to them. According to Amelia, once inside the *maison close,* "our clothes were taken away, and we were tricked out with silk dresses and other finery" as a way of forcing a debt on them and making it impossible for them to leave without being accused of theft. Amelia was told that she owed her madam eighteen hundred francs, both for the clothing she was compelled to wear and "the cost of the commission for being brought over." She was instructed that once she had paid down this sum by entertaining gentlemen, she might be free to leave, but she soon learned that this too was impossible: "When the account shows that you have only four or five hundred francs against you, the mistress sets to work to induce you, by cozening, cajoling, or absolute fraud, to accept other articles of clothing. Thus you go on month after month."[17]

Such ruses had been common practice in brothels for centuries and were just as likely to catch seasoned sex laborers off guard as they were to entrap the novice. Those involved in international sex trafficking worked discreetly and in advance, plotting out their maneuvers, so that a woman destined for overseas trade would not guess what awaited her. It is probable that Mary Jane's French landlady had some role in sending her to Paris and colluded with "the gentleman" to place her in a brothel there. Whatever the case, she seemed certain enough that Marie Jeanette would have no need for her trunk of pretty gowns when she arrived at the *maison close*.

Once inside, life within these houses was tightly regulated. To keep the streets free of the nuisance of prostitution, the law restricted the women's movements in and out of a *maison close*. They were permitted in public only during certain hours and even then were not allowed to congregate in groups, loiter near the door, or even make themselves visible through the window; a brothel's windows had to remain shuttered. Additionally, all new recruits were expected to register with the Police de Moeurs (the regulating authority) and submit to twice-weekly examinations for venereal disease. If indebtedness to the brothel was not enough to break the will of a trafficked woman, the strict code governing her personal freedom would have done that on its own. Once caught within the rigid jaws of a foreign *maison close,* a woman, with no friends and unable to communicate in French, had little hope of escape.

Mary Jane must have sensed this. She later explained the situation to Joe Barnett by telling him that she had gone to Paris, but since she "did not like the part," she did not stay. Barnett seemed to indicate that by "part," she meant "the purpose" of her journey there. She returned after no more than a fortnight. How she managed to wriggle free from the snare is another mystery altogether. As Sallecartes mentioned in his interview with Stead, it was not unusual for girls to "have their suspicions aroused" and "take alarm" after they arrived abroad. If Mary Jane was as well educated as has been suggested, she would have had at least a basic grasp of French, which perhaps gave her an advantage. A madam knew that if one of her "human parcels," as they were called, was able to communicate with the police, she could pose a real threat. However, even after the captive had been delivered to her destination, dangers for the traders and the brothel keepers remained. According to statute, anyone (and often it was an amenable customer of the *maison close*) who suspected illegal trafficking might appeal to the Police de Moeurs, who were "bound by law to release any English girl detained in a brothel against her will, even if she has not paid her debt."[18] Setbacks such as these were not taken lightly by the traffickers or the brothel, both of whom would be out of pocket when a girl was released. Perhaps more troubling to them still, there would be a young woman at large who could attest to their crimes.

As Stead was keen to point out, international slave traders were not people with whom to trifle. These rings were managed by extremely dangerous men, mostly "ex-convicts, who know too well the discomforts of the *maison correctionelle*." They would feel no compunction at "removing an inconvenient witness" in order to escape another conviction.[19] Although Mary Jane had not intended to do so, by fleeing her captors she had made some fearsome enemies. Although she managed to outrun them in Paris, she would never again find life easy in London.

THE GAY LIFE

DURING THE SUMMER months, ships from the northern French port of Boulogne, carrying travelers from Paris, landed at St. Katherine's Wharf, beside the Tower of London. Disembarking passengers coming down the gangway were more likely to turn west toward the center of the city, rather than cross the road and turn east. Just beyond the confusion of the docks — the piles of luggage and cargo, the blasts of steam, and the smell of ship's tar — rattled the constant traffic of the Ratcliff Highway. At first sight, the road seemed a bustling center of maritime business, stuffed with marts offering ship utensils, lamp depots, seamen's outfitters, and a few dingy gin palaces. But farther along the thoroughfare, the area's true character became obvious. Cheap lodging houses replaced the shops of ship chandlers; beer houses nestled beside pubs and music halls, thrumming with the sounds of sin.

The Ratcliff Highway was as much a neighborhood as it was a road, bearing its own identity and an economy fueled largely by the steady influx of ships and sailors who stalked its streets in search of drink and sex. At the end of the century it still retained the reputation for violence it had acquired in 1811 when seven people were murdered in their beds in one of England's first serial killings. In spite of the blazing gaslights and the bouncy polka melodies, the Ratcliff Highway was a dark and miserable place. The smashing of glass and of jaws, the spilling of drink and of blood, occurred regularly among the multilingual customers who filled the music halls and drinking cellars. Late into the night, as merrymakers stumbled about in search of unlicensed pubs and opium dens, the highway and the surrounding streets echoed with shrieking, arguing, singing, and copulating.

Mary Jane Kelly certainly did not intend that her life should take her to the Ratcliff Highway, but the situation in which she had found herself left her little choice. Had it been safe to return to the West End, she might have continued to do business in her former manner. Prostitutes at the middle to upper end of the trade did not work in isolation; they would have acquired networks of friends and knowledge of other landlady-procuresses whom they could contact when in need of a new situation. It was also not uncommon for such women, in a pinch, to call upon good clients or former lovers for assistance. Mary Jane would have had a number of people to whom she might have turned and easily resumed her place in the promenade of the Alhambra and the dining room of the Café de l'Europe, had she believed there was no risk of being discovered there by someone who might harm her. Instead, she chose to turn east from St. Katherine's Dock, for the Ratcliff Highway.

Little more than a ten-minute walk from the dock stood 79 Pennington Street, on the corner of Breezer's Hill. Until 1874, the soot-covered brick building, which faced onto warehouses, had been the Red Lion public house. Only recently converted into a home, in 1885 it was inhabited by the Millers, a German family of tailors, and a Dutch couple, Eliesbeth Boekü and Johannes Morgenstern, and their twin infant daughters.

Mrs. Boekü, as she called herself, had been born in the Netherlands as Eliesbeth Bluma, the daughter of a sugar-baking family who appear to have immigrated and settled on Pennington Street during her youth. Eventually, Eliesbeth married a man from the Dutch community, Louis Boekü, who claimed to be a gas fitter. However, rather mysteriously for one earning a laborer's wage, Mr. Boekü began to acquire property. By 1880, if not earlier, 79 Pennington Street came into his possession. Boekü apparently rented the former Red Lion to the Millers, who, under his authority, took to subletting rooms to prostitutes. This was not an uncommon practice; rents could be easily collected by simply turning a blind eye to the activities of one's tenants. While the Millers tended to his dirty work, Louis Boekü was content to live elsewhere, with his wife and family. However, following his death in 1882, Eliesbeth decided to take control of her husband's investment and, along with her new common-law partner, Johannes Morgenstern, moved into 79 Pennington Street, upstairs from the Millers.

When Mrs. Boekü and Morgenstern assumed residence in the former Red Lion, it would have been with a view to making a career from the sex trade. Seventy-nine Pennington Street was likely to have been only one of several similar properties that Louis Boekü had acquired for this purpose. Interestingly, at about the same time that Eliesbeth and Johannes moved to Pennington Street, Johannes's brother, Adrianus Morgenstern, moved to a property in Poplar with a woman named Elizabeth Felix. According to Adrianus's descendant, this house was also used as a brothel.[1] While Mrs. Boekü was evidently a determined entrepreneur, it was only with the assistance of the Morgensterns that this endeavor truly became a family enterprise.

While the Boekü-Morgensterns occupied at least one of the upstairs rooms at number 79, the former pub had several more to rent. In 1881, three young women — Mary Beemer and Ada King, both twenty-one, and twenty-year-old Emily Challis — were living there. According to the census, they were engaged in entertaining two visiting sailors at the time the enumerator called. When Mary Jane, a pretty twenty-two-year-old "gay girl," turned up at the door, she was just the sort of lodger that Mrs. Boekü would have been seeking. It is unknown how much of her past she revealed to her new madam, but if the name Kelly was not her real one, then it is likely she adopted it at this point. Upon her return from France, Mary Jane did not wish to be found and if her pursuers were hunting for a Welsh woman, then it would have behooved her to have become Irish by assuming one of the country's most ubiquitous surnames and slipping into anonymity.

If Mary Jane had arrived at 79 Pennington Street penniless, Mrs. Boekü could be assured that she would soon earn the price of her rent, though the establishments, the clientele, and even the practices along the Ratcliff Highway were somewhat different from those of Picca-dilly. "Ratcliff and Wapping have ways of their own," wrote the social reformer Edward W. Thomas, "and in no particular could this be bet-ter illustrated than in the conduct of the sailors and the women . . ."[2] During a visit to the area, Thomas observed that a certain protocol existed among prostitutes when it came to recruiting customers. The women and their pimps and procuresses kept abreast of when the ves-sels were due into port, and "when a ship arrives in the docks, so many of the women as are disengaged go down to the entrance, and there and then endeavor to inveigle the seamen . . ." These attachments would become binding for the duration of a sailor's time ashore. Ac-cording to Thomas, mariners had a custom of selecting their "partic-ular girl," and the Ratcliff Highway sex trade used this fully to its ad-vantage. A sailor's chosen "girl" would then "accompany him hither and thither, always in the neighbourhood, carousing by night . . . and sleeping by day" with her in her bed. During this time, should his in-terest wane, "he is fought for by his paramour, as long as his money remains unexhausted."[3] When his purse was empty or his shore leave had ended, there was always the next shipload of seamen or the usual methods of trade to fall back on: streetwalking and attracting business in one of the many public houses, gin palaces, or music halls.

As moralists noted, women from the Ratcliff Highway seemed to tout for trade more brazenly than those in the West End and other parts of the city. Given that the demand for commercial sex quite liter-ally swelled with the tide, the police found it difficult to regulate pros-titution and restrain the proliferation of brothels there. "Gay women" walked the streets openly, without much fear of the authorities. Thomas observed that "not a bonnet or head-dress of any kind . . . nor indeed any superfluous clothing," even on the coolest nights, could be seen as these women passed by for an evening stroll.[4] He further re-marked that "many of them were remarkably well-clothed," though their low-necked gowns, which "were equally limited in length," and their "jewelry of a cheap and flashy kind" made them "very conspicu-ous."

The better sort of "gay women," those who were young, or at least bore a youthful appearance, could be found in the public singing-rooms. To draw in seafaring custom, most of these smoke-filled drinking dens were decorated with a nautical theme, their walls daubed with crude seascapes, anchors, and mermaids. Dancers with rouged faces, dressed in diaphanous material, performed amid wooden waves, while singers melodramatically reminisced about lovely lasses left on shore. With the exception of the women and a few locals, most of the audience spoke Swedish, Danish, German, Portuguese, Spanish, or French, and didn't understand a word of what was being sung. Still, they were happy to slump on the wooden benches, quaff the bar dry, and fondle their girls until a fight broke out.

As in the more expensive West End, an evening's entertainment along the Ratcliff Highway revolved around drink. However, the savvy women in the sex trade tippled with care. Unfamiliar customers, whether sailors or swells, could be dangerous. To fill one with a bottle of champagne or several glasses of gin was like placing a bullet in one of the chambers of a gun and spinning it. A woman could never predict what sort of john he would be once intoxicated (or even while sober). If she was fortunate, he might slip into a stupor; if she was less so, he might beat her senseless. Her best defense was to remain clearheaded, which could prove difficult if her customer constantly refilled her glass. One of the era's ladies of pleasure wrote that when she was with a client, "It was seldom necessary to drink." She would only "touch the glass to the lips" before discreetly depositing the contents elsewhere.[5] However, drink also offered a convenient escape from a miserable existence. It dulled the fear of unwanted pregnancy and disease, a very real possibility in every penetrative encounter. It obliterated the horrors of intimacy with a man who was physically repellent, and it quieted, even for a short time, feelings of self-loathing, guilt, and pain, and traumatic memories of violence. Mary Jane Kelly was likely to have drunk throughout her career in the sex trade, but after her return from France, this habit seems to have grown into a bad one. Mrs. Boekü's "sister-in-law," Elizabeth Felix (or Mrs. Phoenix, as she was erroneously called in the papers), observed Mary Jane's behavior firsthand. She was "one of the most decent and nicest girls [you could meet] when sober," Felix stated, but became "very quarrelsome and

abusive when intoxicated."⁶ Even for a family like the Boekü-Morgensterns, who would be accustomed to such conduct among many of
their soul-dead, disillusioned boarders, Mary Jane's "indulgence in in-
toxicants" had started to make her "an unwelcome friend."⁷ Eventually,
either Mary Jane herself or her landlords decided it was time for her to
leave. However, when she did go, it wasn't very far.

Next door to the former Red Lion was 1 Breezer's Hill, a boarding
house that belonged to Mrs. Rose Mary (or Mary Rose) McCarthy and
her husband, John. The McCarthys' establishment, like 79 Pennington Street, provided beds for women like Mary Jane and their guests.*
They were also running an unlicensed public house on the premises,
which not only sold alcohol unlawfully, but used prostitutes to inveigle
"sailors and other unwary persons into these places," where they were
then robbed.⁸ Whether Mary Jane was involved in these activities is
unknown, but presumably in such an environment, the McCarthys
were not as concerned about her angry drunken antics, so long as she
was capable of paying her rent.

Whether Mary Jane was able to comfortably discharge her debts
to landlords and landladies is questionable, particularly where the
Boekü-Morgensterns were concerned. Mrs. Felix recalled an incident
that she claimed occurred shortly after Mary Jane arrived at 79 Pennington Street. Whether it was because Mary Jane was in desperate
need of funds or because Mrs. Boekü had convinced her she had nothing to fear, the two women decided they would attempt to reclaim
Mary Jane's trunk of expensive dresses from her former landlady in
Knightsbridge. Although undoubtedly eager to have her possessions
once again, Mary Jane could not have felt easy about returning to a
part of London where she was known. In an attempt to reassure her
boarder and perhaps demonstrate to the French madam that Mary
Jane was now under the protection of the Morgensterns, Mrs. Boekü
traveled with her across town on this errand. It was likely to have been

---

* The census enumerator in 1891 accidentally indicated that the three female boarders at 1
Breezer's Hill in their twenties were "unfortunates," or prostitutes, before crossing out this
indiscretion.

the first time since her return from Paris that Mary Jane had seen these familiar streets, and trepidation must have gnawed at her.

In the end, there is nothing to suggest that the mission was successful. If "the French Lady" was as sharp as Mrs. Boekü and other women in her position, she would have sold on Mary Jane's valuable belongings long before her former girl showed her face again in Knightsbridge. To worsen matters, this venture into the west of London was perhaps indeed ill-judged.

Apparently at some point after Mary Jane's visit to her former landlady, a man came to the Ratcliff Highway in search of her. According to Joseph Barnett, to whom she told the story, a middle-aged man, calling himself "her father," "tried to find her." He must have been fairly determined, asking after her in the various pubs and drinking establishments and making inquiries among the young women who plied the streets. Eventually, she "heard from her companions that he was looking for her." Mary Jane knew that this man was trouble and went out of her way to hide from him.[9] Whatever his identity, he was almost certainly not Mary Jane Kelly's father. Mrs. Felix insisted that Mary Jane had no contact with her family, "who had discarded her," and Barnett too stated that "she saw none of her relations." At the inquest in 1888, Barnett claimed that Mary Jane did harbor fears for her safety, though she never articulated who or what may have caused this anxiety.

If Mary Jane was beginning to weary of life on the Ratcliff Highway and her arguments with her landladies, then this alarming visit may have compelled her to begin considering her future. Then, at some point between late 1886 and early 1887, what must have seemed the perfect solution to her problems appeared: someone fell in love with her. Young, pretty, and sexually alluring, Mary Jane would have had no shortage of admirers and, despite the area's constantly shifting population, a number of regular clients. One of them was a twenty-seven-year-old plasterer from nearby Bethnal Green, called Joseph Fleming (or Flemming). As a laborer in the building trade, Fleming was not financially secure, and certainly far less comfortably off than the men whose hearts she might have captured in the West End. However, according to Mrs. McCarthy, whose house she left to live with Fleming, he was smitten and "would have married her." It appears that Mary Jane reciprocated his feelings and confided her fondness for him to her female acquaintances.[10] For a handful of months at most, the couple lived in what was probably no more than a single furnished room on Bethnal Green Road, or Old Bethnal Green Road, before the relationship fell apart.* The reason for this is unclear; Mary Jane's friend Julia Venturney suggested that Fleming may have been violent and "ill used" Mary Jane.[11] The first Mrs. McCarthy heard of Mary Jane's change in circumstances was when her former lodger appeared at her door at two o'clock in the morning. She had come in search of a bed for herself and a male companion. The landlady seemed somewhat puzzled and asked "if she was not still living with the man who took her from the neighbourhood." Mary Jane replied that the relationship had ended and that she had returned to soliciting. Mary McCarthy said no more, but took two shillings from her for the convenience of a room.[12]

When Mary Jane parted with Joe Fleming, she did not wish to remain in Bethnal Green, nor did she want to return to the Ratcliff Highway. Instead she moved somewhere entirely new, to Spitalfields. Here she is said to have taken residence at Cooley's lodging house on Thrawl Street and worked a patch around Aldgate. In his shamelessly romanticized memoirs of his tenure in the Metropolitan Police, Detective Chief Inspector Walter Dew claimed that he often caught sight of Mary Jane "parading along Commercial Street, between Flower-and-Dean Street and Aldgate, or along Whitechapel Road." He asserted that she was always "fairly neatly dressed and invariably wearing a clean white apron, but no hat" as she promenaded down the road "in the company of two or three of her kind."[13] Dew's comments about her outward appearance and demeanor were echoed by many who knew

---

* In his testimony, Joseph Barnett stated that Mary Jane lived with a man called Morgenstern (a reference to Mrs. Boekü's husband, Johannes) and also Joe Fleming. His statement is a very confused one. At one point he mentioned that Mary Jane lived near Stepney gasworks, or a gasworks, with one of these two men. As Pennington Street is not near a gasworks and there is no evidence that she lived with Adrianus Morgenstern, it is more likely he was referring to Fleming. The eastern part of Old Bethnal Green Road faces onto what was once Bethnal Green gasworks.

her. "She was one of the smartest, nicest looking women in the neighbourhood," commented a missionary who was interviewed by the *Evening News*. She never failed to be "neatly and decently dressed, and looked quite nice and respectable." Her neighbors too were charmed by her humor and kindness, claiming she was "a good, quiet, pleasant girl" and "well liked." According to several, Mary Jane enjoyed singing and telling stories, especially about her time in the West End; now living in rough, filthy surroundings, she must have longed for her former locale. She "made no secret" about her previous adventures and regaled her companions with tales of how she drove about in carriages and "led a life . . . of a lady"; she even boasted that she had been to Paris. These stories, along with her fantasies about Ireland and "returning to her people," seemed to capture the imagination of those she met. Yet these affectionate portraits of Mary Jane illustrate how well she had become adept at masking her feelings, an essential accomplishment for a so-called "gay woman." In a rare moment of openness, she spoke candidly to her neighbor, twenty-year-old Lizzie Albrook, who seemed enchanted by Mary Jane's worldliness. Mary Jane warned her off embarking upon a similar career, remarking that, in truth, "she was heartily sick of the life she was leading."[14]

Intriguingly, another description of Mary Jane Kelly exists that is much at variance with these generous comments. Tom Cullen, when researching his book on the murders in 1965, spoke with Dennis Barrett, who had been a boy in 1888 and claimed to remember Mary Jane. Barrett, who knew her as "Black Mary," described her as "a bit of a terror." When it came to soliciting trade outside the Ten Bells pub, she was as fierce as a bulldog. "Woe to any woman who tried to poach her territory . . . such a woman was likely to have her hair pulled out in fistfuls," he remarked.[15] Of course, Barrett's boyhood identification of Mary Jane may be confused, but if this account is to be believed, then it presents two very disparate sides to her character. Mary Jane may have been skilled at presenting a sweet façade, but her internal life was one of turmoil and distress.

A streetwalking existence in the East End could not have afforded Mary Jane much solace. The brief period of settled domesticity that she experienced with Joseph Fleming, however imperfect, must have come as a relief from the unpredictability and ever-present danger of soliciting. Not long after she and Fleming parted, she began to search for a similar but more stable arrangement. It soon presented itself as she touted for custom on Commercial Street, around March 1887.

Joseph Barnett, the primary narrator of Mary Jane's history, shot into her life like a comet, or so it appears from his one-sided description of their meeting. It occurred on a Thursday night, near Easter. Joseph was instantly taken with Mary Jane, whom he "picked up with" and invited for a drink at a public house. He discreetly omitted any mention of paying for sex with her, stating instead that he "arranged to see her the next day." Not forty-eight hours into the relationship, Barnett was a man in love. By Saturday he had proposed that they move in together, and Mary Jane agreed. Joseph immediately secured a room in nearby George Street. "I lived with her from then, till . . . the other day," he told the coroner eighteen months later.[16]

In November 1888, as he stood before a judgmental middle-class coroner's jury, Joseph Barnett did not leave the best impression of himself. Having been interviewed by the police for four hours, he was utterly terrified as he took the stand. His testimony was earnest but fraught, and he stammered and repeated his words. This was not the man whom Mary Jane Kelly had known, who was confident and determined when it came to acquiring what he desired.

The Joseph Barnett she had met that night on Commercial Street was a twenty-nine-year-old blue-eyed, fair-haired Whitechapel man who had been born into an Irish family and who sported a fashionable mustache. Like many children of his class and era, Joseph had lost both of his parents by the age of thirteen and was raised by his older siblings. His brother introduced him at Billingsgate fish market and assisted him in getting a job as a porter, a specialist trade that required a license to transport goods to the vendors. This coveted position could earn a man a good living, if he was quick and strong. Joseph, who is described as being five foot, seven inches, and of a medium build, certainly seemed physically equipped for the work. Notwithstanding this, the couple still struggled for money. Both of them enjoyed a drink, and this habit was perhaps the source of the problem. In the roughly eighteen months they were together, Joseph Barnett and Mary Jane Kelly moved four times. They left their shabby room on George Street for another one on Little Paternoster Row, from which they were evicted for drunkenness and failing to pay their rent.[17] From there they took up residence on Brick Lane before moving again, this time to a single room in Miller's Court around March 1888.

Miller's Court, in the earlier part of the century, had consisted of two adjoining gardens belonging to 26 and 27 Dorset Street. This space had later been developed and turned into a set of cramped workers' cottages in which thirty people lived, sharing three public toilets at one end of the courtyard. As the downstairs back parlor of number 26 faced onto a rather disagreeable view of a squalid yard, it was partitioned off from the rest of the house and rented out as 13 Miller's Court. For the cost of four shillings and six pence a week, Mary Jane and Joseph made a home of this ten-by-twelve-foot space at the end of a dark alley. It was no better or worse than any of the other wretched hovels found along Dorset Street and contained only the sparsest of furnishings: a bed, a table, a disused washstand, a chair, and a cupboard. Someone, at some stage, attempted to brighten the grimy, bare surroundings by tacking a print titled "The Fisherman's Widow" to a wall.

Unfortunately, like everything contiguous to it, the gloom of Miller's Court and the misery of those who inhabited it were inescapable. The owner, a slumlord known as John McCarthy (no relation to the McCarthys of Breezer's Hill), described as "a bully" and one who swindled "poor people out of small sums," appeared to favor compromised, lone women as tenants.[18] Elizabeth Prater, who lived upstairs from number 13, had been deserted by her husband. Julia Venturney, at number 1, was a widow in her late forties working as a charwoman, while Mary Ann Cox, who called herself a "widow and an unfortunate," resided at number 5. Although Mary Jane claimed that Barnett promised he would never "let her go on the streets" while she lived under his care, she apparently took on the rental of number 13 in her own name.[19] McCarthy must have known that women, especially those who were known prostitutes, would always be able to make good on outstanding sums. The true test of this arrangement came in the late summer, when Joseph lost his job at Billingsgate. The reasons for this are unknown, but if the couple drank heavily enough to warrant eviction from their previous home, alcohol may have played a role in this misfortune too. With Barnett out of work, the debts to McCarthy, who also ran the adjoining chandler's shop where tenants bought groceries, candles, and other necessities on credit, soon began to mount. By the beginning of November 1888 the couple had fallen six weeks behind in their rent and owed twenty-nine shillings to their landlord.

It may have been McCarthy who had a word with Mary Jane about a return to soliciting. She would not have embraced this prospect willingly after more than a year of sharing a bed with only one, familiar partner. For nearly eighteen months she had not needed to inspect a strange man for signs of syphilis. She had not wondered how she would manage if she found herself pregnant. She had not stood hungry on a corner in the rain without a hat or shawl, smiling. She did not have to consider what she might do if the unwashed man she had just pleasured refused to pay her. It was Barnett who had insisted that she need not solicit while they lived together, that he would provide for them, and the anger and resentment she must have felt at him for having failed her would have been palpable. Unfortunately, however Joseph tried, he was unable to find any work other than odd jobs, which did not cover the cost of the rent. The couple began to argue, frequently and furiously. On one occasion while drunk, Mary Jane broke a pane of glass in the window beside their door. She stuffed it full of rags to stop the draft, but now damaged, it was not to be repaired.

Although Joseph had met Mary Jane in the course of practicing her trade, after he had settled down with her, he did not wish to be reminded of her past. By contrast, Mary Jane was unashamed of it, though she did tread carefully around Barnett, who may have harbored a jealous streak. While Mary Jane lived at Miller's Court, it is said she received letters from Ireland, which she claimed were from her mother, or possibly her "brother." Interestingly, from August 1888, the 2nd Battalion of the Scots Guard was based in Dublin, and it is equally probable that she was receiving correspondence, and possibly small sums, from a former paramour in the regiment.[20] She also remained in contact with Joseph Fleming, who, according to Julia Venturney, visited her on occasion and "used to give her money."[21] Joseph Barnett was not aware of this and might not have taken kindly to their continued meetings. Apparently, Mary Jane was known to taunt him by mentioning his predecessor, of whom she stated "she was very fond." However, what seemed to anger Barnett the most was Mary Jane's frequent association with prostitutes, whom she brought into their home. This outrage was probably on account of his frustration at Mary Jane's return to streetwalking, rather than a genuine annoyance at sharing his space with Mary Jane's friends. As their disagreements continued to rage, Mary Jane eventually sent Joseph a very clear message: she valued her friendship with "gay women" more than she did her relationship with him.

By October, Jack the Ripper's killing spree was the talk and terror of everyone in Whitechapel. The residents of Dorset Street and Miller's Court, home to so many vulnerable women, were especially anxious. Joseph claimed that during those tense months he and Mary Jane read the newspapers daily, hoping to learn that the murderer had been caught. However, while the criminal remained at large, Mary Jane decided to offer sanctuary to acquaintances who might otherwise have had to solicit or sleep rough. The first of these women was a prostitute known only as "Julia."* Shortly after this, Mary Jane took in Maria Harvey, an unmarried laundress who hadn't enough money for a bed and who left behind a litter of clothing in the room. These nocturnal guests were the last straw for Barnett. Although he recognized that Mary Jane had been moved by compassion, her actions were also obviously designed to push him out. He left her on October 30, though not without a great deal of remorse.

In spite of their difficulties, Joseph obviously cared for Mary Jane. He took a bed at Buller's Boarding House on the corner of Bishops-

---

* The identity of this first woman is unknown. The name Julia appeared in *Lloyd's Weekly Newspaper* on November 11, but the journalist may have mistakenly inserted the name of Julia Venturney, who appeared before Maria Harvey at the inquest into Mary Jane's death.

gate Street but made certain to look in on her. He also continued to search for work and hoped that they could be reconciled. In the early evening of Thursday, November 8, he rapped on her door. The window that had been shattered was still plugged with rags, and a coat that Maria Harvey had left in the room was hung across it as a makeshift curtain. On that night, Joseph might have pulled out the rag stopper and unlatched the door from within, as he and Mary Jane had done after losing the key, but this was likely to seem too forward. A candle was burning inside, and he noted that Mary Jane was not alone. She had been chatting with Lizzie Albrook, and when he arrived, Mary Jane's neighbor excused herself. Mary Jane had only recently returned from drinking in the Ten Bells with a friend, Elizabeth Foster, but Barnett claimed that she was perfectly sober when he came to see her.

The couple were together for about an hour. They may have conversed softly, or quarreled, or given in to their desires, but whatever occurred failed to shift the impasse. In the end, Joseph rose to leave and with sadness apologized to Mary Jane. "I told her that I had no work, and that I had nothing to give her," he repeated at the coroner's inquest, "for which I was very sorry."[22] Mary Jane, in a worn black velvet bodice and skirt, which had once been made of a fine material, watched him go.

If Mary Jane Kelly was in any way heartbroken by the loss of her relationship with Joseph Barnett, she did not confide her sadness to any of her friends. Instead, she drew the customary mask over her face and carried on with her life, as she had done before.

No one is absolutely certain where Mary Jane went after she bid farewell to Joseph Barnett. Mary Ann Cox, her neighbor at number 5, believed she saw Mary Jane with a man turn from Dorset Street into Miller's Court at around 11:45. She thought Mary Jane was very drunk, but none of the publicans in the area claimed that they had seen her or served her that night. According to Cox, Mary Jane and her male guest then disappeared into her room, but before they did, Mary Jane warned Cox that she was "going to have song." The door then banged shut, and a glimmer of light began to shine from behind her crudely curtained window. After a moment or so of silence, Cox heard Mary

Jane's voice rise into the first verse of "A Violet Plucked from My Mother's Grave When a Boy":

Scenes of my childhood arise before my gaze,
Bringing recollections of bygone happy days.
When down in the meadow in childhood I would roam,
No one's left to cheer me now within that good old home,
Father and Mother, they have pass'd away;
Sister and brother, now lay beneath the clay,
But while life does remain to cheer me, I'll retain
This small violet I pluck'd from mother's grave.

Only a violet I pluck'd when but a boy,
And oft'time when I'm sad at heart this flow'r has giv'n me joy;
So while life does remain in memoriam I'll retain,
This small violet I pluck'd from mother's grave.

Well I remember my dear old mother's smile,
As she used to greet me when I returned from toil,
Always knitting in the old arm chair,
Father used to sit and read for all us children there,
But now all is silent around the good old home;
They all have left me in sorrow here to roam,
But while life does remain, in memoriam I'll retain
This small violet I pluck'd from mother's grave.

Cox seemed fairly certain that she heard Mary Jane singing at least until around 1 a.m., but as with so many of the witness testimonies in all five of the cases, there are omissions, questions, and inconsistencies.[23] What precisely had happened to Mary Jane's male customer over the course of this concert, lasting an hour and fifteen minutes, is anyone's guess.

Elizabeth Prater, who lived upstairs from Mary Jane, claimed she could hear most sounds clearly through the thin partition wall and floor. At 1:30 a.m. nothing was stirring in Mary Jane's room.

At some point in the very early hours of November 9, Mary Jane decided to bring an end to the day and retire to sleep. She removed her clothes piece by piece, a few shabby items of a once resplendent wardrobe diminished by wear; the hems had been dragged along the uneven sidewalks of Dorset Street, and the fabric splashed with beer and gin. In spite of each article's poor condition, she folded it neatly and placed it on her chair. The flame of her only candle, which she had balanced on a broken wineglass, guttered and bobbed until snuffed out. Enveloped in darkness, she slid under her bed sheet and pulled it snugly around her, protecting herself from the night.

Joseph Barnett was the nearest thing Mary Jane Kelly had to a family member, and even he never knew the true identity of the woman who was placed in the casket. Because she called herself Mary Jane Kelly and claimed she had been born in Ireland, she was interred at a Catholic cemetery: St. Patrick's in Leytonstone. But if she was as Welsh as everyone else attested, Mary Jane might well have been buried by Methodists.

Mary Jane was whatever she wished to be, and in the wake of her death, she became whatever Joseph Barnett wished to commemorate. It was he who insisted that the name on her brass coffin plate read "Marie Jeanette Kelly," a moniker brimming with all the flounce and flamboyance of a Saturday night in the West End.

Following her death, Mary Jane, an otherwise anonymous resident of Spitalfields, also became what Whitechapel imagined her to be: a local heroine who had suffered at the hands of a monster still on the loose. Her open hearse, her two mourning carriages, and her polished oak-and-elm coffin, decorated with two floral wreaths and a cross of heartseed, became a show of defiance. It also became an excuse to gawk and drink and exclaim at the carnival of mourning that passed through the streets, trailed by publicans and their best customers, as well as the sort of females that the newspapers called "unfortunates." Women with infants on their hips watched from the doorsteps, men removed their hats as she passed by.

"God forgive her!" they were said to have cried out, through their sobs. "We will not forget her!"

CONCLUSION:
"JUST PROSTITUTES"

The loss of these five ... lives is clearly a tragedy ... You may
view with some distaste the lifestyles of those involved ...
whatever drugs they took, whatever the work they did, no-one
is entitled to do these women any harm, let alone kill them.

— Mr. Justice Gross, *R v. Steven Gerald James Wright*
(the "Suffolk Strangler"), 2008

Shortly after the death of Annie Chapman, Mr. Edward Fairfield, a senior civil servant at the Colonial Office and a resident of the upmarket South Eaton Place, in London's Belgravia, was moved to pick up
his pen and write a letter to the *Times*. He was particularly concerned
about the series of Whitechapel murders. The actual deaths of "the
vicious inhabitants of Dorset Street and Flower and Dean Street"
were not what was bothering him. Edward Fairfield was far more anxious that in the wake of this disturbance, women like Annie Chapman
would be displaced from their hellish hovels in Spitalfields and make
their way into his neighborhood, carrying their "taint to the streets
hitherto untainted." "The horror and excitement caused by the murder of the four Whitechapel outcasts imply a universal belief that they
had a right to life," continued this representative of the government.

... If they had, then they had the further right to hire shelter from the
bitterness of the English night. If they had no such right, then it was,
on the whole, a good thing that they fell in with the unknown surgi-

cal genius. He, at all events, has made his contribution towards solving, "the problem of clearing the East-end of its vicious inhabitants."[1]

While today we are likely to shiver at such a comment, Edward Fairfield was simply expressing what would have been, if not a widely held sentiment, then one that he did not feel was inappropriate to discuss openly in 1888. Fairfield was a bachelor, a man who spent a good deal of time at his club, where he was noted for his "slightly flippant, slightly dissipated personality."[2] When he was not there, he was cared for by a cook and a parlor maid and regularly hosted intimate dinners for his male friends. Fairfield, like most of the literate public, had learned all he needed to know about the "vicious inhabitants" of the East End from the newspapers. He had been educated about their disgusting, impoverished, drunken lives from the snippets of information he had read. Whatever gaps remained in his understanding of slum-dwelling women would have been filled in by that which was "common-knowledge": they were all desperate, filthy, foul-mouthed prostitutes. Sadly, what he and the rest of the readership of the *Times* failed to realize was that there was much more to the story of "the typical Annie Chapman," as he called women of her ilk, than what appeared in the press. Little did Edward Fairfield know that Annie Chapman had already "carried her taint" into his part of town, because Annie Chapman had spent a good part of her life there. Annie Chapman's family lived a fifteen-minute walk from Fairfield's front door, and in her final years, ragged, sick, dejected, "vicious" Annie came there to visit her sisters. Edward Fairfield may have even passed her on the Brompton Road, on his way to Harrods.

The truth of these women's lives was not simple, and the sensationalist nineteenth-century press was certainly not telling the whole story to readers like Edward Fairfield. Neither did the editors nor the journalists covering this story deem it necessary, worthy, or interesting to delve into the biographical details of the victims. Ultimately, no one really cared about who they were or how they ended up in Whitechapel.

The cards were stacked against Polly, Annie, Elisabeth, Kate, and Mary Jane from birth. They began their lives in deficit. Not only were most of them born into working-class families; they were also born female. Before they had even spoken their first words or taken their first steps, they were regarded as less important than their brothers and more of a burden on the world than their wealthier female counterparts. Their worth was compromised before they had even attempted to prove it. They would never earn the income of a man; therefore, their education was of less importance. What work they could secure was designed to help support their families; it was not intended to bring them fulfillment, a sense of purpose, or personal contentment. The golden ticket for working-class girls was a life in domestic service, where it might become possible, after a number of years of back-breaking work, to rise in station and become a cook, a housekeeper, or a lady's maid. There were no desk jobs for poor girls like Kate Eddowes or Polly Nichols, though both were literate, but many that involved twelve-hour days stitching trousers in a sweatshop, working in a factory, or gluing together matchboxes for a wage that barely paid for bed and board. Poor women's labor was cheap because poor women were considered expendable and because society did not designate them as a family's breadwinner. Unfortunately, many of them had to be. If a husband, father, or partner left or died, a working-class woman with dependents would find it almost impossible to survive. The structure of society ensured that a woman without a man was superfluous.

A woman's entire function was to support men, and if the roles of their male family members were to support the roles and needs of men wealthier than them, then the women at the bottom were driven like piles deeper and harder into the ground in order to bear the weight of everyone else's demands. A woman's role was to produce children and to raise them, but because rudimentary contraception and published information about birth control was made virtually unavailable to the poor, they, like the women of the Eddowes family, like Annie Chapman's mother, and like Polly Nichols, had no real means of managing the size of their families or preventing an inevitable backslide into financial hardship. The inability to break this cycle — to better their own prospects and those of their children — would have been soul crushing, but borne with resignation.

Atop this heap of burdens placed on a woman's shoulders was balanced the most cumbersome one of all: the ideal of moral and sexual immaculacy. As a woman was the keystone at the center of family life, her character must be unimpeachable; if it were not, it was she who was responsible for the ruin of others. Her circumspection and self-sacrifice calibrated the moral compass of her children; her dedication to her husband's needs kept him from sin — away from the public houses and other women. The double standard ensured that although it might not be entirely acceptable for a man to seek sexual relations with a number of women, it was completely understandable, and even normal. A woman, on the other hand, could have sex with a man only if she was legally married to him. The all-pervasiveness of these ideals meant that even in the more permissive working-class communities, where couples frequently had sex outside of wedlock, didn't marry, split up, and recoupled at regular intervals, women still bore the brunt of moral judgment, especially when it came from mainstream, middle-class Victorian society. In the narrow-eyed, censorious gaze of the moral arbiters, Polly and Annie were fallen women the moment they parted with their husbands and threw in their lot with other men. Kate was deemed as dissolute as Mary Jane for living out of wedlock with two partners, and Elisabeth was ruined twice: once in Gothenburg, when her name went on the register of public women, and a second time after her marriage failed, when she supported herself through soliciting. The double standard rendered life in black and white. Missionaries offered pity and promises of redemption to those who had taken the wrong path, but usually applied this balm after years of shame and condemnation had rubbed a woman's self-esteem raw. Is it any wonder that Polly fled the comforts of the Cowdrys' home, that Annie could not bear to tell her sisters where she lived, that Elisabeth never let anyone truly know her, that Kate fell out with her children, and that by age twenty-five Mary Jane had become an angry drunk?

At the time of the murders, the belief that "Jack the Ripper was a killer of prostitutes" helped reinforce this moral code. However, while it served an agenda in 1888, this often repeated line fails to serve any immediately obvious purpose today. Nevertheless, it is still the one "fact" about the murders upon which everyone can agree, and yet it does not bear scrutiny.

From the introduction of the Contagious Diseases Acts in the 1860s through the period of the Whitechapel murders, very few authorities, including the Metropolitan Police, could agree as to what exactly constituted a "prostitute" and how she might be identified.[3] Was a prostitute simply a woman like Mary Jane Kelly who earned her income solely through the sex trade and who self-identified as part of this profession, or could the term *prostitute* be more broadly defined? Was a prostitute a woman who accepted a drink from a man who then accompanied her to a lodging house, paid for a bed, had sex with her, and stayed the night? A woman who occasionally masturbated men behind the pub for money but didn't have intercourse with them? A woman who let a man put his hand up her skirt for three pence? A woman who had sex for money twice over the course of a week, before finding work in a laundry and meeting a man whom she decided to live with out of wedlock? A woman who used to work in a brothel but then left to become the kept mistress of one of her clients? A woman who tramped and agreed to have sex with a man because otherwise she felt threatened and alone? A young factory worker who had sex with the boys who courted her and bought her gifts? A woman with a "free and easy" reputation who stayed out late at night, carousing in pubs? A woman with three children by three different fathers who lived with a man simply because he kept a roof over their heads?

Some of these women might be classed as professional or "common prostitutes," while others might be called "casual prostitutes" or just women who, in accordance with the social norms of their community, had sex outside of wedlock. But as the Metropolitan Police came to recognize, the lines separating these groups were often so blurred that it was impossible to distinguish between them.

The question of who could or couldn't legitimately be called a prostitute came to a head in July 1887, after Elizabeth Cass, a dressmaker who had gone out on her own one evening to buy a pair of gloves and view the Golden Jubilee illuminations on Regent Street, was erroneously arrested as a streetwalker. The resulting trial and acquittal of Cass forced the police to reexamine their assumptions about the morals of women who appeared alone in public and to think twice before slapping the label of "prostitute" onto all of them. Sir Charles Warren's order of July 19, 1887, was issued in an attempt to make an official clarification of how the police were to formally define a prostitute. It was stated that "a Police Constable should not assume that any particular woman is a common prostitute" and that the police were not "justified in calling any woman a common prostitute unless she so describes herself, or has been convicted as such . . ." Furthermore, in order to charge a woman with being a prostitute, proof was required in the form of a formal statement by a person who had been "annoyed or solicited."[4] A year later, Warren was equally cautious about identifying "prostitutes" among the Whitechapel lodging-house population and acknowledged that there were "no means of ascertaining what women are prostitutes and who are not."[5] After having their fingers burned in 1887, police officials were forced to recognize that the intersection between working-class women who were not part of the sex trade and those who were, was so seamlessly interwoven as to make them impossible to isolate into distinct groups. However, this did not always prevent police constables from ignoring these orders and doing whatever their prejudices dictated.

In the absence of any evidence that Polly, Annie, and Kate had ever engaged in common prostitution, many have taken to claiming that these women participated in "casual prostitution," a blanket term cast over the ambiguities of the women's lives that is steeped in moral judgment. It ascribes guilt by association: because a woman was poor and an alcoholic, because she left her children, because she had committed adultery, because she had children out of wedlock, because she lived in a lodging house, because she was out late at night, because she was no longer attractive, because she didn't have a settled home, because she begged, because she slept rough, because she broke all the rules of what it meant to be feminine. This line of reasoning also explains why Polly, Annie, and Kate's homelessness was entirely overlooked as a factor in their murders; a "houseless creature" and a "prostitute" by their moral failings were one and the same. There were many reasons why an impoverished working-class woman may have been outdoors during the hours of darkness, and not all of them were as obvious as street soliciting. Those without homes or families, those who drank heavily, and those who were dispossessed did not lead lives that adhered to conventional rules. No one knew or cared about what they did or where they went, and for this reason, rather than for a sexual motive, they would have appealed to a killer.

If the official criteria established by the commissioner of the Metropolitan Police for defining the term "prostitute" is applied to Polly, Annie, and Kate, it immediately becomes obvious that they cannot be identified as such. Even when relying on inquest testimony, there exists no proof to support these assertions. Similarly, there is no absolute proof that Elisabeth Stride returned to prostitution in the period prior to her murder. Quite simply, there is no evidence that any of these women self-identified as prostitutes and no evidence that anyone among their community regarded them as part of the sex trade. Furthermore, on the nights they were killed, no one came forward to state that they had been solicited by Polly, Annie, Kate, or Elisabeth. After the coroners had heard the evidence provided by all of the witnesses, they made their absolute conclusions as to the victims' identities. These were recorded as "occupation or profession" on the women's death certificates. Mary Ann Nichols was described as the "Wife of William Nichols, Printing Machinist." Annie Chapman was identified as the "widow of John Chapman, a coachman." Elisabeth Stride was recorded as the "widow of John Thomas Stride, carpenter," and Catherine Eddowes as a "Supposed single woman." Only Mary Jane Kelly, who admitted openly to working in the sex trade, was described as a "Prostitute."[6] These official pronouncements must be taken as the final word on whether or not we are justified in claiming that "Jack the Ripper was a killer of prostitutes." To insist otherwise is to fall back on arbitrary supposition informed by Victorian prejudice.

Today there is only one reason why we would continue to embrace the belief that Jack the Ripper was a killer of prostitutes: because it supports an industry that has grown, in part, out of this mythology. There's no doubt that the story of Jack the Ripper is a good yarn. It's a gothic tale of a monster on the loose, stalking the dark streets of foggy London. It contains suspense and horror, and an element of sexual titillation. Unfortunately, this is also a one-sided story, and the hunt for the killer has taken center stage. Over the centuries, the villain has metamorphosed into the protagonist; an evil, psychotic, mysterious player who is so clever that he has managed to evade detection even today. In order to gawp at and examine this miracle of malevolence we have figuratively stepped over the bodies of those he murdered, and in some cases, stopped to kick them as we walked past. The larger his profile grows, the more those of his victims seem to fade. With the advance of time, both the murderer and those he murdered have become detached from reality; their experiences and names have become entwined with folklore and conspiracy theories. To some merchandisers, the victims are no longer human beings, but rather cartoon figures, whose bloody images can be printed on T-shirts, whose deaths can be laughed about on postcards, and whose entrails decorate stickers. Is it any wonder that there has been no public appetite to examine the lives of the canonical five, when they have never seemed real or of any consequence to us before?

Insisting that Jack the Ripper killed prostitutes also makes the story of a vicious series of murders slightly more palatable. Just as it did in the nineteenth century, the notion that the victims were "only prostitutes" perpetuates the belief that there are good women and bad women, madonnas and whores. It suggests that there is an acceptable standard of female behavior, and those who deviate from it are fit to be punished. Equally, it reasserts the double standard, exonerating men from wrongs committed against such women. These attitudes may not feel as prevalent as they were in 1888, but they persist. They may not be expressed freely in general conversation, as they would have been in Edward Fairfield's day; rather, they have been integrated subtly into the fabric of our cultural norms. The threads become apparent in court cases and in politics; they are found interwoven in the statements of the powerful. They can be spotted in instances like *People v. Turner* (2015), which saw Brock Turner, a Stanford University student charged with the rape and sexual assault of a heavily intoxicated woman, receive a reduced prison sentence of six months, which his father complained "was a steep price to pay for 20 minutes of action."[7] They are manifest when it becomes necessary for the judge in the trial of the Suffolk serial killer, Steve Wright, to instruct the jury to lay aside their prejudices against the five victims, four of whom were sex workers, before making their decision about the guilt of the defendant. In a statement chillingly resonant with the echoes of 1888, he reminded the jurors, "You may view with some distaste the lifestyles of those involved . . . whatever drugs they took, whatever work they did, no-one is entitled to do these women any harm, let alone kill them."

When a woman steps out of line and contravenes accepted norms of feminine behavior, whether on social media or on the Victorian street, there is a tacit understanding that someone must put her back in her place. Labeling the victims as "just prostitutes" permits those writing about Polly, Annie, Elisabeth, Kate, and Mary Jane even today to continue to disparage, sexualize, and dehumanize them; to continue to reinforce the values of madonna/whore. It allows authors to rank the women's level of attractiveness based on images of their murdered bodies and to declare "Pulchritude was, it appears, of no interest to the Whitechapel Murderer," before concluding, "Mary Jane Kelly was pretty, Stride, lively and . . . at least attractive . . . Otherwise, his victims were gin-soaked drabs."[8] This attitude gives such authors free rein to speculate pruriently on how frequently these women had sex before they were murdered. It makes it acceptable to dismiss these daughters, wives, and mothers as "a few moribund, drunken trug-moldies," which "all [Jack] did was execute, [and] then gralloch."[9] It elevates the murderer to celebrity status and confers favor on his victims: because they "got intimate with one of the most famous men on earth."[10] At its very core, the story of Jack the Ripper is a narrative of a killer's deep, abiding hatred of women, and our culture's obsession with the mythology serves only to normalize its particular brand of misogyny.

We have grown so comfortable with the notion of "Jack the Ripper," the unfathomable, invincible male killer, that we have failed to recognize that he continues to walk among us. In his top hat and cape, wielding his blood-drenched knife, he can be spotted regularly in London on posters, in ads, on the sides of buses. Bartenders have named drinks after him, shops use his moniker on their signs, tourists from around the world make pilgrimages to Whitechapel to walk in his footsteps and visit a museum dedicated to his violence. The world has learned to dress up in his costume at Halloween, to imagine being him, to honor his genius, to laugh at a murderer of women. By embracing him, we embrace the set of values that surrounded him in 1888, which teaches women that they are of a lesser value and can expect to be dishonored and abused. We enforce the notion that "bad women" deserve punishment and that "prostitutes" are a subspecies of female.

In order to keep him alive, we have had to forget his victims. We have become complicit in their diminishment. When we repeat the accepted Ripper legend in newspapers, in television documentaries, and on the Internet, when we teach it to schoolchildren without questioning the origins of the story and its sources, without considering the reliability of the evidence or the assumptions that contributed to forming it, we not only assist in perpetuating the injustices committed against Polly, Annie, Elizabeth, Kate, and Mary Jane, but we condone the basest forms of violence.

It is only by bringing these women back to life that we can silence the Ripper and what he represents. By permitting them to speak, by attempting to understand their experiences and see their humanity, we can restore to them the respect and compassion to which they are entitled. The victims of Jack the Ripper were never "just prostitutes"; they were daughters, wives, mothers, sisters, and lovers. They were women. They were human beings, and surely that in itself is enough.

Following their discovery, Polly, Annie, Elisabeth, Kate, and Mary Jane's bodies were removed by the police from the scenes of the crime. Their bodies were then stripped of their clothing and whatever small artifacts they had stowed on themselves for safekeeping. As the first four victims had been found outdoors, inventories were made of their possessions. A similar list was not made for Mary Jane Kelly, who had been killed in her bed.

These objects offer a final imprint of a life: a humble snapshot of what each woman valued and what she felt she could use to assist her through her uncertain days.

Polly

- ➤ Black straw bonnet trimmed with black velvet
- ➤ Brown ulster [overcoat] with seven large buttons bearing the pattern of a man standing beside a horse
- ➤ Linsey frock
- ➤ White flannel chest cloth
- ➤ Blue ribbed wool stockings
- ➤ Two petticoats, one gray wool, one flannel. Both stenciled on bands "Lambeth Workhouse"
- ➤ Brown [corset] stays (short)
- ➤ Flannel drawers
- ➤ Men's elastic (spring) sided boots with the uppers cut and steel tips on the heels

> A comb
> A white pocket handkerchief
> A piece of a looking glass

Annie

> Long black figured coat that came down to her knees
> Black skirt
> Brown bodice
> Another bodice
> Two petticoats
> A large pocket worn under the skirt and tied about the waist with strings
> Lace-up boots
> Red-and-white-striped woolen stockings
> Neckerchief, white with a wide red border
> Scrap of muslin
> One small-tooth comb
> One comb in a paper case
> Scrap of envelope containing two pills, bearing the seal of the Sussex Regiment and post-stamped "London, 28, Aug., 1888"

Elisabeth

> Long black cloth jacket, fur trimmed around the bottom, with a red rose and white maidenhair fern pinned to it
> Black skirt
> Black crepe bonnet (the back stuffed with newspaper)
> Checked neck scarf knotted on left side
> Dark brown velveteen bodice
> Two light serge petticoats
> One white chemise
> White stockings

- Spring sided boots
- Two handkerchiefs
- A thimble
- A piece of wool wound around a card
- A key (as of a padlock)
- A small piece of lead pencil
- Six large buttons and one small one
- A comb
- A broken piece of comb
- A metal spoon
- A hook (as from a dress)
- A piece of muslin
- One or two small pieces of paper

Kate

- Black straw bonnet trimmed in green and black velvet with black beads. Black strings, worn tied to the head
- Black cloth jacket trimmed around the collar and cuffs with imitation fur and around the pockets in black silk braid and fur. Large metal buttons
- Dark green chintz skirt, three flounces, brown button on waistband. The skirt is patterned with Michaelmas daisies and golden lilies
- Man's white vest, matching buttons down front
- Brown linsey bodice, black velvet collar, with brown buttons down front
- Gray stuff petticoat with white waistband
- Very old green alpaca skirt (worn as undergarment)
- Very old ragged blue skirt with red flounces, light twill lining (worn as undergarment)
- White calico chemise
- No drawers or stays
- Pair of men's lace-up boots, mohair laces. Right boot repaired with red thread

- One piece of red gauze silk worn as a neckerchief
- One large white pocket handkerchief
- One large white cotton handkerchief with red and white bird's eye border
- Two unbleached calico pockets, tape strings
- One blue stripe bed ticking pocket
- Brown ribbed knee stockings, darned at the feet with white cotton
- Two small blue bags made of bed ticking
- Two short black clay pipes
- One tin box containing tea
- One tin box containing sugar
- One tin matchbox, empty
- Twelve pieces white rag, some slightly bloodstained (menstrual rags)
- One piece coarse linen, white
- One piece of blue and white shirting, three cornered
- One piece red flannel with pins and needles
- Six pieces soap
- One small tooth comb
- One white handle table knife
- One metal teaspoon
- One red-leather cigarette case with white metal fittings
- One ball hemp
- One piece of old white apron with repair
- Several buttons and a thimble
- Mustard tin containing two pawn tickets
- Portion of a pair of spectacles
- One red mitten

ACKNOWLEDGMENTS

Writing this book has taken me on an incredible journey, both intellectually and emotionally, and I am indebted to a number of people who have assisted me at various stages along the way. From the outset, Claire McArdle and Julia Laite have been two invaluable sounding boards and have not only contributed to my knowledge but helped me to consolidate my ideas. The same can be said of both Daniel Olsson and Stefan Rantzow, who have each offered their invaluable insights into Elisabeth Stride's world as well as their assistance in helping me acquire and understand much of the material in Sweden. Helena Berlin and Arne and Olaf Jacobson in Gothenburg are also deserving of my thanks.

It was a great pleasure to meet and exchange thoughts and research with Neal and Jennifer Shelden, who first ventured into the archives many years ago and began piecing together the basic information about the lives of the five women. Anyone who has had an interest in Polly, Annie, Elisabeth, Kate, and Mary Jane will be indebted to them. I'm grateful to Melanie Clegg for facilitating this connection, as well as to Adam Wood and Frogg Moody, who helped me make contact with people within the Ripperology community.

My research schedule was intense, and the volume of material I had to cover in the preparation of this book was daunting. The assistance offered by Lucy Santos, Phoebe Cousins, and Wendy Toole has been of great value to the project, as have the eagle-eyed contributions of Sarah Murden and Joanne Major. I owe Hannah Greig and the University of York a debt for sending me the diligent and skilled historian Sarah Murphy as an intern. I am also grateful for the expertise offered by Anthony Rhys, Lindsey Fitzharris, Anthony Martin, and Drew Grey, while Christine Wagg at Peabody, Mark and Wendy at the LMA, and Sister Elizabeth Jane at the Community of St. Mary the Virgin were especially generous with their time. It would be negligent of me if I did not also thank the London Library for providing such a reliable resource and a perfect place to work.

Finally, those who cheered me on from the inception of this book cannot go unmentioned: my agents, Sarah Ballard, and her assistant, Eli Keren, as well as Yasmin McDonald at United Agents, and Eleanor Jackson at Dunow, Carlson & Lerner. They have been a dream team. Similarly, this book would not have come into being without the vision and tireless enthusiasm of the editorial teams in the UK and the United States. Jane Lawson, my editor at Transworld, has been an absolute star (as usual), as has Nicole Angeloro at Houghton Mifflin Harcourt. Sophie Christopher, Emma Burton, Kate Samano, Richenda Todd, and many others at Transworld and HMH, including Lisa Glover and Susanna Brougham, have had a hand in bringing this book into being, and for that I am truly grateful.

Authors, who lead most of their lives in their heads, would be nothing without those who pull them forcefully back into reality. My husband has endured my temporary transformation into an obsessive Ripperologist, and I am certain that I have bored my family and friends with lengthy discourses on my latest research. To you, my most beloved and cherished, I offer not only my heartfelt gratitude but, equally, my sincerest apologies.

NOTES

Introduction: A Tale of Two Cities

1. Howard Goldsmid, *A Midnight Prowl Through Victorian London* (London, 1887).
2. *Sheffield Daily Telegraph*, 20 July 1887.
3. PRO: Metropolitan Police Files: file 3/141, ff. 158–59.
4. Ibid.

The Blacksmith's Daughter

1. Max Schlesinger, *Saunterings in and About London* (London, 1853), p. 89.
2. John Hollingshead, *Ragged London* (1861), pp. 39, 282.
3. *First Report of the Commissioners for Inquiring into the State of Large Towns and Populous Districts,* vol. 1 (London, 1844), pp. 111–13.
4. George R. Sims, *How the Poor Live* (London, 1883), p. 12.
5. *First Report of the Commissioners for Inquiring into the State of Large Towns and Populous Districts,* vol. 1 (London, 1844), pp. 111–13.
6. *Coventry Standard,* 27 June 1845.
7. LMA: London Parish Register: P69/BRI/A/01/MS6541/5. I am indebted to Neal and Jennifer Shelden for this discovery.

The Peabody Worthies

1. Franklin Parker, *George Peabody: A Biography* (Vanderbilt University Press, 1995), p. 126.
2. *London Daily News,* 29 January 1876.
3. "New Peabody Buildings in Lambeth," the *Circle,* 11 April 1874.
4. Ibid.
5. Phebe Ann Hanaford, *The Life of George Peabody* (Boston, 1870), p. 133.
6. *Daily News,* 29 January 1876.
7. Hanaford, *The Life of George Peabody,* p. 137.
8. *Daily Telegraph,* 24 December 1878.

9. LMA: Stamford Street Registers Acc/3445/PT/07/066.

10. Ibid.

11. Ancestry.com, *Glasgow, Scotland, Crew Lists, 1863–1901.*

An Irregular Life

1. LMA: Board of Guardian Records, 1834–1906; Church of England Parish Registers: 1754–1906, P 73/MRK2/001.

2. LMA: Holborn Union Workhouse records: HOBG 510/18 (Examinations). Records for Renfrew Road for the period in which Polly claimed to enter the workhouse in Lambeth are missing; however, her name does not appear in the 1880 records of the union's other workhouse on Prince's Road.

3. G. Haw, *From Workhouse to Westminster: The Life Story of Will Crooks* (London, 1907), p. 109.

4. Report HMSO, *Royal Commission on Divorce and Matrimonial Causes* (London, 1912b and c), pp. 291, 318.

5. John Ruskin, "Sesame and Lilies," in *Of Queens' Gardens* (London, 1865).

6. George C. T. Bartley, *A Handy Book for Guardians of the Poor* (London, 1876), pp. 152–53.

7. Ibid., p. 59.

8. LMA: Holborn Union Workhouse records HOBG 510/18 (Examinations).

9. Charles Booth, *Life and Labour of the People in London: The Trades of East London* (London: Macmillan and Co., 1893), p. 295.

10. C. Black, *Married Women's Work* (London: Virago, 1983), p. 35.

11. Ancestry.com: New South Wales, Australia, Unassisted Immigrant Passenger Lists: 1826–1922. Woolls immigrated to Australia on board the P&O steamer *Barrabool.*

12. *East London Observer,* 8 September 1888.

13. *Daily Telegraph,* 3 September 1888.

14. Ibid.

15. Booth, *Life and Labour of the People in London,* pp. 55–56.

"Houseless Creature"

1. *Pall Mall Gazette,* 5 August 1887.

2. *Evening Standard,* 26 October 1887.

3. Ibid.

4. *Daily News,* 26 October 1887.

5. Ibid.

6. *Evening Standard,* 26 October 1887.

7. LMA: Lambeth Board of Guardians Creed Registers, X113/011.

8. Peter Higginbotham, http://www.workhouses.org.uk/Stallard/ (retrieved 16 January 2018).

9. George Augustus Sala, *Gaslight and Daylight* (London, 1859), p. 2.

10. William Booth, *In Darkest England and the Way Out* (London, 1890), p. 30.

11. Numbers are all taken from Margaret Harkness, *Out of Work* (London, 1888), p. 171; Rodney Mace, *Trafalgar Square: Emblem of Empire* (London, 2005), p. 171; Booth, *Darkest England,* p. 30.

12. Booth, *Darkest England,* pp. 26–27.

13. Peter Higginbotham, http://www.workhouses.org.uk/Higgs/TrampAmong Tramps.shtml, from Mary Higgs, *Five Days and Nights as a Tramp* (London, 1904).

14. Higginbotham, http://www.workhouses.org.uk/Stallard/ from J. H. Stallard, *The Female Casual and Her Lodging* (London, 1866).

15. J. Thomson and Adolphe Smith, "The Crawlers," in *Street Life in London* (London, 1877), pp. 116–18.

16. George R. Sims, *Horrible London* (London, 1889), pp. 145–48.

17. *Evening Standard,* 26 October 1887.

18. Mitcham Infirmary is now London's Whittington Hospital.

19. LMA: Holborn Union Workhouse records: HOBG 510/18 (Settlement Examinations).

20. Neal Stubbings Shelden, *The Victims of Jack the Ripper* (Knoxville, Tennessee, 2007), p. 8.

21. *East London Observer,* 8 September 1888; *Morning Advertiser,* 4 September 1888; *Exmouth Journal,* 8 September 1888. Holland was said to claim that she knew Polly for both six weeks and three weeks. This could be the result of inconsistencies in reporting, or it is possible that Polly may have taken up residence at Wilmott's shortly after leaving the Cowdrys.

22. *East London Observer,* 8 September 1888.

23. *Western Daily Press,* 4 September 1888.

24. The *Star,* 1 September 1888.

25. *East London Observer,* 8 September 1888.

26. Ibid.

27. *Evening Standard,* 4 September 1888. More recently, many books on Jack the Ripper have deliberately rewritten this quote to read "a house where men and women were allowed to sleep together."

28. *East London Observer,* 8 September 1888.

29. Ibid.

30. *Manchester Guardian,* 8 September 1888.

31. *Morning Advertiser,* 3 September 1888; *Evening Standard,* 3 September 1888; *Illustrated Police News,* 8 September 1888.

32. *Daily News,* 3 September 1888.

33. *East London Observer,* 8 September 1888.

34. *London Times, Daily Telegraph, St. James Gazette,* 1 September 1888.

35. Ibid.

36. The *Times,* 3 September 1888.

Soldiers and Servants

1. *Morning Chronicle,* 11 February 1840.

2. Henry Mayhew, "Soldiers' Women," in *London Labour and the London Poor,* vol. 4: *Prostitution in London* (London, 1862).

3. Ibid.

4. Myrna Trustram, *Women of the Regiment and the Victorian Army* (Cambridge, UK, 1984), p. 106.

5. *Windsor and Eton Express,* 24 April 1830.

6. C. Davis, ed., *Memorials of the Hamlet of Knightsbridge* (London, 1859), pp. 103, 144.

7. *Chester Chronicle,* 20 June 1863.

8. Isabella Beeton, *Mrs. Beeton's Book of Household Management* (London, 1861).

9. *The Duties of Servants: A Practical Guide to the Routine of Domestic Service, by a Member of the Aristocracy* (London, 1894), pp. 49–50.

10. Ibid.

11. *Chester Chronicle,* 20 June 1863.

12. GRO: Death certificate for George Smith, 13 June 1863, Wrexham.

Mrs. Chapman

1. Shelden, *Victims*, p. 15.

2. William Lee, *Classes of the Capital: A Sketch Book of London Life* (Oxford, 1841), p. 43.

3. Berkshire Record Office: St. Leonard's Hill Estate Sale Catalogue, D/EX 888/1, Illustrated Sales Catalogue with plan of the St. Leonard's Hill Estate, D/EX 1915/5/11/1-2.

4. *Evening Standard,* 11 September 1888.

5. The *Court,* 18 June 1881.

6. *Penny Illustrated Paper,* 18 June 1881.

Demon Drink

1. *Pall Mall Gazette*, 1 May 1889.

2. I am indebted to Neal and Jennifer Shelden for this information.

3. "Inebriety and Infant Mortality," *Journal of Inebriety,* March 1878, vol. 2, p. 124.

4. "Visitor's Day at Spelthorne," *Woman's Gazette,* December 1879.

5. *Windsor and Eton Gazette,* 15 September 1888.

Dark Annie

1. http://booth.lse.ac.uk: Charles H. Duckworth's Notebook, Police District 23, Booth/B/359, p. 143.

2. "The Female Criminal," *Female's Friend,* 1846.

3. *Daily News,* 11 September 1888.

4. http://booth.lse.ac.uk: Interview with Sub-division Inspector W. Miller . . . Booth/B/355, pp. 166–85.

5. "The Worst Street in London," *Daily Mail,* 16 July 1901.

6. *Evening Standard,* 11 September 1888.

7. Shelden, *Victims*, p. 18.

8. *Daily News,* 11 September 1888.

9. Ibid.

10. *Penny Illustrated Paper,* 22 September 1888.
11. The *Star,* 10 September 1888; the *Times,* 20 September 1888. In other versions of this interview, the engagement ring is described as "an oval."
12. PRO Home Office papers: HO 45/9964/x15663.
13. PRO Home Office papers: HO 144/221/A49301C f 136, ff. 137–45.
14. The *Times,* 20 September 1888. Again, to confuse matters further, there are several versions of this statement. The *People* claims Cooper said, "Bring men *into* the lodging house," while various other papers, such as the *Freeman's Journal* on the same date, claimed she said that Annie "used to bring them to the public house," which holds different implications altogether.
15. *Daily Telegraph,* 11 September 1888.
16. The *Star,* 27 September 1888.
17. *Daily Mail,* "The Worst Street in London," 16 July 1901.
18. *Manchester Courier,* 11 September 1888. The many varying newspaper reports of this conversation claim that Annie went to either the infirmary or the casual ward.
19. M. A. Crowther, *The Workhouse System, 1834–1929: The History of an English Social Institution* (Athens, GA, 1982).
20. Howard Goldsmid, Chapter 7, in *Dottings of a Dosser* (London, 1886).
21. Metropolitan Police Files (PRO); 3/140 ff. 9–11.

The Girl from Torslanda

1. Orvar Lofgren, "Family and Household: Images and Realities: Cultural Change in Swedish Society," in *Households: Comparative and Historical Studies of the Domestic Group,* ed. Robert McNetting et al. (1984), p. 456.
2. SE/GLA/13186/E I/1 Image 17, SE/GLA/13566/B/2 (1835–1860).
3. SE/GLA/13566/B/2 (1835–1860), SE/GLA/13186/A I/30 (1858–1864), p. 141.
4. Therese Nordlund Edvinsson and Johan Söderberg, "Servants and Bourgeois Life in Urban Sweden in the Early 20th Century," *Scandinavian Journal of History,* vol. 35, no. 4 (2010), pp. 428–29.
5. Christer Lundh, "Life-cycle of Servants in Nineteenth-Century Sweden: Norms and Practice," in *Domestic Service and the Formation of European Identity* (Bern, Switzerland: Peter Lang, 2004), p. 73.
6. SE/GLA/13186/B I/3.

Allmän Kvinna 97

1. Françoise Barret-Ducrocq, *Love in the Time of Victoria* (London, 1991), p. 60.
2. Yvonne Svanström, *Policing Public Women: The Regulation of Prostitution in Stockholm, 1812–1880* (Stockholm, 2000), pp. 146–47.
3. SE/GLA/12703 D XIV a.
4. SE/GLA/12703 D XIV a.
5. SE/GLA/13566/F/H0004.
6. SE/GLA/12703 D XIV a.
7. SE/GLA/12703 D XIV a.
8. Ibid.

9. SE/GLA — Holtermanska (Kurhuset records, uncatalogued papers — original document has been lost).
10. I am indebted to Stefan Rantzow for this information.
11. Göteborgs Domkyrkoförsamling (O)–B:7 (1861–79) and Emigranten Populär 2006/Gustafsdotter/Elisabet (Emibas).

The Immigrant

1. *Maidstone Telegraph,* 2 March 1861. Daniel Elisha Stride eventually married and became a pharmacist, though he ended his life in an asylum in 1900.
2. George Dodds, *The Food of London* (London, 1856), pp. 514–15.
3. Ulrika Elenora Församling (UT) HII:1, image 2110. I am indebted to Daniel Olsson for the discovery of this document in the Gothenburg Archives.
4. Walter Dew, *I Caught Crippen* (London, 1938).
5. The *Times,* 4 October 1888; *Daily Telegraph,* 4 October 1888.
6. An ad for Goffrie's lessons at 67 Gower Street appears in the *Daily Telegraph,* 19 January 1869.
7. Jerome K. Jerome, *My Life and Times* (London, 1927), p. 38.
8. Charles Dickens, *Household Words* (London, 1852).
9. Alfred Fournier, *Syphilis and Marriage* (London, 1881), p. 157.
10. *Sheerness Times and General Advertiser,* 13 September 1873.
11. Probate Wills; William Stride the Elder of Stride's Row, Mile Town, Sheerness, proven 30 September 1873.

Long Liz

1. LMA: Stepney Union; Bromley and Hackney Union Workhouse records: Admissions and Discharge Registers; SH BG/139/003, STBG/L/133/01.
2. *Evening Standard,* 31 December 1878.
3. *Reynolds' Newspaper,* 29 September 1878.
4. Goldsmid, *Dottings of a Dosser* (Kindle loc. 1250).
5. *Birmingham Daily Post,* 2 October 1888.
6. "Nooks and Corners of Character, The Charwoman," *Punch,* January–June 1850.
7. Daniel Olsson, "Elizabeth Stride: The Jewish Connection," *Ripperologist* no. 96 (October 2008).
8. *Evening Standard,* 3 October 1888.
9. LMA: Thames Police Court Ledgers PS/TH/01/005.
10. G. P. Merrick, *Work Among the Fallen as Seen in the Prison Cells* (London, 1890), p. 29.
11. LMA: Thames Police Court Ledgers PS/TH/A01/008.
12. The *Times,* 4 October 1888.
13. *Daily Telegraph,* 2 October 1888.
14. *Bath Chronicle and Weekly Gazette,* 4 October 1888.
15. *Evening Standard,* 3 October 1888.
16. Ibid.
17. *Lloyd's Weekly Newspaper,* 7 October 1888.
18. *Londonderry Sentinel,* 2 October 1888.

19. *Evening Standard,* 6 October 1888.
20. The *Times,* 9 October 1888.
21. *Illustrated Police News*, 13 October 1888.
22. *North London News,* 6 October 1888.

Seven Sisters

1. *Wolverhampton Chronicle and Staffordshire Advertiser,* 4 March 1840.
2. Ibid., 15 February 1843.
3. W. H. Jones, *The Story of Japan, Tin-Plate Working, and Bicycle and Galvanising Trades in Wolverhampton* (London: Alexander and Shepheard, 1900), p. 15.
4. *W.C. & S.A.*, 25 January 1843.
5. Ibid., 29 March 1843.
6. Ibid.
7. Margaret Llewelyn Davies (ed.), *Maternity: Letters from Working Women* (London, 1915), p. 5.
8. For national illiteracy figures circa 1841, see Pamela Horn, *The Victorian Town Child* (Stroud, Gloucestershire, 1997), p. 73.
9. LMA: Bridge, Candlewick and Dowgate Schools, Minutes: CLC/215/MS31.165.
10. *Manchester Weekly Times,* 6 October 1888.
11. *Gloucestershire Echo,* 5 October 1888.
12. LMA: Bridge, Candlewick and Dowgate Schools, Minutes: CLC/215/MS31.165.
13. Clement King Shorter (ed.), *The Brontës Life and Letters*, vol. 2 (Cambridge, 2013; originally published in 1908).
14. *Morning Advertiser,* 27 June 1851.
15. That George Eddowes contracted tuberculosis from his wife is suggested by Neal Shelden in *The Victims of Jack the Ripper* (2007).
16. *Manchester Weekly Times,* 6 October 1888.
17. LMA: Bermondsey Board of Guardians, Settlement Examinations: Indexed, 1857–59; Reference Number: BBG/523: Workhouse examination for the Eddowes children, Alfred, George, Thomas, Sarah Ann, and Mary, on December 16, 1857.

The Ballad of Kate and Tom

1. Charles Dickens, *The Old Curiosity Shop* (London, 1840–41), p. 71.
2. *Shields Daily Gazette and Shipping Telegraph,* 4 October 1888.
3. Ibid. "Mrs. Croote's" version of events is recounted in this issue.
4. *Bell's Life in London and Sporting Chronicle,* 18 September 1866.
5. Pierce Egan, *Boxiana; or, Sketches of Ancient and Modern Pugilism* (London, 1824), pp. 285, 293.
6. There is some dispute about the actual date and place of Conway/Quinn's birth. I'm using the information cited by Anthony J. Randall in *Jack the Ripper: Blood Lines* (Gloucester, 2013). Conway's army medical records suggest he was twenty-four in 1861 and born in Kilgeever, near Louisburgh, County Mayo.
7. PRO (Discharge papers for Thomas Quinn) WO97/1450/058 (Royal Hospital Kilmahain: Pensioner Register) WO118/33.

8. WO22/180 Monthly ledger for Kilkerry District, Ireland 1861; WO23/57 Yearly ledger 1855–64 for Royal Chelsea Hospital; WO23/57 Yearly ledger 1864–74 for Royal Hospital Chelsea.

9. See WO22/23 for Thomas Quinn's pension records.

10. http://www.attackingthedevil.co.uk/ Andrew Mearns, *The Bitter Cry of Outcast London: An Inquiry into the Condition of the Abject Poor* (London, 1883).

11. Unfortunately, most ballads and chapbooks were written anonymously and so, with a rare exception, it is virtually impossible to trace the authors of these works.

12. *Sheffield Independent,* 10 January 1866.

13. Jarett Kobek, the author of "May My End a Warning Be: Catherine Eddowes and Gallows Literature in the Black Country" (https://www.casebook.org/dissertations/dst-kobek.html), builds a case for attributing the ballad to Kate Eddowes and Thomas Conway.

14. *Black Country Bugle*, January 1995.

Her Sister's Keeper

1. Montagu Williams, Chapter 5, "Down East: Griddlers or Street Singers," in *Round London: Down East and Up West* (London, 1894).

2. http://www.workhouses.org.uk/WHR.

3. Nancy Tomes, "A Torrent of Abuse," *Journal of Social History,* vol. 11, no. 3 (March 1978), pp. 328–45.

4. Ibid.

5. *Daily News,* 4 October 1888.

6. Ibid.

7. LMA: GBG/250/12 Greenwich Workhouse Admissions and Discharge Registers.

8. *Manchester Courier and Lancashire General Advertiser,* 6 October 1888.

9. *Hull Daily Mail,* 4 October 1888.

10. Goldsmid, Chapter 3, "Cooney's," in *Dottings of a Dosser*.

11. *Manchester Weekly Times,* 6 October 1888; *MC & LGA,* 6 October 1888.

12. *MC & LGA,* 6 October 1888.

13. Ibid.

14. LMA: CLA/041/IQ/3/65/135: John Kelly statement (Catherine Eddowes Inquest Records), the *Times,* 5 October 1888; *Evening News,* 5 October 1888.

15. Ibid.

"Nothing"

1. The *Echo,* 5 September 1888.

2. Ibid.

3. *Wolverhampton Chronicle and Staffordshire Advertiser,* 6 October 1888.

4. Sidney and Beatrice Webb, eds., *The Break Up of the Poor Law* (London, 1909).

5. *Daily Telegraph,* 5 October 1888.

6. The *Times,* 5 October 1888.

7. LMA: CLA/041/IQ/3/65/135: Frederick William Wilkinson, Statement.

8. Ibid.; *Daily Telegraph,* 5 October 1888.

9. Goldsmid, Chapter 7, "No Doss Money," in *Dottings of a Dosser.*
10. *Daily Telegraph,* 3 October 1888.
11. LMA: CLA/041/IQ/3/65/135: George Henry Hutt.
12. LMA: CLA/041/IQ/3/65/135: James Byfield.
13. LMA: CLA/041/IQ/3/65/135: Hutt.

Marie Jeanette

1. "Walter," *My Secret Life,* vol. 10 (London, 1888).
2. LMA: MJ/SPC NE 1888 Box 3, case paper 19, Inquest statement of Joseph Barnett, 12 November 1888.
3. The *Echo,* 12 November 1888.
4. *Evening News,* 12 November 1888; the *Star,* 10 November 1888.
5. *Morning Advertiser,* 12 November 1888; *Eddowes Journal and General Advertiser for Shropshire and the Principality of Wales,* 14 November 1888.
6. *Evening News,* 12 November 1888.
7. "Walter," *My Secret Life,* vol. 11.
8. Daniel Joseph Kirwan, *Palace and Hovel: Phases of London Life* (London, 1878), p. 466.
9. Ibid., pp. 467–78.
10. Ibid., p. 474.
11. "Walter," *My Secret Life,* vol. 10, pp. 642–43.
12. Julia Laite, *Common Prostitutes and Ordinary Citizens: Commercial Sex in London, 1885–1960* (London, 2012) (Kindle loc. 1656).
13. W. T. Stead, "The Maiden Tribute of Modern Babylon IV: The Report of Our Secret Commission," *Pall Mall Gazette,* 10 July 1885.
14. Sallecartes was the source interviewed in part IV of Stead's "Maiden Tribute."
15. Bridget O'Donnell, *Inspector Minahan Makes a Stand* (London, 2012), p. 71.
16. "The Maiden Tribute," *Pall Mall Gazette.*
17. Ibid.
18. Ibid.
19. Ibid.

The Gay Life

1. Neal Shelden, *The Victims of Jack the Ripper: The 125th Anniversary* (n.p., 2013). Adrianus's daughter, Wilhelmina, claimed that she grew up in a brothel in Poplar between 1884 and 1891.
2. Edward W. Thomas, *Twenty-Five Years Labour Among the Friendless and the Fallen* (London, 1879), p. 36.
3. Ibid.
4. Ibid., p. 37.
5. Madeleine Blair (anonymous), *Madeleine: An Autobiography* (London, 1919).
6. *Morning Advertiser,* 12 November 1888.
7. The *Echo,* 12 November 1888.
8. *Evening Standard,* 10 May 1891; also see Neal Shelden, *Mary Jane Kelly and the Victims of Jack the Ripper: The 125th Anniversary* (2013).

9. *Daily Telegraph,* 12 November 1888.
10. LMA: MJ/SPC NE 1888 Box 3, case paper 19, Julia Venturney.
11. Ibid.
12. *Evening Star,* 12 November 1888; the *Echo,* 12 November 1888.
13. Dew, Chapter 1, "The Hunt for Jack the Ripper," in *I Caught Crippen.*
14. *Pall Mall Gazette,* 12 November 1888.
15. Paul Begg, *Jack the Ripper: Just the Facts* (London, 2004).
16. LMA: MJ/SPC NE 1888 Box 3, case paper 19, Inquest statement of Joseph Barnett, 12 November 1888.
17. Begg, *Jack the Ripper.*
18. Ibid. The term "bully" might be read in two ways here — the conventional definition, or in reference to the sex trade. A bully was also another name for a pimp.
19. LMA: MJ/SPC NE 1888 Box 3, case paper 19, Julia Venturney.
20. Begg, *Jack the Ripper.*
21. LMA: MJ/SPC NE 1888 Box 3, case paper 19, Julia Venturney.
22. Ibid., Joseph Barnett.
23. LMA: MJ/SPC NE 1888 Box 3, case paper 19, Inquest Statement of Mary Ann Cox, 9 November 1888.

Conclusion: "Just Prostitutes"

1. The *Times,* 1 October 1888.
2. John Holland Rose (ed.), *The Cambridge History of the British Empire,* vol. 1 (Cambridge, UK, 1940), p. 745.
3. Nina Attwood, *The Prostitute's Body: Rewriting Prostitution in Victorian Britain* (London, 2010), pp. 51–54.
4. PRO Home Office papers: HO 45/9964/x15663.
5. PRO: Metropolitan Police Files: file 3/141, ff. 158–59.
6. GRO: Death Certificate for Mary Ann Nichols: 1888, J-S Whitechapel 1c/219, Annie Chapman: 1888, J-S Whitechapel 1c/175, Elizabeth Stride: 1888 O-D St George in the East, 1c/268, Catherine Eddowes: 1888 O-D London City 1c/37, Mary Jane "Marie Jeanette" Kelly: 1888 O-D Whitechapel 1c/211.
7. *Washington Post,* 6 June 2016; *Huffington Post,* 7 June 2016.
8. Maxim Jakubowski and Nathan Braund (eds.), *The Mammoth Book of Jack the Ripper* (London, 2008), p. 470.
9. Mickey Mayhew, "Not So Pretty Polly," *Journal of the Whitechapel Society* (April 2009); Mark Daniel, "How Jack the Ripper Saved Whitechapel," in *The Mammoth Book of Jack the Ripper,* Maxim Jakubowski and Nathan Braund, eds. (London, 2008), p. 140.
10. Mayhew, "Not So Pretty Polly."

SOURCES

PRIMARY SOURCES

HO: Home Office
MEPO: Metropolitan Police
PCOM: Home Office and Prison Commission
WO: War Office

Public Records Office, Kew (PRO)

HO 45/9964/x15663: Police Correspondence, Charles Warren
HO 144/221/A49301C: Police investigation; Elizabeth Stride
MEPO 3/140, Police investigation; Polly Nichols, Annie Chapman, Mary Jane Kelly
MEPO 3/141, MacNaghten Report into the murders
PCOM2/284, 288, Wandsworth Prison, Surrey: Register of Prisoners
WO22/23 Thomas Quinn pension records
WO22/180 Monthly ledger for Kilkerry District, Ireland, 1861
WO23/57 Yearly ledgers 1855–64, 1864–74, for Royal Chelsea Hospital
WO 97/1274/160, 166 Discharge papers, Thomas Smith, George Smith
WO97/1450/058 Discharge papers for Thomas Quinn
WO118/33 Royal Hospital Kilmahain Pensioner Register
WO 400/81/523 Soldiers Documents, Household Cavalry, 2nd Life Guard: George
     Smith

London Metropolitan Archives (LMA)

ACC/3445/PT/07/066 (Peabody Trust: Stamford Street)
BBG/523 (St. Mary Magdalen Bermondsey Settlement Records)
CLC/215–11, CLC/215/MS31165 (Sir John Cass Foundation: Bridge, Candlewick and
     Dowgate Schools, meetings and minutes)
GBG/250/008–013 (Greenwich Woolwich Road Workhouse Admissions and Dis-
     charge)
HABG/308/001 (Hackney Workhouse Admission and Discharge)
HOBG/510/18, HO/BG/535/21 (Holborn Union Workhouse Settlement Examinations)

HOBG/535/020–023 (Holborn Union Workhouse Admissions and Discharge)
LABG/044, 047, LABG/056/001 (Lambeth Board of Guardians, minutes)
LABG/162/008–014 (Lambeth Princes Road Workhouse Admissions and Discharge)
POBG/169/05–12 (Poplar Workhouse Creed Registers and Admission and Discharge)
PS/TH/A/01/005, 008, 007, 011, 003 (Thames Magistrate Court Registers)
SOBG/100/013–019 (Southwark Workhouse Admissions and Discharge)
STBG/SG/118/025–043 (Stepney Workhouses Admission and Discharge)
WEBG/ST/135/001 (Edmonton Workhouse/Strand Union/Westminster Admission and Discharge)
X020/413, X100/072, 073, 070 (Brighton Road School and South Metropolitan District School, microfilm)

London Metropolitan Archives — Inquest Documents

CLA/041/IQ/3/65/135 (Eddowes inquest records)
MJ/SPC/NE/376/1–11 (Mary Jane Kelly inquest records)

London Metropolitan Archives (via www.ancestry.com)

London Church of England Parish Registers: 1754–1906
London Church of England Marriages and Banns: 1754–1921
London Church of England Deaths and Burials: 1813–1980
London Church of England Births and Baptisms: 1813–1917
London Poor Law and Board of Guardian Records: 1834–1906
London Workhouse Admission and Discharge Records: 1659–1930
United Kingdom Census Records: 1841–1911
Crew Lists, Glasgow, Scotland: 1863–1901
New South Wales, Australia, Unassisted Immigrant Passenger Lists: 1826–1922

Berkshire Record Office

D/P39/28/9, 11 (National School Admission Registers & Log-Books 1870–1914)
D/EX 888/1 (St. Leonard's Hill Estate Sale Catalogue, 1869)
D/EX 1915/5/11/1–2 (Illustrated Sales Catalogue with plan of the St. Leonard's Hill Estate, 1923)

Göteborg Lansarkivet, Gothenburg, Sweden

SE/GLA/12703 D XIV (Police Registers of "Public Women")
SE/GLA/13186/A I/30 (1835–60 Employment Records)
SE/GLA/13186/E I/1 (Marriage Records)
SE/GLA/13187/P/10 (Uncatalogued Parish Records)
SE/GLA/13566/B/2 (1835–60 Gothenburg Censuses)
SE/GLA/13566/F/H0004 (Kurhuset Records)

(Available as digitized records through Göteborg Lansarkivet)

Emigration Records:
Emigranten Populär 2006

Göteborgs Domkyrkoförsamling (O)–B:7 (1861–79)
Swedish Church in London Records:
Ulrika Eleonora församling (UT) H II

Library and Archive of the Convent of St. Mary the Virgin, Wantage

Logbooks: Spelthorne Sanatorium

City of Westminster Archive Centre

St. Margaret and St. John, Westminster, rate books (Knightsbridge)

London Guildhall Library and Archive

Kellys Directories, 1861–78

General Register Office (GRO)

Birth records
Death certificates

Wills and Probate (www.Gov.uk)

Probate Wills; William Stride the Elder of Stride's Row, Mile Town, Sheerness, proven
30 September 1873

BOOKS

Ackroyd, Peter. *London: The Biography* (2000)
Acton, William. *Prostitution considered in its moral, social, and sanitary aspects, in London and other large cities and garrison towns: With proposals for the control and prevention of its attendant evils* (1870)
Alford, Stephen. *Habitual Drunkards' Act of 1879* (1880)
"A Member of the Aristocracy," in *The Duties of Servants: A practical guide to the routine of domestic service* (1894)
Arthur, Sir George. *The Story of the Household Cavalry*, vol. 2 (1909)
Ashton, John R. *A Short History of the English Church in Gothenburg, 1747–1997* (1997)
———. *Lives and Livelihoods in Little London: The Story of the British in Gothenburg, 1621–2001* (2003)
Atkinson, David, and Steve Rond (eds.). *Street Ballads in Nineteenth-Century Britain, Ireland, and North America* (2014)
Attwood, Nina. *The Prostitute's Body: Rewriting Prostitution in Victorian Britain* (2010)
Bakker, Nienke, and Isolde Pludermacher (eds.). *Splendeurs & Misères: Images de la Prostitution, 1850–1910* (2015)
Barnsby, George J. *Social Conditions in the Black Country* (1980)
Barret-Ducrocq, Françoise. *Love in the Time of Victoria* (1991)
Bartley, George C.T. *A Handy Book for Guardians of the Poor* (1876)
Bartley, Paula. *Prostitution: Prevention and Reform in England, 1860–1914* (1999)
Bateman, John. *The Great Landowners of Great Britain and Ireland* (2014)

Bates, Barbara. *Bargaining for Life: A Social History of Tuberculosis, 1876–1938* (1992)

Beaumont, Matthew. *Night Walking: A Nocturnal History of London* (2015)

Beeton, Isabella. *Mrs. Beeton's Book of Household Management* (1861)

Begg, Paul. *Jack the Ripper: Just the Facts* (2004)

Begg, Paul, and John Bennett. *The Complete and Essential Jack the Ripper* (2013)

Begg, Paul, Martin Fido, and Keith Skinner (eds.). *The Complete Jack the Ripper A to Z* (2015)

Benjamin, Walter. *A Short History of Photography* (1972; originally published 1931)

Berg, William. *Contributions to the History of Music in Gothenburg, 1754–1892* (1914)

Black, C. *Married Women's Work* (1983)

Blaine, Delabere Pritchett. *An Encyclopaedia of Rural Sports: Or, a Complete Account, Historical, Practical, and Descriptive, of Hunting, Shooting, Fishing, Racing, and Other Field Sports and Athletic Amusements of the Present Day*, vol. 1 (1840)

Blair, Madeleine. *Madeleine: An Autobiography* (1919)

Booth, Charles. *Life and Labour of the People in London: The Trades of East London* (1893)

———. *Life and Labour of the People in London: Religious Influences* (1902)

Booth, William. *In Darkest England and the Way Out* (1890)

Bowley, A. L. *Wages in the United Kingdom in the Nineteenth Century* (1900)

Bradlaugh, Charles, and Annie Besant. *The Fruits of Philosophy* (1891)

Bumstead, Freeman J. *The Pathology and Treatment of Venereal Diseases* (1861)

Burnett, John. *Plenty and Want: A Social History of Food in England from 1815 to the Present Day* (2013)

Butler, Josephine Elizabeth. *Rebecca Jarrett* (1886)

Bynam, Helen. *Spitting Blood: The History of Tuberculosis* (1999)

Carlsson, A. *Göteborgs Orkesters Repertoar* (1996)

Chandler, David, and Ian Beckett (eds.). *The Oxford History of the British Army* (1994)

Chisholm, Alexander, Christopher-Michael DiGrazia, and Dave Yost (eds.). *The News from Whitechapel: Jack the Ripper in the* Daily Telegraph (2002)

Clark, Anna. *The Struggle for the Breeches: Gender and the Making of the British Working Class* (1997)

Clarke, Edward T. *Bermondsey: Its Historic Memories and Associations* (1901)

Clayton, Antony. *London's Coffee Houses* (2003)

Clowes, W. B. *Family Business, 1803–1953* (1969)

Cohen, Deborah. *Family Secrets: Living with Shame from the Victorians to the Present Day* (2013)

Covell, Mike. *Annie Chapman: Wife, Mother, Victim* (2014)

Crompton, Frank. *Workhouse Children* (1997)

Crowther, M. A. *The Workhouse System, 1834–1929: The History of an English Social Institution* (1982)

Cunnington, Phillis, and Catherine Lucas. *Charity Costumes* (1978)

Curtis, Perry L., Jr. *Jack the Ripper and the London Press* (2002)

Curtis & Henson. *Royal Windsor: Illustrated particulars of the St. Leonards Hill Estate originally part of Windsor Forest . . . for sale by private treaty* (1915)

Davidson, Roger, and Lesley A. Hall. (eds.). *Sex, Sin, and Suffering: Venereal Disease and European Society Since 1870* (2003)

Davin, Anna. *Growing Up Poor: Home, School, and the Street, 1870–1914* (1996)

Davis, C. (ed.). *Memorials of the Hamlet of Knightsbridge* (1859)

Dew, Walter. *I Caught Crippen* (1938)

Dickens, Charles. *Dombey and Son* (1846–48)

———. *The Old Curiosity Shop* (1840–41)

Dickens, Charles, Jr. *Dickens's Dictionary of London* (1879)

Dodds, George. *The Food of London* (1856)

Downes, Miles Henry. *Pugilistica: The History of English Boxing* (1966)

Egan, Pierce. *Boxiana; or, Sketches of Ancient and Modern Pugilism* (1824)

English Heritage. *Kent Historic Towns' Survey: Sheerness — Kent Archaeological Assessment Document* (2004)

Evans, Stewart P., and Keith Skinner. *The Ultimate Jack the Ripper Sourcebook* (2001)

Fauve-Chamoux, Antoinette (ed.). *Domestic Service and the Formation of European Identity* (2004)

First Report of the Commissioners for Inquiring into the State of Large Towns and Populous Districts, vol. 1 (London, 1844)

Fournier, Alfred. *Syphilis and Marriage* (1881)

Frost, Ginger. *Living in Sin: Cohabiting as Husband and Wife in Nineteenth-Century England* (2008)

———. *Promises Broken: Courtship, Class, and Gender in Victorian England* (1995)

Frost, Rebecca. *The Ripper's Victims in Print: The Rhetoric of Portrayals Since 1929* (2018)

Fryer, Peter (ed.). *The Man of Pleasure's Companion: A Nineteenth-Century Anthology of Amorous Entertainment* (1968)

Garcia, Magaly Rodriguez, Lex Heerma van Voss, and Elise van Nederveen (eds.). *Selling Sex in the City: A Global History of Prostitution, 1600s–2000* (2017)

Gavin, Hector. *Unhealthiness of London: The Habitations of Industrial Classes* (1847)

Gay, Peter. *The Cultivation of Hatred: The Bourgeois Experience, Victoria to Freud* (1993)

Gibson, Clare. *Army Childhood: British Army Children's Lives and Times* (2012)

Gibson, Colin S. *Dissolving Wedlock* (1994)

Goldsmid, Howard. *Dottings of a Dosser* (1886)

———. *A Midnight Prowl Through Victorian London,* Peter Stubley, ed. (2012)

Gordon, Mary Louisa. *Penal Discipline* (1922)

Gorham, Deborah. *The Victorian Girl and the Feminine Ideal* (2012)

Gray, Drew D. *London's Shadows: The Dark Side of the Victorian City* (2010)

Greenwood, James. *The Seven Curses of London* (1869)

Gretton, George Le Mesurier. *The campaigns and history of the Royal Irish regiment from 1684 to 1902* (1911)

Hadfield, Charles. *Canals of the West Midlands* (1966)

Hanaford, Phebe Ann. *The Life of George Peabody* (1870)

Harkness, Margaret. *A City Girl* (1887)

———. *Out of Work* (1888)

———. *Toilers in London; or, Inquiries concerning female labour in the metropolis* (1889)

Hart, H. G. *Hart's annual army list, special reserve list, and territorial force list* (1857)

Hartley, Jenny. *Charles Dickens and the House of Fallen Women* (2012)

Haw, G. *From Workhouse to Westminster: The Life Story of Will Crooks* (1907)

Heise, Ulla. *Coffee and Coffee Houses* (1999)

Higginbotham, Peter. *The Workhouse Encyclopedia* (2012)

Higgs, Mary. *Five Days and Nights as a Tramp* (1904)

Hiley, Michael. *Victorian Working Women: Portraits from Life* (1979)

HMSO (Her Majesty's Stationery Office). *Royal Commission on Divorce and Matrimonial Causes* (1912)

Hollingshead, John. *Ragged London* (1861)

Horn, Pamela. *The Rise and Fall of the Victorian Servant* (1975)

——. *The Victorian Town Child* (1997)

Howarth-Loomes, B.E.C. *Victorian Photography: A Collector's Guide* (1974)

Hughes, Kathryn. *The Victorian Governess* (2001)

Jakubowski, Maxim, and Nathan Braund (eds.). *The Mammoth Book of Jack the Ripper* (2008)

Jerome, Jerome K. *My Life and Times* (1927)

Jesse, John Heneage. *London: Its celebrated characters and remarkable places* (1871)

Jones, W. H. *The Story of Japan, Tin-Plate Working, and Bicycle and Galvanising Trades in Wolverhampton* (1900)

Kelly's Directory of Berkshire (1883)

Kirwan, Daniel Joseph. *Palace and Hovel: Phases of London Life* (1878)

Knight, Charles. *London* (1841)

Koven, Seth. *Slumming: Sexual and Social Politics in Victorian London* (2004)

Laite, Julia. *Common Prostitutes and Ordinary Citizens: Commercial Sex in London, 1885–1960* (2012)

Larkin, Tom. *Black Country Chronicles* (2009)

Lee, William. *Classes of the Capital: A Sketch Book of London Life* (1841)

Lindahl, Carl Fredrik. *Svenska millionärer: Minnen och anteckningar* (1897–1905)

Lindmark, Daniel. *Reading, Writing, and Schooling: Swedish Practises of Education and Literacy, 1650–1880* (2004)

Llewelyn Davies, Margaret (ed.). *Maternity: Letters from Working Women* (1915)

Lloyds Insurance. *Lloyds Register of British and Foreign Shipping* (1874)

Lock, Joan. *The* Princess Alice *Disaster* (2014)

Lofgren, Orvar. "Family and Household: Images and Realities: Cultural Change in Swedish Society," in *Households: Comparative and Historical Studies of the Domestic Group*, ed. Robert McNetting et al. (1984)

Longmate, Norman. *The Workhouse: A Social History* (2003)

London, Jack. *People of the Abyss* (1903)

Lundberg, Anna. *Care and Coercion: Medical Knowledge, Social Policy, and Patients with Venereal Disease in Sweden, 1785–1903* (1999)

Mace, Rodney. *Trafalgar Square: Emblem of Empire* (2005)

Macnaghten, Melville. *Days of My Years* (1914)

Mason, Frank. *The Book of Wolverhampton: The Story of an Industrial Town* (1979)

Mason, Michael. *The Making of Victorian Sexuality* (1995)

Mayhew, Henry. *London Labour and the London Poor* (1862)

McNetting, Robert, Richard Wilk, and Eric J. Arnold (eds.). *Households: Comparative and Historical Studies of the Domestic Group* (1984)

Mearns, Rev. Andrew. *The Bitter Cry of Outcast London: An Inquiry into the Condition of the Abject Poor* (1883)

Merrick, G. P. *Work Among the Fallen as Seen in the Prison Cells* (1890)

Metropolitan Board of Works. *Minutes of Proceedings of the Metropolitan Board of Works* (1880)

Miltoun, Francis. *Dickens' London* (1908)

Mirbeau, Octave (trans. B. R. Tucker). *A Chambermaid's Diary* (1900)

Morrison, Arthur. *Tales of Mean Streets* (1895)

Nicholls, James. *The Politics of Alcohol: A History of the Drink Question in England* (2013)

Nokes, Harriet. *Twenty-Three Years in a House of Mercy* (1886)

O'Donnell, Bridget. *Inspector Minahan Makes a Stand* (2012)

O'Neill, Joseph. *The Secret World of the Victorian Lodging House* (2014)

Palmer, Dennis, and Giselle Pincetl (trans.). *Flora Tristan's London Journal: A Survey of London Life in the 1830s* (1980)

Parker, Franklin. *George Peabody: A Biography* (1995)

Parochial Council, Saint Paul, Parish of Knightsbridge. *Report upon the poor of the Parish of St. Paul's Knightsbridge, receiving legal and charitable relief, by a Sub-Committee appointed by the Parochial Council* (1872)

Pearsall, Ronald. *The Worm in the Bud: The World of Victorian Sexuality* (2003)

Pickard, Sarah (ed.). *Anti-Social Behaviour in Britain* (2014)

Prynne, G. R. *Thirty-Five Years of Mission Work in a Garrison and Seaport Town* (1883)

Randall, Anthony J. *Jack the Ripper: Blood Lines* (2013)

Reynardson, C.T.S. Birch. *Down the Road; or, Reminiscences of a gentleman coachman* (1875)

Ribton-Turner, C. J. *A History of Vagrants and Vagrancy* (1887)

Richter, Donald C. *Riotous Victorians* (1981)

Roberts, Henry. *The dwellings of the labouring classes, their arrangement and construction: with the essentials of a healthy dwelling* (1867)

Robinson, Bruce. *They All Love Jack: Busting the Ripper* (2015)

Robinson, Sydney W. *Muckraker: The Scandalous Life and Times of W. T. Stead, Britain's First Investigative Journalist* (2012)

Rose, John Holland (ed.). *The Cambridge History of the British Empire* (1940)

Rose, Lionel. *Rogues and Vagabonds: Vagrant Underworld in Britain, 1815–1985* (1988)

Royal Commission on the Ancient and Historical Monuments of Scotland. *The Francis Tress Barry Collection* (1998)

The Royal Windsor Guide, with a brief account of Eton and Virginia Water (1838)

Rule, Fiona. *Streets of Sin: A Dark Biography of Notting Hill* (2015)

———. *The Worst Street in London* (2010)

Rumbelow, Donald. *The Complete Jack the Ripper* (2004)

Ruskin, John. *Of Queens' Gardens* (1865)

Russell, William Howard. *My Diary in India in the Years, 1858–59* (1960)

Rutherford, Adam. *A Brief History of Everyone Who Ever Lived* (2016)

Sala, George Augustus. *Gaslight and Daylight* (1859)

Schlesinger, Max. *Saunterings in and About London* (1853)

Schlör, Joachim. *Nights in the Big City: Paris, Berlin, London, 1840–1930* (1998)

Scott, Christopher. *Jack the Ripper: A Cast of Thousands* (2004)

Scott, Franklin D. *Sweden: The Nation's History* (1978)

Shelden, Neal. *Annie Chapman, Jack the Ripper Victim: A Short Biography* (2001)

———. *Catherine Eddowes: Jack the Ripper Victim* (2003)

———. *Mary Jane Kelly and the Victims of Jack the Ripper: The 125th Anniversary* (2013)

———. *The Victims of Jack the Ripper: The 125th Anniversary* (2013)

Shelden, Neal Stubbings. *Kate Eddowes, 2007 Conference Tribute* (2007)

———. *The Victims of Jack the Ripper* (2007)

Sherwood, M. *The Endowed Charities of the City of London* (1829)

Short History of the Royal Irish Regiment (1921)

Simonton, Deborah. *A History of European Women's Work: 1700 to the Present* (1998)

Sims, George R. *How the Poor Live* (1883)

——. *Horrible London* (1889)

Smith, Charles Manby. *The Working Man's Way in the World: Being an Autobiography of a Journey Man Printer* (1854)

Souter, John. *The Book of English Trades and Library of the Useful Arts* (1825)

Stallard, J. H. *The Female Casual and Her Lodgings* (1866)

Stanley, Peter. *White Mutiny: British Military Culture in India* (1998)

Stead, W. T. *The Maiden Tribute of Modern Babylon* (1885)

St. Leonard's Hill Estate Sales Catalogue (1907)

Sugden, Philip. *The Complete History of Jack the Ripper* (2006)

Svanström, Yvonne. *Policing Public Women: The Regulation of Prostitution in Stockholm, 1812–1880* (2000)

Swift, Frank. *Crime and Society in Wolverhampton: 1815–1860* (1987)

Thomas, Edward W. *Twenty-Five Years Labour Among the Friendless and the Fallen* (1879)

Thompson, F.M.L. *The Rise of Respectable Society: A Social History of Victorian Britain, 1830–1900* (1988)

Thomson, John, and Aldophe Smith. *Street Life in London* (1877)

Townsend, S., and H. J. Adams. *History of the English Congregation and Its Association with the British Factory in Gothenburg* (1946)

Trout Bartley, Sir George Christopher. *The Parish Net: How it is Dragged, and what it Catches* (1875)

Trustram, Myrna. *Women of the Regiment and the Victorian Army* (1984)

Tweedie, William. *The Temperance Movement: Its Rise, Progress, and Results* (1853)

Valverde, Mariana. *Diseases of the Will: Alcoholism and the Dilemmas of Freedom* (1998)

Vicinus, Martha (ed.). *Suffer and Be Still: Women in the Victorian Age* (1973)

Victoria County History. *A History of the County of Berkshire* (1923), vol. 3

——. *A History of the County of Warwick* (1964), vol. 7

Vincent, Davia. *Literary and Popular Culture: England, 1750–1914* (1993)

Walkowitz, Judith R. *City of Dreadful Delight: Narratives of Sexual Danger in Late-Victorian London* (2013)

——. *Prostitution and Victorian Society: Women, Class, and the State* (1983)

Walsh, J. H. *A Manual of Domestic Economy: Suited to Families Spending from £150 to £1500* (1874)

"Walter." *My Secret Life* (1888)

Warne, Frederick. *The Servant's Practical Guide* (1880)

——. *Warne's Model Housekeeper* (1879)

Warwick, Alexandra, and Martin Willis (eds.). *Jack the Ripper: Media, Culture, History* (2013)

Watson, J.N.P. *Through the Reigns: A Complete History of the Household Cavalry* (1997)

Webb, Sidney and Beatrice (eds.). *The Break Up of the Poor Law* (1909)

Werner, Alex. *Jack the Ripper and the East End* (2012)

Westcott, Tom. *Ripper Confidential: New Research on the Whitechapel Murders* (2017), vols. 1–2

Weston-Davies, Wynne. *Jack the Ripper: A True Love Story* (2015)

White, Jerry. *London in the Nineteenth Century* (2007)

Whitechapel Society (eds.). *The Little Book of Jack the Ripper* (2014)
White-Spunner, Barney. *Horse Guards* (2006)
Whittington-Egan, Richard. *Jack the Ripper: The Definitive Casebook* (2013)
Wikeley, N. *Child Support: Law and Policy* (2006)
Williams, Lucy. *Wayward Women: Female Offending in Victorian England* (2016)
Williams, Montagu. *Round London: Down East and Up West* (1894)
Wise, Sarah. *The Blackest Streets: The Life and Death of a Victorian Slum* (2008)
Wohl, Anthony S. *The Eternal Slum: Housing and Social Policy in Victorian London* (2001)
Wyndham, Horace. *The Queen's Service* (1899)
Yates, Edmund. *His Recollections and Experiences* (1885)
Yost, Dave. *Elizabeth Stride and Jack the Ripper: The Life and Death of the Reputed Third Victim* (2008)

JOURNAL ARTICLES

Arif, Debra. "Goodnight, Old Dear," *Ripperologist*, no. 148, February 2016, pp. 2–8
Blom, Ida. "Fighting Venereal Diseases: Scandinavian Legislation c. 1800 to c. 1950," *Medical History* no. 50, 2006, pp. 209–34
Edwards, C. "Tottenham Court Road: The Changing Fortunes of London's Furniture Street, 1850–1950," *The London Journal*, vol. 36, no. 2, 2011, pp. 140–60
"Inebriety and Infant Mortality," *Journal of Inebriety*, vol. 2., March 1878, p. 124
Lundberg, Anna. "The Return to Society, Marriage, and Family Formation After Hospital Treatment for Venereal Disease in Sundsvall, 1844–1892," *Annales de Démographie Historique*, no. 2, 1998, pp. 55–75
Lundh, Christopher. "The Social Mobility of Servants in Rural Sweden, 1740–1894," *Continuity and Change*, vol. 14, no. 1, 1999, pp. 57–89
Mayhew, Mickey. "Not So Pretty Polly," *Journal of the Whitechapel Society*, April 2009
McLaughlin, Robert. "Mary Kelly's Rent," *Ripperana* no. 41, July 2002, pp. 19–22
Mumm, Susan. "Not Worse Than the Other Girls: The Convent-Based Rehabilitation of Fallen Women in Victorian Britain," *Journal of Social History*, vol. 29, no. 3, Spring 1996, pp. 527–47
"Nooks and Corners of Character, The Charwoman," *Punch*, January–June 1850
Nordlund Edvinsson, Therese, and Johan Söderberg, "Servants and Bourgeois Life in Urban Sweden in the Early 20th Century," *Scandinavian Journal of History*, vol. 35, no. 4, 2010, pp. 427–50
Oddy, Derek J. "Gone for a Soldier: The Anatomy of a Nineteenth-Century Army Family," *Journal of Family History*, vol. 25, no. 1, January 2000, pp. 39–62
Olsson, Daniel. "Elizabeth's Story: A Documentary Narrative of Long Liz Stride's Early Life in Sweden," *Ripperologist*, no. 52, March 2003
———. "Elizabeth Stride: The Jewish Connection," *Ripperologist* no. 96, October 2008
———. "Ultimate Ripperologists' Tour: A Journey to Gothenburg," *Casebook Examiner*, no. 11, April 2011
Parlour, Andy. "The Life and Death of William Nichols," *Journal of the Whitechapel Society*, April 2009, pp. 10–12
Pollock, Ernest M., and A. M. Latter. "Women and Habitual Drunkenness," *Journal of the Society of Comparative Legislation*, new series, vol. 2, no. 2., 1900, pp. 289–93

Rantzow, Stefan. "In Memory of Elizabeth Stride," *East London History Society Newsletter*, vol. 3, no. 17, Winter 2013/14, pp. 7–12

Skelly, Julia. "When Seeing Is Believing: Women, Alcohol, and Photography in Victorian Britain," *Queen's Journal of Visual and Material Culture*, vol. 1, 2008, pp. 1–17

"Spelthorne Sanatorium," *Medical Temperance Journal*, vols. 12–13, 1881, p. 7

Tarn, John Nelson. "The Peabody Donation Fund: The Role of a Housing Society in the Nineteenth Century," *Victorian Studies*, September 1966, pp. 7–38

Tomes, Nancy. "A Torrent of Abuse," *Journal of Social History*, vol. 11, no. 3, March 1978, pp. 328–45

Weld, C. R. "On the Condition of the Working Classes in the Inner Ward of St. George's Parish, Hanover Square," *Journal of the Statistical Society of London*, vol. 6, no. 1, April 1843, pp. 17–23

Wilcox, Penelope. "Marriage, Mobility, and Domestic Service," *Annales de Démographie Historique*, 1981, pp. 195–206

ONLINE SOURCES

British-History.ac.uk (British History On-Line)

Ditchfield, P. H., and William Page (eds.). "Parishes: Clewer," in *A History of the County of Berkshire*, vol. 3 (1923)

Greenacombe, John (ed.). "Knightsbridge Barracks: The First Barracks, 1792–1877," in *Survey of London: Volume 45, Knightsbridge* (2000)

———. "Knightsbridge Green Area: Raphael Street," in *Survey of London: Volume 45, Knightsbridge* (2000)

———. "Montpelier Square Area: Other Streets," in *Survey of London: Volume 45, Knightsbridge* (2000)

Malden, H. E. (ed.). "Parishes: Bermondsey," in *A History of the County of Surrey*, vol. 4 (1912)

Sheppard, F.H.W. (ed.). "Brompton Road: Introduction," in *Survey of London: Volume 41, Brompton* (1983)

Casebook.org/dissertations

DiGrazia, Christopher-Michael. "Another Look at the Lusk Kidney"

Kobek, Jarett. "May My End a Warning Be: Catherine Eddowes and Gallows Literature in the Black Country"

Marsh, James. "The Funeral of Mary Jane Kelly"

Rantzow, Stefan. "Elisabeth Gustafsdotters' Last Stride: In the Memory of Elizabeth Stride — Jack the Ripper's Third Victim"

Sironi, Antonio, and Jane Coram. "Anything but Your Prayers: Victims and Witnesses on the Night of the Double Event"

Wescott, Tom. "Exonerating Michael Kidney: A Fresh Look at Some Old Myths"

Charles Booth's London (https://booth.lse.ac.uk/)

Maps Descriptive of London Poverty
Inquiry into Life and Labour in London (notebooks)

Victorianweb.org

Diniejko, Dr. Andrzej. "Arthur Morrison's Slum Fiction: The Voice of New Realism"
McDonald, Deborah. "Clara Collet and Jack the Ripper"
Skipper, James, and George P. Landow. "Wages and Cost of Living in the Victorian Era"
Zieger, Dr. Susan. "The Medical 'Discovery' of Addiction in the Nineteenth Century"

W. T. Stead Resource Site (https://attackingthedevil.co.uk/related/narrative.php)

"Rebecca Jarrett's Narrative" (c. 1928), Salvation Army Heritage Centre

Wolverhampton History and Heritage

http://www.wolverhamptonhistory.org.uk/work/industry/
http://www.historywebsite.co.uk/Museum/OtherTrades/TinPlate
http://www.historywebsite.co.uk/articles/OldHall/Excavation.htm
http://www.historywebsite.co.uk/Museum/metalware/general/perry.htm

CONTEMPORARY NEWSPAPERS AND PERIODICALS

Bath Chronicle and Weekly Gazette
Bell's Life in London and Sporting Chronicle
Bilston Herald
Birmingham Daily Post
Black Country Bugle
Chester Chronicle
The *Circle*
The *Court*
Coventry Standard
Daily Mail
Daily Telegraph
East London Observer
Eddowes Journal and General Advertiser for Shropshire and the Principality of Wales
Evening News
Evening Standard
Evening Star
Exmouth Journal
Female's Friend
Freeman's Journal
Gloucestershire Echo
Göteborgsposten
Hull Daily Mail
Illustrated Police News
Lloyd's Weekly Newspaper
London Daily News
Londonderry Sentinel
Maidstone Journal and Kentish Advertiser
Maidstone Telegraph

Manchester Courier and Lancashire General Advertiser
Manchester Guardian
Manchester Weekly Times
Manitoba Daily Free Press
Morning Advertiser
Morning Chronicle
North London News
Pall Mall Gazette
Penny Illustrated Paper
The *People*
Reading Mercury
Reynolds' Newspaper
Sheerness Guardian and East Kent Advertiser
Sheerness Times and General Advertiser
Sheffield Daily Telegraph
Sheffield Independent
Shields Daily Gazette and Shipping Telegraph
The *Star*
St. James Gazette
The *Sun*
The *Times*
Western Daily Press
Windsor and Eton Express
Windsor and Eton Gazette
Wolverhampton Chronicle and Staffordshire Advertiser
Wolverhampton Evening Express and Star
Woman's Gazette

INDEX